CHRIST
CENTERED
LEADERSHIP

CHRIST
CENTERED
LEADERSHIP

THRIVING IN BUSINESS BY
PUTTING GOD IN CHARGE

Perry Pascarella

PRIMA PUBLISHING

Prima Publishing and colophon are registered trademarks of Prima Communications, Inc.

Library of Congress Cataloging-in-Publication Data

Pascarella, Perry.
  Christ-centered leadership : thriving in business by putting God in charge / Perry Pascarella.
    p.   cm.
  Includes bibliographical references and index.
  ISBN 0-7615-2106-2
  1. Leadership—Religious aspects—Christianity. 2. Business—Religious aspects—Christianity. I. Title.
BV4597.53.L43P37   1999
248.8'8—dc21   99-28046
                                                           CIP

99 00 01 02 HH 10 9 8 7 6 5 4 3 2 1
Printed in the United States of America

HOW TO ORDER
Single copies may be ordered from Prima Publishing, P.O. Box 1260BK, Rocklin, CA 95677; telephone (916) 632-4400. Quantity discounts are also available. On your letterhead, include information concerning the intended use of the books and the number of books you wish to purchase.

Visit us online at www.primalifestyles.com

To Frank Walter

*Frank was a doer, a man of action, a man of God;
but for the last ten years of his life here, as illness ate
away at his body, his courage, his love for others, and
his faith in God shone more brightly than ever.*

*He left his family, friends, and business associates
two priceless gifts:*

1. *The reminder that life itself is a gift;*
2. *The reminder that, while it is important to live
   out our faith in action, it is through our very
   being—what we see, what we believe, and how
   much we love—that we reflect the God who gave
   us that life.*

CONTENTS

While I appreciate a quality product and a good return on my investments, I have always suspected that business exists for something beyond just *things*—for something more human, for some higher purpose. Now that the *management* of business organizations is becoming more a matter of *leadership* and more concerned with people than with things, we should all wonder why management does not lead in ways that reflect what people really are—spiritual beings. Why do we adhere to the assumption that, in business, it is mandatory to avoid matters of the spirit? That denial of what we really are restricts our economic activities to using only part of ourselves and serving only part of us. As a result, we shortchange ourselves both economically and spiritually.

My puzzlement has become even more pronounced as management began struggling over the past decade to generate such things as spirit and teamwork. This trend coincides with the increase in Americans' interest in spirituality—or at least their talk about it. Unfortunately, most of the spirit and spirituality talk related to business has been guarded, so that we do not discuss the source of that spirituality. Why is this happening in a nation that considers itself religious, in fact, dominantly Christian? There are millions of Christians in the workplace playing by the rules of the business game, but there seems to be little Christian influence at the top permitted to set those rules.

I have long known top executives who are successful in business and Christian in their personal lives. What really intrigued me, however, was the possibility that there are a significant number who really walk the Christian talk in their business leadership roles. If we could find them and learn something about them, perhaps they could offer us meaningful insights into leadership and the role of business in our lives.

So I made a commitment to track down these walkers and research a book on them, to answer a long list of questions, such as: How do Christians who are company executives or owners conduct their business according to their faith? Does their behavior enhance their companies' profitability or harm it? How do they treat their customers, vendors, and employees? What are some of the specific things these executives do, and how do they do them in a way that does not offend others or cross legal limits?

Often, when I told friends I was working on a book about Christians in business leadership, they seemed to think it had to be a work of fiction. "Have you found any yet?" they would ask. Or they would snicker, "Christian executives? That's an oxymoron!" Some assured me, "You won't find any in our company!"

I did manage to find them, however. In every case, I first verified with others that the person I would study was truly walking his or her faith, not simply talking about it. I was seeking leaders who were Christ-centered, and that meant bypassing many who were Christians only because they said so or thought so.

Then I conducted in-depth interviews across the country with more than forty such executives in small, family-owned companies and publicly owned corporations with billions of dollars in sales. None were advertising their faith, but all were willing to spend considerable time with me in one or more conversations about it. Not one of these executives requested anonymity. Rarely did they ask that any portion of our discussion be off the record. I have, however, bestowed anonymity when I thought a comment might cause embarrassment to the individual or to some other person mentioned.

As I progressed in my research and reflected on it, I realized that the outward behavior of Christian executives does not get at the heart of the vital truth to be revealed. It is their inner faith, the worldview by which these executives operate, which causes them to see things differently from the way most of us see things, and then to exhibit different behavior from the rest of us. I found that they approach life and work from a biblical perspective and yet operate successfully in the secular realm, as they take leadership roles in restoring the world that God saw as good. Because they see the spiritual and secular "worlds" as one, they tap into the power of our interconnectedness on both the spiritual and physical planes. This, I came to discover, was only one of the many paradoxes that characterize these executives.

A growing number of leading thinkers are calling for us to rise to a higher consciousness and break out of the dualistic thinking that separates the spiritual from the secular. These Christ-centered executives demonstrate that it is possible to make a profound shift in mindset. They offer us the hope that we can undergo transformation individually so we can link together and work to change the world for the better.

Someone once suggested to me once that the first Reformation put the Bible in the hands of lay people and the second Reformation will put the *work* of God in the hands of lay people. I believe that the next Reformation will be led, in large part, by the business community. I believe that the Spirit of God is moving among people in the business world as much as or more than in any sector of our society. No one knows whether there are more Christian executives in the late 1990s than there were ten years ago or twenty years ago, but more and more leaders are openly expressing their beliefs and striving to follow biblical principles as they lead their companies.

By no means have I written this book to help anyone succeed in business by simply copying the behavior of the leaders about whom I am writing. In the first place, I am more concerned about our being successes in *life*. Second, my objective is not to present the exterior manifestations of the Christian faith as elements from which to model business leadership, but to describe the faith and the frame of reference that allows some leaders to be successful in life as well as in work. Perhaps, after learning what goes on in the hearts and minds of these leaders, the reader will come to wonder how any leader of the future could succeed without being grounded in the spiritual. Business leaders may come to appreciate that the values and principles they would like to see guiding their organizations come not from management seminars but from the spiritual realm.

It is my hope that a look at the faith in action of successful Christian leaders will help young men and women who are trying to reconcile their faith with the demands of their work. I hope, too, that top executives and middle managers will come to realize that it is possible to blend their spiritual and secular lives and step out in faith to do God's work.

There are no prescriptions in the following pages. At best, you may come to identify what is wrong with our prevailing attitudes about faith and business and then search for your own route to spiritual health. The road is not an easy one.

The people we study here have not chosen some vague, self-centered spirituality to make themselves feel good. The lives they have undertaken are highly demanding, because the people themselves are responding to a high calling.

ACKNOWLEDGMENTS

As I was completing work on an earlier book, I was also considering several ideas for future books. But which idea should I develop next? I posed this dilemma to John Willig, my friend and literary agent. "This is the one you're most clearly focused on and committed to. Go for it," he urged.

At the same time, several good friends with whom I had shared the idea of writing a book on Christian business executives urged me to do it, and to go beyond merely reporting. "You are writing this book because it's important to you," one pointed out. "You should express your views—what you have observed in business, in the church, and elsewhere."

Encouragement came from non-Christians as well as from Christians. I found that the truly spiritual are eager to hear others' expressions of faith.

So I committed to seeking out these executives. Several persons recommended that I meet Don Kline, a vice president of the Fellowship of Companies for Christ International (FCCI). During our first meeting, he invited me to an FCCI meeting in Florida the following week. I didn't know the content, exact dates, or the hotel at which the event was being held. When I told my wife, Carol, about the invitation, her first words were, "You've got to go!" I booked my flights and gambled on getting to the right place on the right dates. The three-day immersion into this group got me rolling.

From there it has been a whirlwind of meeting people who in turn put me in contact with others. For those leads I am deeply thankful. And I cannot thank enough those busy persons I interviewed. They were most gracious in setting appointments and sharing their deepest thoughts with me.

All along, my wife, Carol, continued to give her support for my travel, telephone interviews, reading, and writing.

Don Kline was kind enough to read the first draft of the manuscript closely and offer constructive criticism and encouragement.

David Krueger read some of the early chapters and offered valuable suggestions.

John Willig never let up on giving good advice and encouragement as he worked his way to the folks at Prima Publishing, who were daring enough to produce a book that straddles that fence between secular and religious publishing.

My friend and supporter Frank Larkin made many phone calls from Atlanta and sent many e-mail messages to offer ideas and show my own thoughts back to me in a new light.

Shawana Johnson generously shared her research on Gordon Heffern, as well as her own views on faith and business.

Along the way, numerous synchronicities occurred in the creation of this book: attendance at a yearlong class at church that grounded me in the biblical explanation of humanity's need for work, years of participation in a weekly Bible study group that sensitized me to the challenges that men and women of faith encounter in business, books and articles recommended by friends, new books that I stumbled across, old books on my shelves that I dug back into and found passages I had marked years earlier. (The many references listed in the bibliography represent very little deliberate research on my part. All but a few were books with which I had become acquainted in my "normal" course of reading.)

I did not write this book alone. Thank God.

Note: All biblical quotations are from the New International Version, Zondervan Publishing House.

PART I

Reuniting the Sacred and the Secular

ONE

The Fruits
of Their Faith

In all of history, there has never been a nation that generated the material wealth that America does today. Yet we suffer from widespread poverty–not only the very apparent economic poverty of millions of people, but the less obvious spiritual poverty of perhaps many millions more.

In an˙era when our chief resources are our brains and our hearts, we seem to have unlimited potential to increase our economic power. We will never match our economic performance with our economic needs, however, unless we first attend to our spiritual poverty. This would involve changing our perceptions of our needs and the means with which we meet them. Unfortunately, we are restrained by a corporate and societal environment that obscures our spiritual reality and prevents us from fully engaging our hearts and minds.

No amount of technique, training, or tinkering will create a healthy economy atop a society that is not healthy in human terms. No amount of analyzing the world from a business point of view will substitute for establishing a sound worldview and then making business serve it.

No amount of management effort to "empower people" or build teamwork will offset an employee's lack of trust of the company and the hundreds of subtle ways that organizations reveal a fundamental disrespect for the humanity of the employee and even the customer. Furthermore, regardless of the environment, people can empower themselves only when they come to an understanding of who they really are, what their purpose is, and what they really value.

SPIRITUAL FOUNDATION

Many executives have worked hard during recent years to change their worldviews; attach themselves to deeper, more lasting values; and build more productive work communities. A few of them have succeeded in doing so when they were able to remain in touch with their spiritual dimension in their daily work. They then found themselves in a good position to make the best use of what we have learned intellectually about creating effective organizations. In 1998, Bernie Nagle and I published *Leveraging People and Profit*. We described a person we dubbed "the altrupreneur—one who conducts the affairs of an enterprise with conspicuous regard for the welfare of others." We explored what makes these people tick, and found it was that spiritual dimension that gave them an other-centeredness.

People can empower themselves only when they come to an understanding of who they really are, what their purpose is, and what they really value.

While we found that a fundamental spirituality drives these leaders, we did not address the questions: How do you acquire that drive that emanates from outside the material world? How do you acquire a worldview that leads you to be other-centered? How can you rise to a worldview that elevates other people, that instills the values that make the world go 'round and even help business succeed? How can you come to the point where you are constantly driven to do what is right? And how can you hold to that worldview no matter what the day-to-day circumstances?

Most American business managers do not approach their work from a spiritual perspective. They take, instead, a business point of view. They think in Cartesian dualistic terms, and thereby separate the physical world from the spiritual realm. They also employ Newtonian thinking and see the world as a machine made up of separate, distinct parts. Operating, then, in a separatist, individualistic mode, they regard people as things—as parts of an economic machine. This view is self-limiting, however. No matter how much they may spend on management improvement techniques, they never really grapple with the full realities of what it means to be human and to create organizations of human beings.

Many of us refrain from giving our business organizations all that we can, and our organizations are failing to allow us to *be* all we can.

As a result, business in general is not addressing the real issues of being stewards of the universe. Not surprisingly then, many of us refrain from giving our business organizations all that we can, and our organizations are failing to allow us to *be* all we can. We are not meeting the deepest needs of all our stakeholders. We fail to commit to issues such as hunger, environmental harm, and personal dysfunction—not because of a lack of capabilities but because our worldview causes a clash in intentions, and values, and priorities.

A more limited number of managers, however, have worldviews that provide the proper foundation for improvement techniques and enable them to use these tools effectively over the long term. One of those worldviews is that of certain Christians. Yes, we *can* find in business Christian managers who live out their faith in loving action. They are successes, first in human terms, and second in business terms. They approach all aspects of business leadership dramatically differently from those who put business success first.

We have long regarded business as a world unto itself; we have separated it from the spiritual and, especially, the sacred. Even the Christian church has contributed to this division of upper world versus lower world over the centuries with its preachings and teachings that range from advocating avoidance of secular matters to merely coping with them.

Some Christians, however, see the secular as created by God with the intention that humankind will be stewards of it—lead it, not ignore it. They do not buy into the common dualism. They are not on the fence between the two worlds; for them, there is no fence; there is no need to "balance" their lives. They do not withhold themselves from the "secular world"; they are proactive in making the secular a reflection of the sacred. Rather than rejecting the world that humans have fabricated and letting it go at that, their faith drives them to work at co-creating the world that God wants. When they hear Christ's admonition to be "in the world but not of it," they understand both parts. He directs His followers to avoid the ways that humans have established in the world, but He does not suggest that they remove themselves from it.

They do not ask the question, "Is there a place for spirituality in business?" Instead, they define the role that business is to play in the world by allowing knowledge of the sacred to provide the "why"—the purpose—for their being in this world. Their role is to be the salt that changes the character of the world or the light that shows the better way.

For more than thirty-five years, I have been studying management—overtly as a business magazine editor, and less obviously, as a member of upper management. At the same time I have been a member of Bible study groups, church discussion groups, spiritual formation groups, and men's retreat staffs. In business, I became well acquainted with executives who showed no signs of letting any awareness of their spiritual dimension affect their business behavior. I was excited more and more frequently in recent years, however, to find some managers who expressed a deep sense of spirituality—spirituality in a broad sense of the word. The word may relate to the spirit or the unseen as opposed to the material; it may refer to fundamental, universal principles or a set of morals; it may include thoughts and emotions.

WALKERS VERSUS TALKERS

But were Christians among these spiritual managers? Sure, in the management ranks there are many people who regularly attend church, yet some of them fall into that group that shows no sign of letting their faith affect their business behavior. "Not all Christians walk the faith. Sometimes you find more integrity in the secular community," admits Dick Leggatt, vice president of the Ohio Roundtable, a group that works to restore traditional principles to public policy. While they may temper their competitiveness and or their scramble for material gain, they are still locked in the sacred/secular dilemma. They may turn their Christianity on to help them, or they may turn it off so it doesn't get in their way. Wearing a removable badge of Christianity, they listen to the message on Sunday, but whether they practice it Monday through Friday depends on the situations they encounter or the roles in which they find themselves.

Daniel Hanson, president, Fluid Products Division, Land O'Lakes, Inc., asks the crucial question: "People can say the right words, but are they living the values? If they are Christians, are they showing it in their actions?"

Yes, there are Christian executives who, like nominal Christians in all walks of life, fail to live out the central Christian message of love. They pay their vendors late, if at all; take unfair advantage of customers; or show disregard for the welfare of others as they pursue their own gain. Or they permit their employees to do so. At the other end of the spectrum, we find Christians who go overboard in expressing their religious views and even politicizing them. Whether they are liberals taking to the streets to make militant demands on society or conservatives walling themselves off against anyone with different beliefs, neither type displays the integrity that others expect of the fully Christian person.

Added to these two extremes, by default, are those people who are simply overwhelmed by rules of the "secular world" and lack the confidence to live out their faith or express it verbally.

Through all of its history, Christianity has suffered the sins of those who have done things in the name of Christ without really living in the spirit of His message or revealing His spirit at work in them. Yet I suspected that there were Christians who really walk the talk, who succeed in spanning both the material and spiritual realms and living out their faith in all aspects of their lives, rather than insisting that spirituality and the world of business be kept separate.

So, over a two-year period, I conducted a deliberate search for and conducted interviews with executives who are Christ-centered and live out the Christian message in their personal and professional lives. We might say they are *in the company of Christ* for two reasons: (1) They believe their organization—like all things—is ultimately owned by Christ and is in the service of Christ; and (2) they are in a personal relationship with Christ—they walk in His company.

This means we will be looking at just a segment of a broad array of Christians who have many differing beliefs and practices. I am writing about a minority (by nature of their faith and lifestyles as well as their corporate positions), but an increasingly vocal minority with growing influence on the world around them. In this book, we will look at what distinguishes them from would-be or self-anointed Christians who are not truly Christian in their daily business conduct.

CHRIST-CENTERED LEADERS

From the outside, we see these Christ-centered leaders as focused on Christ, conducting themselves as though they see themselves working *beside* Christ. Internally, they see themselves as having Christ in the center of their consciousness, perhaps in the center of their very being. Christ is there, working *through* them.

> Christ-centered leaders see themselves as having Christ in the center of their consciousness, perhaps in the center of their very being. Christ is there, working *through* them.

They do not admire or worship Christ from afar. They open themselves to the substance of Christ; they do not simply copy His style. They say, "Christ, here is a new me. Make me what You will; work through me." They do not say, "Here I am. Now what shall I borrow from Christ's model?"

Christ, not their egos, is the center for their lives. They do not patch on certain behaviors they have learned from Christ; they are reflecting His presence. They do not use Christ to further their ego needs.

Christ-centered people are not all alike, nor do they look alike. The blend of the human and Divine takes different forms, creates different gifts or skills, and prepares them for different roles. When their role is that of a leader, they demonstrate love and concern for their followers, win others to a common cause, and lead to the unknown rather than maintaining the status quo.

These Christian business leaders have their feet on the ground. While they are deeply spiritual, they involve themselves actively in the secular world. Their lives—business and personal—are centered on Christ and His work and clearly demonstrate what they believe. Some of them are highly visible as they speak their views at company meetings, head up charitable efforts, or write books. Others are a little harder to spot unless you work for them or do business with them and witness the quiet actions that distinguish them. They work at disciplining themselves in order to align themselves with God in everything they do.

Carole Hamm, one of the owners of Country Cupboard Inn and restaurants, which employ 350 persons in Lewisburg, Pennsylvania, says that when she was new in her faith in Christ someone asked her, "Do you have to see Christianity in *everything*?" She recalls that even then she thought that was important to the integrity of her faith. "I was so new in my faith at the time I wasn't sure what the answer was supposed to be, but I said, 'I think you do. Because I think if you don't then it doesn't connect for myself and those things that I do.' This is not a faith of weakness. This is not a faith of convenience. This is difficult work."

In her study of evangelical Christian executives, Laura Nash found three types of responses to the moral conflicts in business: *generalists* who ignore the conflicts, *justifiers* who deny them, and *seekers* who are aware of them and are somehow a mediating factor "in the ongoing tensions between the musts of religion and the musts of business. The seekers reject the idea of business success as an ultimate value, and yet they are extraordinarily able to manage their business activities so that the result is economic success" (Nash 1994, p. xiii).

It is in this group of seekers you will find the Christ-centered leaders I am writing about. Nash, too, finds that this group "provides the best example of active faith." The seeker "confronts the tensions between Christian belief, human failing, and economic practicality" and "seeks out a course of action consistent with Christianity" (p. 45).

I must point out that the people I'm talking about don't like to label themselves. C. William Pollard, chairman of the $6 billion ServiceMaster Company, says, "I don't like to label people. When I talk about my faith I like to describe it as the fact that I'm a follower of Jesus Christ." It's important to note, too, that these executives seldom, if ever, refer to their faith as *religion*. Those whom I have interviewed are less concerned about doctrine and ritual than they are about having a *relationship* with Christ.

John Shumate, who heads up Shumate Development Company in Columbus, Ohio, says, "People think I am a religious person. Far from it. I have a relationship with Christ Jesus, not a religious experience. Do you have a wedding ring on? Would you go home to your wife after a hard day's work and be *religious* to her, or would you go home and have a genuine one-on-one relationship with her? That's all God wants to do with us—have a one-on-one relationship from the heart. That's why He created us."

FINDING GENUINE SUCCESS

The purpose of this book is not to relate one financial success after another or to offer up a carrot for adopting Christianity as a means of achieving business success. It is, rather, to show how some executives have found a higher order of success and avoided the confusion and disorientation of trying to live in two separate worlds. It is about soul, not stock options. And yet, it will offer some insight as to why leaders who deal at the soul level and, therefore, address fundamental issues are building successful new millennium enterprises.

For Christ-centered leaders, the *sacred* is not some vague spiritual notion, but a very real force that they allow to shape their lives. They do not pick and choose their values to fit secular needs, but live them out in response to commandments. They do not borrow the teachings of Christ to be more effective leaders; they are effective leaders because they live out the teachings of Christ and work to fulfill His purpose for them. Because they are very much at home in the world that God created, it should not be surprising that they can succeed in it.

To understand their personal and business successes, we have to appreciate the fact that these business leaders do not gauge their success in secular terms. They measure success in terms of how well they are fulfilling God's expectations of them as individuals who are called to shape the secular world according to spiritual principles. They are successes, not as a matter of where they are, but of knowing why they are there. Their expectations of themselves are based on being effective as stewards of a world created by a sacred being and of the talents and situations presented to them for doing so.

Let's examine Christ-centered business leaders to see what we can learn from them. Let's not simply look for models to copy superficially, but learn what makes them fundamentally different in worldview from the many who fail to address human needs and from those who engage in trial-and-error searches for something that will provide meaning as they lose themselves in the secular realm.

> The fruits of their faith show up not in just their individual lives but in the lives of others in their organizations— their customers, their suppliers, their stockholders—and the communities around them.

I do not claim that the number of executives who walk in the company of Christ is soaring. I am convinced, however, that more and more of them are becoming visible, that they are coming forth with actions that testify to their faith and serve the temporal and eternal needs of those who are touched by their lives.

The fruits of their faith show up not in just their individual lives but in the lives of others in their organizations—their customers, their suppliers, their stockholders—and the communities around them. We see more and more cases of company prayer meetings and Bible study. We see mission statements that are openly Christian. We know there are Christians in the workplace—but in the upper ranks of companies? Yes! In the following chapters, we will explore how some top executives and company owners live out Christian values as they lead their organizations, shape the values by which those companies operate, and show us what it takes to meet our deepest needs.

TWO

The Soul's Hunger

We are a nation in need—a deep-seated need for *something*, the lack of which prompts us to come up with endless wish-lists and to-do lists. In some ways, we live in a wonderful country. We have unmatched freedoms. We have an economic machine that lavishes upon us a seemingly endless flow of products and experiences. Yet, we have a deep sense that something is missing. We need something that our economy does not, and, we suspect, cannot supply. That something is about relationship—relationship with oneself or one's soul, relationships with other persons, and a relationship with a higher being or greater purpose.

The "relationship from the heart" to the people around us that John Shumate spoke of in chapter 1 is out of place in many quarters today, especially in corporate environments. We are more likely to find people working halfheartedly, managers with hard hearts or no heart, and workers at all levels who are softhearted but ineffective. We cannot dismiss this truth by saying, "That's too bad." The absence of strong relationships, those that come from the heart, constitutes the reason for many of the problems in our personal and corporate lives and makes our freedom of little value. The absence of relationships that come from the heart diminishes our freedom to be what we were intended to be.

IN SEARCH OF THE L-WORD

Relationships from the heart are *love* in its broadest sense. The Christian concept of love is not a matter of chemistry, magic feelings, sentimentality, or intimacy. It is *agape*—a noble form of love. It does not begin with feelings or emotions; in fact, they may even be absent. We sometimes have to lift ourselves from apathy or negative feelings to generate concern for the interests of other persons and to demonstrate as much concern for them as for ourselves.

Michael Prewitt, chairman of Dana Communications and a student at the Princeton Theological Seminary, says, "Love is an act of will. It's often counterintuitive. We're human beings. We are not God's children 100 percent of the time. What we think of as love and those warm feelings may not have anything to do with our doing God's will in the world and being the love of God in the world." We are, after all, commanded by God to love others. We have the freedom to obey that command, to make the decision to love others.

Loving others has to do with the oneness of the universe. Since we are made in the image of God, we are connected not only to God but to one another and to the entire Creation. What the scientist might call "connectedness" is what the Christian calls "love." Love is a matter of caring, concern, compassion, and connectedness. Love is a matter of the will, which rules the heart and, therefore, it does not just *happen*.

The Bible contains many romantic love stories. Yet the love story that best exemplifies what Christ meant when He commanded us to love God and to love others is the familiar one of the Good Samaritan. When a man was felled by robbers and lay on the side of the road, both a priest and a Levite (a high-ranking servant of the temple) passed by him. Only a Samaritan, an undesirable in the eyes of the Jews of the time, stopped to care for the man. Christ asked, "Which of these three was a neighbor to the man who was felled?" Helping a fallen stranger, the Samaritan was not *in* love with him but acted out of love *for* him.

Love for others leads one to dealing honestly, with a sense of fairness and justice, and with humility and self-discipline—values taught by all the world's major religions. When we love, we are directed by the values on which our nation and even our economy were built. In his book *Rediscovering American Values,* Dick DeVos, president of Amway Corporation, reminds us of these essential values. In addition to honesty, fairness, humility, and self-discipline, he speaks of such values as reliability, compassion, courage, service, cooperation, forgiveness, and stewardship.

In leadership positions, the challenge to love everyone becomes magnified by the number of persons who have a stake in or are affected by the organization. As we shall discuss in chapter 14, there are times when we must choose between the interests of an individual and those of the group. Some stakeholder groups are more vocal or more attractive than others. Some individuals are easier to like than others. The choices are not always simple, but the leader must rise above favoritism and apply the same standards to all. Even at that, he or she may have to suffer the pain of making choices when there is no clear-cut right or wrong.

It is fairly obvious, however, that business today is not being driven by these values or by sensitivity to the dilemmas they may create. Not only do we lack a base of love for our business organizations, many of us would scoff at the notion that love applies to business. This lacking is "built in," Kevin Cashman, president of LeaderSource, told me as we sat on the patio outside his office in Minneapolis. "We have banned the 'L-word' from business—the substance that unifies teams, builds cultures, fosters commitment, and bonds people to an organization."

Through our lawmaking, regulation setting, and management practices, we are institutionalizing the opposite of love—indifference. We feel compelled to refrain from expressing our concern, our love, or—God forbid—our faith, lest we lose our jobs or even be sued. (But it's not "God forbid"; it's *we* forbid.)

We are beginning to rebel against indifference, however. We long for relationships. We are not searching simply for someone to love us; we are searching for ways to express the love that is within us. We are filled with the energy that love is. "Love is not a passive state. It is an active force. It is the force of the soul," says Gary Zukav. "It brings a different way of being in the world. It brings harmony and an active interest in the well-being of others. It brings concern and care. . . . It washes away the concerns of the personality" (Zukav 1989, p. 231).

We are not searching simply for someone to love us; we are searching for ways to express the love that is within us.

Love comes from a deeper level than the emotions. It is an outpouring of the energy of our souls. Rather than simply an emotional reaction to something, it releases emotions such as joy, excitement, conviction or sense of purpose, and compassion for others. Regrettably, our institutionalized society restricts the flow of this energy.

TOXIC ME-ISM

Love supports the health and well-being of the object of love and of the one who loves. It cements relationships. When it is lacking, we feel the pain of being outside the world rather than being part of it. Without love, we cannot build genuine community.

Especially when we are at work, more and more of us are realizing that not only is something missing, but that the environment has turned toxic. Countless conversations, Internet chat rooms, and even newspaper comics reveal our concern about "a toxic work environment." Several years ago, when my wife had cancer, only one of my nine top management colleagues asked—beyond the first time—how she was doing during the long months of surgery and radiation treatments. I realized that I, too, was in a toxic environment. This indifference was the stuff that was driving the organization, allowing—or causing—it to fall far short of the wonderful work that could come from its more than 1,000 members. Management, with its efforts to drive the numbers up a few percentage points here or there, was totally oblivious to the immeasurable potential that it was failing to tap.

A cancer has spread throughout business—in fact, throughout our society. Fear, mistrust, and even terror suppress the spirit within us. One company drastically reduced the number of jobs in a particular department and restructured it, putting the leftover people into a short-term "pool" from which other departments might select them for new jobs. "Sure there have been a lot of tears around here," says the department head, who was out of town when top management began the restructuring! "What you see now is people—even those who kept their jobs—walking around with terror on their faces." Management's lack of compassion and civility created a bad situation for those who retained their jobs or found new ones internally as well as for those who were put out on the street. All were victims of management's lack of "relationship from the heart."

Referring to the sweeping restructuring and downsizing of the 1990s, one professional worker, who elected to leave the corporate world after working for a series of toxic bosses and go into business for herself, says, "All the people who have lost their jobs or who are still frightened and trying to keep their jobs were feeling terrible pain as all this wonderful restructuring was taking place."

The organization suffers pain and loss, too. When management tries to change the environment by restructuring or downsizing, it is likely to do more than displace the individual. Because people insistently and covertly build community, management's ax-swinging injures the communities that are creating the wealth. Ironically, management has often engaged in elaborate attempts to build teamwork at the very time it is killing off community.

> Management has often engaged in elaborate attempts to build teamwork at the very time it is killing off community.

When we don't have love, we turn inward. We become selfish. We hold back from our neighbors. We don't give our best to the organization. Envy and greed take over our lives. We view the world around us in terms of what it can do for us. Since we are determined to get what we can for ourselves, not surprisingly we then see the world as a competitive, if not hostile, place. We teach our children to look out for Number 1 and spread the toxicity of me-ism farther and farther.

In the workplace, we perform only for a paycheck, and our managers see us only as recipients of the paychecks they reluctantly sign. Any productivity or quality improvements are mere fractions of what fully committed people could achieve. In the long run, our selfishness restricts what we are, what we do, and what we become—as individuals and as members of organizations.

Selfishness breeds selfishness. Because of that, we have the added problem of toxic organizations weakening good people. Even if we do not want to play the organizational game, we are affected by it anyway. It can lead us to be less than we can be or want to be. Without realizing it, we may attempt to fit in with the environment, either for personal comfort or to be positioned politically to do what we think we must do—or perhaps both. We make compromises. We display bad behavior and become persons we didn't intend to be. We become victims of our own negative emotions.

By overvaluing our individuality, we allow marketers to exploit our self-oriented values. By being concerned more about ourselves than about others, we don't even know how to approach the Divine. Looking out at the world as though each of us is the center, we cannot grasp the truths about the world we live in.

We have made so much of individualism that we forget the Americans before us who built this nation in community. People used to be born into large families and small towns. They were in community whether they liked it or not. Even in the Wild West, people relied on neighbors and government infrastructure to open the frontier. Today, we are in smaller families, if any at all, and our neighborhoods are often not really communities. Whether we are in community with others largely depends on our deliberately *choosing* to join and taking steps to create the bonds of community, whether it be in the neighborhood, the church, the social group, or the workplace.

We speak of corporate culture, but that is often a superficiality, a contrivance. Culture is not as rich or as deeply meaningful as genuine community. We talk, too, of networking, of making a series of connections with people to engage in projects together. Networking may be an exciting new way of doing business, but it is not based on relationships that come from the heart. In management circles, we speak of creating teamwork, without truly recognizing that we are interdependent to begin with.

SEEKING SPIRITUALITY

Restructuring and downsizing notwithstanding, all the activity around worker participation, teamwork, and empowerment has opened the door to people's seeing the need to be and the possibility of becoming what they want to be. As more and more people work toward self-development and self-actualization, they will explore the ethical and spiritual considerations of life. As American business began exploring quality circles and other forms of worker participation in the early '80s, I could see that the resultant personal growth would inevitably lead to questions of who one is and why one exists. It would lead to questions beyond the self. (Pascarella 1984, p. 184)

Millions of Americans now seem to be thinking, "All these material things are great, but I want something more out of life!" But many of them realize that they stand naked, with neither spiritual connection nor social agreement to give purpose to their lives and, especially, their work. Surveys show that one of the prime needs that people want to address in their lives is that of intimacy, of belonging. They want relationships and love. They are turning to spirituality in search of genuine connections.

In all ages and most places humankind has sensed and, at times, been driven by a spiritual dimension, a sense of the sacred. Despite the various manifestations and means of expression, this reality of the species has persisted. "Spirituality, by definition, addresses the world of spirit, the soul, and the sacred. . . . It is fostered by certain beliefs, attitudes, and behaviors. We see indications of our spiritual development in our relationship with the material world," writes Dorothy Marcic in *Managing with the Wisdom of Love* (1997, p. 2). "The spiritual laws that govern human behavior have been articulated for thousands of years by all the world's religions and schools of philosophy, with remarkable consistency. At the core of all these guiding principles is one fundamental law from which all others spring: love your neighbor," says Marcic (p. 3).

Since they do not accommodate this love for our neighbors, we have to conclude that our business institutions are not being shaped by spiritual laws. There are very few, if any, corporate mission statements, values declarations, or codes of behavior that make any reference to love, spirituality, or the sacred. We don't talk spirituality in management meetings, and it's seldom the topic of conversation around the water cooler.

Yet spirituality is here among us. For some people, their spirituality shapes their lives. For others, spirituality haunts them, as they reject twinges of conscience and behave as they think they must in the "business world." And others are unaware, unconcerned. Yet, I am convinced the overwhelming majority of us fall into the first two groups. Even in the toxic workplace, we can find pockets of love and spiritual health, but they are underground; they don't fit the prevailing corporate culture.

Awareness and concern are on the rise, however. Our spirituality is always present, but spiritual awareness or searching has been surging in the United States since the mid-1980s. More and more of us are willing to peel back the secular surface and confront the difficult questions: "What is life?" and "What is the good life?" We know, or at least suspect, that our quality of life and our personal well-being depend at a deep level on interpersonal relationships and spiritual connection.

In its October 6, 1997 issue, *Time* magazine ran a cover story on the Promise Keepers' huge "Stand in the Gap" gathering in Washington. In its very next issue, the magazine ran a cover story on Buddhism. Something is going on! Dr. Kenneth Goodpaster, professor of business ethics at the University of St. Thomas, says that the school has designed a new MBA course on spirituality and the modern manager. He explained to me that the course is a response to students' search for "balance in their lives." At St. Thomas, he estimates, about 70 percent of the undergraduates and 30 percent of the graduate students are Catholic. Greater numbers are Christians in general; perhaps

95 percent arc believers of some kind. Across the country we find people who want to learn how to relate their faith to the hard realities they the encounter in business. Is there a corresponding rise in interest from the corporate side? "No question about it," he said.

Although religion is more than a source of guidance for moral behavior, the moral dilemmas we are creating for ourselves are prompting more and more people to look to religion as the only way out. Max Stackhouse, professor of Christian ethics at Princeton Theological Seminary, believes we are seeing an upsurge of Christian evangelicalism, Roman Catholicism, Hinduism, Islam, Buddhism, and Confucianism "not simply because people are fearful of change and are seeking old-fashioned certitudes in the face of new insecurities." The upsurge reflects "a profound doubt that we can treat moral issues . . . without reference to a . . . right order of things and a vision of divine purpose to the gifts of creation" (Stackhouse 1997, p. 42).

POP SPIRITUALITY

There is a danger that we will look to spirituality merely to extend our secular power or to compensate for disappointment in our secular mess. I would call some of the spirituality being espoused, especially in business management books, "pop spirituality." As someone has warned, "Spirituality is spreading, but it may not be deepening."

While we may welcome the spread of spiritual awareness, we must pause and ask some hard questions about what's going on:

- Are people raising their eyes to God? Or are they elevating themselves to Godlike status?
- Are people turning to spirituality for self-satisfaction?
- Is spirituality, in all its forms, a unifying force or is it divisive?
- Is spirituality being used to show us how to live better in the secular world or to escape from it?

"We ought to strike the word *spiritual* from the English language," Michael Prewitt says in an interview.

It now implies some kind of sentimentality, which is the worst possible thing for us to be involved in. We think that somehow, if we're sitting there and very caringly lighting candles and listening to soft music, we're doing God's work.

I think we need to learn about the great mystical tradition, but frankly I think the mystical tradition would say the same thing—it's not about me or my deep feelings. It's about the fact that some huge outside force overwhelmed me and I was, due to God's grace, receptive to it. It's not that I went deep down inside myself, got quiet and meditated, and there was some feeling of God. But isn't that the way to reach God—"Be still and know that I am God"? Yes, but we have taken that and turned it into a kind of New Age individualistic pursuit of spiritualism which is just not where we need to be.

Even if we look to the growing *religious* aspect within the more general spiritual movement, we might find some of it *pop religion*. We must ask, "Are the people involved because they are searching for what *they* want or for what *God* wants for them? Are they changing their lives to meet God's commandments, or are they exercising their American individualism to design a god that fits their needs?"

We may be tempted to use religion to cope with our personal problems, seek what we want, justify our ungodly actions, or salve our conscience as we "love mankind" while being indifferent to the individuals around us. In a self-oriented society, we are inclined to extend our egos rather than position ourselves in relationship to a supreme being, to seek what we want rather than what God wants.

Thomas Merton warned more than three decades ago: "The mere fact that men are frightened and insecure, that they grasp at optimistic slogans, run more frequently to Church, and seek to pacify their troubled souls by cheerful and humanitarian maxims, is surely no indication that our society is becoming 'religious.' In fact, it may be a symptom of spiritual sickness" (Merton 1963, p. 14).

In times of illness, there is the danger that we will take the wrong medicine—any that happens to be around. We might assume that all spirituality is created equal. We might brew one concoction after another. But there is a critical difference between constructing a religion and responding in faith to God.

WALLING OFF RELIGION

Many of the people who are writing books on spirituality or speaking about it at business conferences emphasize that they are talking about spirituality in its "broad definition." They insist that we put a wall around religion and stay out of that territory. (I can't help wondering, then, if God isn't doing some head shaking as we bar any discussion of spirituality that has to do with the source of it.)

Yet, this sterile concept of spirituality seems to run counter to widespread religious interest. In survey after survey about 95 percent of Americans say they believe in God. Forty percent or more say they have attended church in the past week. Ninety percent say they pray. (But what they pray for includes such things as good grades, victory in sports, and material possessions.) From 1974 to 1996, the number of religious TV stations grew from 9 to 257. Nearly 90 percent of Americans consider themselves Christians. Sales of "Christ-honoring products" such as books, bumper stickers, and recorded music grew from $1 billion in 1980 to $4 billion in 1996 (*New York Times Magazine*, 1997).

With this sort of base of religious interest and practice, then, why would anyone insist on separating spirituality and religion? Columnist Dick Feagler puts the religion-spiritual contest into a humorous, yet serious, light:

> A national newspaper took a poll and asked Americans how many considered themselves religious. A sizable number said they did. Well, how many considered themselves spiritual? A much larger number said they did.
>
> The results aren't surprising. It is more pleasant to be spiritual than to be religious. Being spiritual means you don't have to follow any rules.
>
> The convenient thing about spirituality is, it isn't about doing. It's about feeling. If you feel spiritual, you can claim you are spiritual. Who's going to call you a liar? Who's going to ask you to prove it? (Feagler 1997, 2A).

There are at least a half dozen reasons why people would want to avoid engaging in discussing religion in business:

1. Religion challenges the foundation as well as the practices of business. It's far easier to manage a business when the business reigns supreme, when it does not have to fit into a more encompassing belief system.

2. Many of the authors who write about spirituality and work strive to be rational, taking a strictly intellectual approach to the world. As they apply only rational processes to what they study, they dissect spirituality from love and the sacred. The business audience to whom spirituality in business writings have been directed are likewise inclined to the rational. They want facts. They want proof. But proof of God lies well outside the realm of our wonderful yet meager rational minds. The basis of all religions is revelation, not reasoning.

3. Many of those who say they believe in God have a tendency to separate God from the world they live in and not let faith or religion interfere with business. "Popular religion in the United States includes at least three perspectives on spirituality, all of which emphasize the separation of the sacred from material life," writes Robert Wuthnow, director of the Center for the Study of American Religion at Princeton University.

> One . . . includes a clear conception of God as a supernatural being and yet removes this God from the day-to-day functioning of most things here on earth. A second view . . . stressing the importance of faith over works, but also making faith so purely a matter of the soul that it seldom has discernible consequences for daily behavior. The third view is a de facto agnosticism that holds forth the possibility of a realm other than one in which we normally live but conceives of this realm with sufficient doubt and in such vague terms that its impact on ordinary conduct is negligible. (Wuthnow, 1996, p. 301)

4. When more than 90 percent of Americans say they believe in God, we don't really know what that means. We have no way of knowing how many simply feel they have to respond that way because they *ought* to believe in God. Their god may represent some vague notion about the possibility that the world was created by a god and the possibility that God may be watching over it or be engaged in it today.

5. Religion can lead to disagreements between adherents of different faiths. It's more efficient to avoid any disagreement about tradi-

tion and ritual than to engage in dialogue about common fundamental principles and values.

6. For many years, the predominant Christian church has made it difficult for outsiders to see a focus on Christ because of *denominational differences*. In addition, mainline churches have been losing ground in recent decades, giving the impression that the faith is failing. Since the Christian body, therefore, seems so divided, it should not be surprising that, to many, it looks too risky to allow it a voice in business.

RENAISSANCE SPIRITUALITY

Within the Christian ranks, the denominations have been softening the lines among themselves. Perhaps this is in response to the fact that many members frankly just don't care about denomination as they shop for churches that meet their needs and interests. Surprisingly, many of the incoming members of the fast-growing, new-style churches reflect less, not more, self-interest than they had prior to their conversion or recommitment. They are interested, rather, in building deep relationships within the family and in the communities around them. While they reject the traditions, hierarchy, and tarnished history of traditional churches, they are digging for the central truths about the Christian faith. They are not simply wallowing in feelings but are engaged in action and playing by some fundamental rules.

Futurist Gerald Celente, in his book *Trends 2000*, wrote in 1997 from the vantage point of the year 2000. Looking back on the '90s, he says,

> A new consciousness was sweeping America, a new spirituality, which was not based upon traditional religion and yet was religious. . . . The new spiritual quest was not in fundamental opposition to traditional organized religion. This new religiosity opposed only the doctrinaire, dogmatic, and authoritarian nature of religions as *institutions*.
>
> Renaissance spirituality was directed toward the attainment of a higher (or divine) state of consciousness. This was originally the basis of all traditional religions. . . . Throughout history, human beings had understood that life had a meaning, collectively and individually. Over the course of the Industrial Age, this understanding had been lost, blurred, or conquered." (Celente 1997, p. 310)

Americans are layered over with organizations for governing, serving, and working. But our organizations too seldom give us meaningful relationships or allow room for our souls. They demand only partial commitment from us and meet only a limited array of our needs. Americans are the beneficiaries of a powerful economic system, but they are learning that the economy does not embrace the ultimate truths of life.

RELIGION CONFRONTS MANAGEMENT

Despite all the troubles we have with religion when it touches our daily lives, we Americans, utilitarians that we are, have managed to fashion a civil religion—one filled with good thoughts and assumptions that we are God-fearing and pursuing a special mission in the world. Yet this self-serving civil religion demands little from us. Furthermore, cautions Stephen Carter, author and professor of law at Princeton University, "Nobody, in the civil religion, is asked to do anything for God" (Stephen Carter 1993, p. 52).

Americans are the beneficiaries of a powerful economic system, but they are learning that the economy does not embrace the ultimate truths of life.

What we are now facing is mounting pressure to go beyond the etiquette of civil religion and to put God in the forefront. For better or for worse, then, religion will be confronting management in the years ahead as people ask of themselves life's big, timeless questions: "Who are we? Why are we here? Where are we going?"

This confrontation can be for the better, under certain conditions. In my book, *The New Achievers*, published in 1984, I looked ahead to what I then detected as a coming surge in spiritual awareness: "If spirituality turns people outward, they will approach their work, their interpersonal relationships, and their institutions with different expectations than people have in recent decades" (Pascarella 1984, p. 77). A sense of becoming and a vision of unity could lead people toward a healthy interdependence" (p. 84).

Today, many of us are scaling the walls between spirituality and religion and between religion and business. We are demanding to express our spirituality at work and build meaningful relationships. We join in discussion groups, Bible reading, and prayer sessions in our workplaces. More and more managers are among those stepping forth to express their faith. People of various religions display not only a recognition of the spiritual but a willingness to make it a central part of their lives.

> Executives who are really Christ-centered do not merely cope with the secular world; they thrive in it. They do not accept it as it is; they know they are commanded to change it.

Among these wall-scalers are Christ-centered executives who regard their faith not as a collection of spiritual ideas or good intentions but a set of convictions to be lived out. While they frequently look inward in reflection, they turn outward for purposeful expression of their faith. The resultant love in action runs counter to the prevailing me-ism and too-narrow definition of what it means to be human.

Although the Christian voice is not often heard in the talk about spirituality that's beginning to make its way into business conferences and literature, these top executives are quietly moving forward day by day with revolutionary ways of doing business.

Although Christianity seems to have been tossed aside in favor of Eastern religions and ideas from new scientific thinking, it is as progressive and relevant to our times as any of them—perhaps more so. In this era of talking about the need for organizational transformation, some Christian executives reveal a dramatically different worldview than that prevailing in the business community as well as in much of American society.

We will see that these leaders, directed by a core of values derived from their different worldview, are able to be far more effective in business than we might expect. Executives who are really Christ-centered do not see two separate worlds—a spiritual one that is good and a secular one that is hopelessly evil. They do not merely cope with the secular world; they thrive in it. They do not accept it as it is; they know they are commanded to change it.

The principles by which they lead are revealed in all the major religions. These rules work in "the real world" because they come from the One who established the rules. It's God's world, God's rules.

THREE

New Corporate Imperatives

The speed and complexity of change in business has escalated to near chaos. It seems the clock is running faster and faster as we near the close of the twentieth century. We are experiencing not only a host of new technologies that are revolutionizing old products and creating new ones, we are facing daily changes in corporate structures and ownership, new ways of relating to one another in organizations, new methods of communicating and learning, new lifestyles—all compounded by the fact that they are increasingly global in origin and reach.

One person alone cannot be aware of all the problems and opportunities that must be addressed if an organization is to reach its goals. Top executives must regard the company's chief assets to be its members' knowledge and ability to learn and adapt. Limits are set more by the mind and heart than by the supply of raw materials. The job of management, then, is to nurture this intellectual capital and apply it to processes, products, and services. And, as we shall see, this is why it is important that a leader adhere to certain universal principles and live by a core of values that will sustain our humanity.

Learning and the ability to solve problems creatively requires widespread collaboration, because significant innovation comes far more often from groups—informal or formal—than from the individual. Whatever their source, innovative ideas do not become implemented solely because of their brilliance. Someone has to make decisions, commit to the idea, and take action. In order to facilitate that process, businesses are struggling to change the content of work and the nature of working relationships.

Since the 1970s American businesses have, for example, made widespread use of teams—quality circles, productivity teams, labor-management participation teams, and so on. The advantage of such teams is that they bring together different knowledge, experience, and viewpoints so that people can build on one another's strengths and come to creative solutions.

If we optimize the management of the new kind of assets—people's knowledge and creativity—collaboration will be the name of the game. Unfortunately, management often lacks experience in fostering collaboration or coaching and providing feedback on performance to develop these most vital assets. That is why we so often hear that managers who say they want quality or excellence or teamwork "don't walk the talk." Management itself hasn't truly bought in to what it advocates.

COMMITMENT, CREATIVITY, COMMUNITY

It is heartening to see that a growing number of managers do regard their jobs as nurturing collaboration, commitment, and creativity. They understand that, more and more often, they will have to call upon people to be flexible and operate in quickly assembled and detached groups. So they are searching for ways to facilitate cooperation and knowledge sharing.

Along the way, they are making some critical observations about leading the new kind of workers and getting results from the new kind of work and working relationships:

1. Collaboration does not come from controlling. The more a job involves service, flexibility, and creativity, the less it is truly control-

lable. Teamwork, therefore, threatens the traditional hierarchy, status, and position power of managers.

2. Employment of teams calls for a new mindset for both worker and manager. The mindset to which we have become accustomed was based on a me-against-the-world attitude; the new one will have to take a we're-in-this-together approach. Instead of paying people for piecework or by the hour, we will have to find ways to pay for cooperative problem solving.

3. Teamwork requires a new kind of compensation. Managers are used to compensating people only in financial terms, so they have to learn to share the

> The quest for quality comes from within the individual, but the attainment of quality often depends on teamwork.

company's financial gains and provide nonfinancial rewards as well. Team participation and inclusion in the corporate decision-making process can provide powerful intrinsic rewards to workers. Participation in teams can be fulfilling, even exciting, as it lifts people to new heights—a step up Abraham Maslow's hierarchy of needs toward fulfillment in nonmonetary terms. But compensating and recognizing people can raise all sorts of questions of fairness, since different people have different wants and needs.

4. Compensating people to participate in teams involves a paradox: The quest for quality comes from within the individual, but the attainment of quality often depends on teamwork. The secret to dealing with this paradox is to remember that teams are not made up of automatons or clones. Teams succeed best when we honor the uniqueness of each member. We innovate, not through groupthink, but through diverse thinking.

5. Leaders have to take the time to confront problems and coach people to top performance. They cannot rely only on financial incentives to entice people to be successful. If leaders do so, they will get some high performance, some low performance, and too much in-the-middle tolerable performance. Leaders have to lead performance upward.

Those of us who have been in the middle-management or lower echelon trenches know how little of our human resources we really bring to bear on our companies' goals. Management often employs the wrong approach to people and sets the wrong objectives. Even when management tries to sustain lofty-sounding programs for empowering people, which it doesn't always do, it can miss the mark.

Daniel Hanson of Land O'Lakes has done a great deal of teaching in business school. The message he gets from his students, most of whom are in the workplace: "On the surface it sounds like organizations are becoming nicer places to work. Down here in the middle of the trenches, they ain't." He says,

> A lot of the students in my classes are forty to sixty years old, and they are the ones who feel the conflict most and want to do something about it. But they don't know where to start, so we have a lot of discussions about starting grassroots movements in organizations and across organizations so that people have somebody to talk to.
>
> There's a frustration with all the programs—people are saturated with them, and they are feeling that the organization is in some ways reverting back to "When the going gets tough the tough get going" and "Let's get back at it here because, after all these programs, we're going to be measured on the next quarter by Wall Street and it isn't going to like our returns if we aren't delivering. And there are still a lot of passive investors out there who don't give a hoot if our values are right."

NEW ASSUMPTIONS ABOUT THE BUSINESS ORGANIZATION

Throughout the industrial age, managers have tried to fit people to organizations. Now, however, we are beginning to struggle with shaping our organizations to fit people. This means we must set aside outdated concepts of the business organization and put new assumptions in their place:

1. An organization's productivity has *human dimensions* beyond simple output-and-input calculations of dollars and things.

2. Productivity reflects the stewardship of our *God-given talents.* It reveals the individual's skills, inventiveness, and accomplishments.

3. The organization serves not just its owners but several *stakeholder groups:* employees, customers, suppliers, and the public.

4. The organization bears considerable responsibility for the *welfare and development* of its members.

5. The organization is involved in the *ethical and moral issues* surrounding it, whether it is so directed by law or not.

6. The organization plays a major role in shaping the *values* of its various stakeholders.

7. Nurturing a *service mentality* produces both a healthier economy and more human growth than nurturing a consumer mentality.

8. Cooperation by *growing persons* is more effective than competition among persons who have been crowded into narrowly defined roles.

9. Work and the work situation can be a rich source of *meaning, identity, personal development,* and a sense of *community.*

> **N**urturing a *service mentality* produces both a healthier economy and more human growth than does nurturing a consumer mentality.

10. Involvement of employees in the decision-making process depends on each organization member's wanting to be part of a *unity* and feeling personally responsible for the welfare of others.

11. Terms like "cooperation" and "teamwork" are no more than slogans unless people genuinely feel a sense of unity and work out of a feeling of *love for all.*

12. Free enterprise is more than competition. It is built primarily on *communities of producers creating value* for communities of customers.

13. Rapid, concurrent changes look like *chaos* to the person who wants to maintain control and stability, but present opportunities for the person who plunges into change and growth with purpose.

14. Corporate purpose begins in the *spiritual* realm with one's worldview and deepest values.

Wayne Alderson, the Christian management consultant who has long advocated "the value of the person," says, "Employees don't want to be regarded as an economic factor" (Alderson 1994, p. 16). The old Theory X and Theory Y management, as well as more modern techniques such as Total Quality Management, are all designed to fit the people to the organization's design; they are confrontational, he says. "Nearly all the people programs in corporations are result-driven." But he believes that people want to contribute unconditionally and therefore he proposes an approach to leadership that is "person-driven" (p. 47). "Many management programs come and go like bouquets of cut flowers, because they have no root—no foundation. Programs bear results, but they do not produce ongoing results unless they are firmly grounded in something basic to human nature: the value of the person" (p. 103).

We have to ask ourselves, "What, then, is the purpose of business?" Business meets secular needs, of course: it provides goods and services for life and it provides livelihood—the wherewithal for purchasing those goods and services. It also meets two spiritual needs: it creates communities of producers, each doing what he or she does best, and enables us to use our skills and knowledge to further the Creation. In short, business is not an end in itself. It is certainly not something to be idolized. It can be a means of being fully human, linking the secular and spiritual into a meaningful whole.

LEADING AT A DEEP LEVEL

The most challenging problems facing corporate leadership involve people's values, feelings, identity, and relationships, but these things are beyond measurement. They are matters not of statistics but of spirit.

Management has begun to use the terms "spirit" and "heart" in discussing what they want from people; however, their interest often comes across as their simply wanting more hustle and commitment. Their discussion seems to reflect something they want to obtain, not to share or nurture.

People demonstrate in many ways that they want work environments that support more concern, more love, more interconnectedness. A sense of purpose burns fiercely in them. Some people express their needs clearly and openly. Others come to work in need of a purpose with which they can identify. Whether it is a deep philosophical inquiry ("What's the purpose of life?") or a more down-to-earth question ("Why am I doing this work?"), people continually express or search for purpose. It is a basic human need that satisfies the search for self-identity and for unity in some larger self. (Pascarella and Frohman 1989, pp. 27–28)

The challenge to management is to relate to what is going on inside people, including themselves, at the deepest levels. Managers may not even realize their tool kits lack the things they need most. Their management techniques aren't working because the techniques are not grounded in what people are all about. Managers are trying to lead their organizations by the numbers, overlooking the essential spirit that drives the people that make up the organization. They fail to deal with the whole person. In fact, they are unable to see the *essential* part of the person.

Despite the disappointments and frustrations we are experiencing, an exciting time could lie ahead. As we move inexorably to widespread participation in decision making, empowerment, and teamwork, we are reaching out and tapping the full potential of what it means to be human. As we search for ways to make greater use of our minds, we inadvertently open the door to our human spirit. That is where we will learn what will fully engage us and what will drive us to accomplishment.

Corporate managers—in fact, most of us—are not comfortable dealing with the human search for significance and relationship in the spiritual realm, and the need to come together in a cooperative community to serve all of an organization's stakeholders. Such challenges certainly don't offer the security of the status quo. They seem to take us into uncharted territory, yet they are the stuff of perennial philosophy and ancient wisdom. People have lived in those realms as far back as history can reveal, but the learning became lost as our secular, Newtonian, industrial paradigm drew a smaller map of reality.

Corporate leaders will have to regain this spiritual ground and rediscover the soul so that they can connect with their true selves and with other people. This is where they will find the fulfillment of what it means to be human. The leaders as well as the led stand at the entrance to a place where we can unleash more of our talents and exercise more of our humanness.

But we have been taught that there's no room for that kind of talk, at least not on company time! Despite all the wealth they generate, our business organizations generally suffer from a poverty of spirit. Workers across the country complain that management doesn't believe in anything but the bottom line and their own compensation packages. Management's belief system has generally come across as little more than the advocacy of free enterprise and individualism. Too often, the manager espousing free enterprise is advocating a negative ideology. It's a me-oriented position with a "leave-me-alone" attitude.

We find it difficult to deal with the spirit issue because our economic system has no spiritual foundation. Despite the fact that many Americans assume a spiritual ethic is built into our political-economic system, the civil religion we have created is not rooted in the spirit or soul.

"The management culture developed during this century has permitted only a rather antiseptic approach to values, morality, and religion. Partly in response to society's insistence that the corporation not interfere with the individual's spirituality, and partly due to scientific management's de-emphasis of the human factors, managers have not had to deal openly with values and beliefs until recently" (Pascarella 1981, pp. 58–59). That's not today's thinking. It's something I wrote at the dawn of the '80s.

MOVEMENT IN MANAGEMENT THINKING

Whenever I get discouraged about the gap between the prevailing management belief system and what I would like it to be, several friends come to my rescue. They embarrass me by pointing out that my own earlier writings reflect how the gap is slowly but surely closing. Those articles and books trace the movement of management thinking toward the desired point of tearing down the walls around values and beliefs and responding to what people want from their economic system and the organizations in which they work.

I realize now that many of my own writings, as well as my selection of other writers' articles to be published in *Industry Week* magazine in the '70s and '80s, reflect three things: my observations of what was going on, my hope for what could be, and my assessment of what a management audience would be willing to read at any given time. To my knowledge, *Industry Week* was one of the first, if not the first, business magazines to deal with such concepts as paradigms, spirituality, and personal breakthroughs. Little by little, management thinking has progressed over the years to the point where we can more comfortably discuss issues and use terms that would not have been acceptable in business discussion a few decades ago.

In the late 1970s, I wrote, "Humanization of the job will progress for two seemingly different yet compatible reasons. It meets the needs of workers—to which a growing number of managers want to respond. It also may be the only means of maintaining or raising productivity levels in a humanizing society" (Pascarella 1979, p. 83). At that time, I was concentrating on appealing to the interest in productivity, although I stressed that productivity had to be measured in human terms.

There are others who now support such thinking. Author Gary Zukav, for example, says, "The 'productivity' of human enterprises will be appraised . . . on their contributions to the spirit" (Zukav 1995, p. 16). Looking ahead, he says,

> When work, like Life, becomes engaging, stimulating, and fulfilling; when fear is absent; when the individual is present by virtue of choice instead of need; when co-workers, with all of their deep difficulties, lessons to learn, and gifts to give, are seen as souls that are learning together how to live and create together in harmony, cooperation, mutual respect, and reverence for Life, business will produce far more than the necessities of physical existence and physical pleasure. It will produce souls of increasing awareness, responsibility, and compassion. (p. 20)

By the early '80s, one could see "the organizational limits we have put on ourselves frequently prevent us from being fully effective in attaining the organization's objectives as well as in realizing our personal goals, but the profession of management was born in hierarchy to master these limitations. So now we find our organizations overmanaged, under-led, and under-achieving" (Pascarella 1981, p. 112). The answer that lay ahead: "The essence of good management is the art of knowing, understanding, and fulfilling human needs" (p. 14).

QUALITY AND CHARACTER

By the mid-1980s, when American management was caught up in cost reduction and productivity improvement, I thought management needed to start thinking about "quality," the buzzword that came along later to capture attention for a decade or more. In a book called *The New Achievers*, published in 1984, I explored what quality would entail on the part of management.

> Both character and quality are based on truth. A person's character is revealed in his or her dedication to all the aspects of quality: the product or service itself, the production and distribution processes and their impact on the environment, the work life of those associated with the product, and the social impact of the product in its usage. If a manager is concerned only about the quality of the product and ignores the quality of the workers' lives or the impact of his business on the environment, he is trying to segment quality. But quality cannot be segmented.
>
> Character has to do with one's search for wholeness, for consistency, for truth, for excellence. Quality of product or service is determined by individuals who can hold out a vision of what can be and then enable others to work toward it. The ability to do that is, in turn, the fundamental measure of the quality of management. American management faces not so much a test of skills as a test of character. (Pascarella 1984, p. 181)

The matter of character would become a critical issue in a few years, as management started slowly began to grapple with the concepts of mission and vision. I have long believed that "we all need a dignity of purpose that we can take into the center of our lives" (Pascarella 1984, p. 23). "People with commitment to values that transcend the economic ones arc those who have proven best at setting out a vision that inspires good economic performance as a by-product of serving some human purpose" (p. 183).

Consistency, truth, and excellence would take us into the realm of ethics, where we have little experience. Yet, I could see that the next breakthrough in management was beginning to take form—"not in some better form of financial analysis or organizational controls" but in the manager's better understanding of what it means to be human (Pascarella 1984, p. 192). This was not just idealism. "Economic necessity will be the flywheel that will maintain the momentum to fashion a new ethical base for the corporation" (p. 101).

Understanding what it means to be human would lead straight through ethics to spirituality because "people are turning inward, reaching outward, and looking upward" (Pascarella 1984, p. 9). "Work may have lost its spiritual aspect in the eyes of many, but people haven't lost their spiritual dimension" (p. 26).

The gap between the corporate way and people's quest for core values and a connection with the Divine means the time is not far off when management will have to deal with spirituality and religious faith. "The workplace is not and should not be a place for sermons and worship, but it will increasingly have to deal with people's ethical, moral, and even spiritual dimension" (Pascarella 1984, p. 101).

It is time to update management science to reflect the truths being reflected by quantum science. It is time to move away from Newtonian thinking.

Would such mushy, touchy-feely stuff undermine the tough management style that we have so carefully developed? "Is the ground swell of management toward purpose and passion a departure from the scientific management that drove American industry to greatness?" I asked in a 1986 article in *Industry Week* (January 6, 1986, pp. 45–50). My answer then (and now): It is time to update management science to reflect the truths being reflected by quantum science. It is time to move away from Newtonian thinking. "Modern science and consciousness theory point toward a new concept of self that is in keeping with many of the world's religions. Concepts of unity of mind and body, of self and others, of self and some greater Self are central to these belief systems."

HIGH LEVEL OF SELFLESSNESS

By the late 1980s, management was tossing around the terms "vision," "mission," and "values." They were writing mission statements and compiling lists of lofty values without getting to the foundation of any of them. They were trying to establish purposeful organizations while holding high the profit motive as the only driving force. There could be no compromise of that purpose, they assumed. They could not engage in anything beyond that. In *The Purpose Driven Organization* (1989), Mark Frohman and I warned, "The sweep of new values will no longer support single-purpose people in single-purpose organizations" (Pascarella and Frohman, 1989, p. 109). We pointed out, too, that leaders could establish meaningful purpose for an organization only if they related to people on a meaningful level and were genuinely concerned about others. "Purpose-driven leaders are trusted because they demonstrate a high level of selflessness. Because their purpose includes serving others, other people are likely to enroll in it" (p. 121).

In 1998, Bernie Nagle and I took that route another mile in writing *Leveraging People and Profit: The Hard Work of Soft Management*. We devoted the entire book to detailing how and why our economic wealth is generated by leaders who are other-centered, not the wheeler-dealers who are the subjects of newspaper articles and novels.

POWER AND GLORY

As we review this progression of management literature, we can see we are on the way to a new type of leader, one who

- embraces wholeness
- reflects good character
- knows what it means to be human

- views the world in a way that incorporates the best scientific thinking
- is driven by a purpose that serves others and, therefore, attracts followers.

A new belief system and a new set of values will have to underlay the character of tomorrow's executives. These attributes are being demonstrated today by the executives who work at putting Christ in the center of all they do. In doing so, they demonstrate that a person can be a successful business leader by leading from the soul.

In business, we tend to measure leadership in terms of power. But these Christian leaders' lives and leadership styles suggest that power is a function of how much they are in touch with their soul, how much they reveal their soul, and how well they engage other souls. In business we are well acquainted with external power, but we know too little about the power of the soul. When we engage ourselves and others at that level, we tap into infinite power, as we shall see in chapter 4.

David Musacchia, owner of a small industrial supply company, says, "In business we think we are in control. We are harried just to keep up because we focus on ourselves and being in control." Over the years, he has learned not to be concerned about losing control or even about losing an occasional customer. "I take what the Lord sets for me today. If my business went under, He would also show me where to go." David sees each day as a gift and every day as an opportunity for ministry. Ray Hinderliter, president of Power Chemicals, Inc., similarly says, "My business is my ministry." He succeeds in business by running it "to glorify God. There are more important things than profit."

Regarding the business as a platform for ministry rather than a battleground for power and control, Christ-centered leaders allow their souls to come forth and engage with others—to truly be alive.

FOUR

Shifting Ground

A llowing the soul to come forth—or allowing ourselves to live at the soul level—rather than being limited by our rational processes requires a dramatic departure from the style with which we have become accustomed to working and leading. After centuries of banning it from business, we would have to give the soul its rightful place in the work environment.

We would first have to acknowledge that we *are* spiritual beings. Such a realization would not be new. Millennia after millennia, people have asserted that part of their reality. "The world we live in is governed not only by physical laws but also by spiritual ones," insists Dorothy Marcic (Marcic 1997, p. 3). And love is the common thread underlying all spiritual laws, she concludes. If spirituality were at work in our organizations, it "would show itself as equitable and just distribution of resources, including removal of most management perks, eliminating abuses of power or privilege, empowering employees by treating them respectfully as adults, and seeing workers as human souls rather than as human resources," she says. Daniel Hanson of Land O'Lakes urges us to think of people as human *sources*, not human resources.

Here and there, we can see changes in our corporate thinking that offer hope that we might move to a loving, caring, perhaps even spiritual state. We could even be at the beginning of a renaissance in corporate thinking that would lead us "toward a compassionate capitalism," believes Gerald Celente, president of the Trends Research Institute. "This renaissance philosophy is not just wishful thinking, but a corporate trend; in its infancy, yes, but visible, vocal and very much alive" (Celente, *Trends Journal* 1997, p. 2).

In this nation that began in faith, we relied on the Protestant ethic to create a society of producers and saver-investors and to influence our behavior in the material world. We eventually abused and then lost touch with that ethic and also lost track of our souls. The Protestant concern for salvation gave way to the liberal notion that society is perfectible through rational development. We shifted our attention from the hereafter to the here and now. In the post–World War II era, says Robert Wuthnow, we were able to reconcile our faith with material pursuits only because our faith no longer focused on a fearsome transcendent being (Wuthnow 1996, p. 308). In effect, we adapted spirituality to American culture to the point where it has little effect on how we work or how we spend our money.

We see now that the spirituality we created, one with no soul or transcendent being, isn't working for us. We languish in the absence of a faith that gives our lives purpose and provides guidance on conducting our lives. As a result, we have worked with our bodies, somewhat with our heads, too little with our spirit, and without love.

Now, coming from different directions, we are seeking the cure for "toxic work environments" and unfulfilling lifestyles as well as more effective organizations. But not all spiritual pursuits will put us on the right track. Love and spirituality don't always go together. Some forms of spirituality turn us outward in love, but others can turn us inward to individual concerns. Some can be self-serving, even isolating. We have to suspect, then, that there is one right spirituality or, at least, that there are some wrong ones.

More and more corporate leaders might exhibit compassion if they could undergo a change in mind and heart. But they cannot rationalize their way through this change; compassion comes only when we reach well beyond our rationality and well beyond some vague spirituality.

THE QUEST FOR TRANSFORMATION

Many of us are asking how we can change the values that drive us individuals, our organizations, and our socioeconomic system. How can we find a core to our being that would turn us outward in love? Many of us recognize we need to shift our entire vision of the world. It's time to refashion our worldview to better match reality. We might reluctantly admit we need a new worldview or paradigm but, unfortunately, too many of us like the paradigm we're using. We like either the material riches we have or the striving for those we don't have.

As much as we might be willing to inch our way to a new worldview, we cannot do so incrementally.

As much as we might be willing to inch our way to a new worldview, we cannot do so incrementally. To begin the leap beyond rational thinking it would help if we understood what our present worldview is and appreciated the fact that other views are possible.

The world is too large and complex for us to know, so we use analogies to represent the truth. Even with the best of analogies, we do not break through to a full understanding of reality. There is more to reality than can be captured in any model devised by the human mind. At present, we are locked into a Cartesian view of man that separates a rational, secular world of the mind and body from a spiritual one. "The world view on which American industrial culture was based emerged from the line of thinking crystallized in the 17th century by Rene Descartes, who viewed the physical world as a great machine and something separate from the intangible world of the mind. This Cartesian dualism of mind versus body led to the separation of science and technology from religion and philosophy. It legitimized the uncoupling of man's actions from his values" (Pascarella 1986, p. 47).

We combine that model with a Newtonian view of the universe that portrays reality as made up of discrete objects drifting in a vast void. We are concerned, therefore, more with separateness than relationship, connectedness, or love. Quantum physics has offered us quite a different analogy, however. It is teaching us that "things" are not separate. In fact, they are not *things*. Scientists believe now that a molecular particle can be both wavelike and particle-like. Some of them suggest that the world is made up of stringlike material. Everything seems to be connected to everything else; all are aspects of the greater whole—of the underlying ground state. It suggests that reality is made up of interconnected elements of a unity—that we are all part of one fabric. We observers, because we are part of the reality we are observing, influence that which we are studying. The answers we get are shaped by the questions we ask. Again, all of us "things" are connected to and acting upon one another.

> From all the sciences today come messages of holism. Physicists speak of the relatedness or unity of all the particles in the universe. Biologists stress the importance of studying the whole organism if one is to understand the part. Medical experts discuss the relationship of mind and body, of getting the patient to join forces with the physician to cure an illness. Psychologists call for an appreciation of both the rational and the intuitive thought processes, of the balance between the conscious and subconscious, of the spiritual as a real dimension of the person. (Pascarella 1986, p. 48)

THE WANTING TO

We may come to recognize our interconnectedness, but be unable to do anything to change our lives accordingly. What we "know" does not always lead to corresponding action. We may analyze scientific laws yet try to defy them. We may study the laws of our state but not necessarily want to live by all of them. We may be aware of spiritual laws but not fully give ourselves over to them. The *wanting to* has to come from outside the laws themselves.

How, then, do we move toward forming a new worldview? What we need is not just a starting point. We need a new *end* point that causes us to *want* to get there. We also need a new process for getting there. Paradigms don't shift. When a new one emerges and then gradually becomes more useful and more convincing, we bridge our way back to the old and backfill the gap as the new view slowly begins to absorb the old.

We may well be seeing two paths leading toward a new paradigm. Our new science offers an analogy that would support the concept of soul in its discussion of connectedness and relationships. At the same time, the rising spiritual awareness represents a search for that same connectedness.

Primitive societies, from the beginning of time to today, have had worldviews of humankind, animals, the Earth, and the heavens all being interconnected.

Primitive societies, from the beginning of time to today, have had worldviews of humankind, animals, the Earth, and the heavens all being interconnected. The ancient biblical analogy teaches the same.

The central message of Christianity, as much as it may have been obscured in many ways over the centuries, is love. The two greatest commandments, said Christ, have to do with loving God and loving others. From this, persons who walk in the company of Christ do so in sharp awareness of connectedness and with a *wanting to* live within spiritual laws. The values they live by emanate from that. They have arrived where others are struggling to get. In chapter 5, we will learn how some Christian business managers who have committed themselves to that message allow it to shape the way they view the world and live in it. We will see that they are in tune with the spiritual laws because they have a different way of knowing. They have faith; they love; and, therefore, they know.

HOW DO WE KNOW WHAT WE KNOW?

As the Garden of Eden story goes, humans separated themselves from God when they ate of the tree of knowledge. They lowered themselves from their special place in Creation to ego, from understanding to intellectualizing. They fashioned myths and sciences, always struggling to understand again. The soul was ever-present but not fully engaged. Both the Old and New Testaments of the Bible tell us again and again that our worldly knowledge is folly.

Dick Leggatt of the Ohio Roundtable points out, "People are trying to analyze spiritual principles through a secular screen, and that's foolishness." Frank Larkin, president of VantagE Business Performance Systems, believes, "Models try to translate reality but lose the meaning. If we stopped rationalizing, we could *realize*."

Throughout her book *ReWiring the Corporate Brain*, Danah Zohar describes three kinds of thinking processes. The first is rational, logical, rule-bound thinking. The second, associative, habit-bound thinking, "gives us pattern-recognizing abilities." She defines a third—what she calls "quantum thinking"; this is the level where one's values and the continual search for meaning kindles creativity.

CORPORATE RIGIDITY

Zohar says the Western model of organization is based on our linear thinking process and the Newtonian concept of a distinct, particle-like self. Conflict is dampened by formal rules and contracts. Its advantages: efficiency and reliability within a given set of rules. Its disadvantages: inflexibility, inability to deal quickly with changes in the rules of the game. She proposes that we leap to a new model of organization based on quantum thinking. The "quantum organization" would function "at the creative edge" between what is and what might be next.

"Organizations interested in transformation have got to touch that level of vision," Zohar told me during an interview while she was visiting the United States from her London base. "Too much transformation talk is just another buzzword. They haven't got the courage and insight to know you have to go down to the spiritual level of the company. I'm talking about the level of meaning, vision, and value: What is this company about? What is it we are really trying to do? What drives us in the morning?"

Despite the need for us to transform ourselves and our organizations to cope with reality, we can see too many cases where leadership's call for corporate transformation is little more than an attempt to get *other* people to change and comply. "Real change . . . is not something we can do in order to 'beat the hell out of the competition,'" Zohar writes (Zohar 1997, p. 2). Unfortunately, our Western, Newtonian organizations are not designed to operate at that level. Therefore, they "have no inner capacity for fundamental transformation" (p. 15). She continues: "All fundamental transformation is ultimately spiritual transformation, spiritual in the very broadest sense as issuing from the level of reflection, meaning, and value" (p. 18).

THE ESSENCE OF WHO WE ARE

"Our mental model of the way the world works must shift from images of a clockwork, machinelike universe that is fixed and determined, to a model of a universe that is open, dynamic, interconnected and full of living qualities," says Joseph Jaworski, founder and chairman of the Centre for Generative Leadership (Jaworski 1996, p. 183).

A small but growing number of business leaders advocate replacing the Newtonian analogy of the organization with a living organism that is built on relationships. They realize that the so-called science of management is self-limiting. It is rational, reductionist, disinterested, control-oriented. It doesn't give space to reflection, meaning, or value. It leads us to insist that the corporation not intrude on individual's values, morality, or religious beliefs. Yet, it would be difficult to find anyone who believes that he or she is part of an organization that is a closed system of lifeless parts. We are more likely to suspect that each of us has a soul that makes us a potentially dynamic, changing force.

We suspect that the soul comes from somewhere else; it began before our time on Earth and may live on afterward. It connects with all others—the entire Creation. Our egos may lead us to fear that we are aliens in the world, but we *are* part of it. We are aliens only in the world that we humans have constructed, because we allowed no spirit in it. Yet we are, after all, spiritual beings.

> The dynamic soul is the essence of who we are. It is immortal. It is not confined to time and space.

The dynamic soul is the essence of who we are. It is immortal. It is not confined to time and space. Only the personality or ego that develops around it dies in time. The ego sees distinctions, pieces, and conflict. It deals in rational thoughts and emotions. The me-ism that troubles our society comes from the ego, not the soul. In the extreme, the ego becomes overly concerned with itself and, in time, thinks it alone deals with reality.

The soul looks at all our experiences in the physical world, offering meaning, interpreting the temporal in light of the eternal. If listened to, it gives rise to our feelings of wanting to be part of something lasting and greater than our physical selves, and directs us to meaningful experiences.

The ego's role is a defensive one, while the soul is proactive. Kay Gilley points out the triple dichotomy of this partnership with "the ego trying to survive versus our divine essence striving to thrive, the practical, feet-on-the-ground, get-the-job-done part of us versus the part of us that wants to soar with the eagles, resignation versus embodiment of our hopes and dreams" (Gilley 1998, pp. 207–8).

The soul knows both the spiritual and secular worlds. Attending to the soul does not mean denying the ego and escaping the physical world to find a state of bliss, but allowing ourselves to exist in both realms. That is the soul's paradox. The soul spans both the unity of the ground state and the disunity of what the ego calls "hard reality." The soul can be obscured by this so-called hard reality of the secular world, if we allow it, but it cannot be destroyed by it. The ego can diffuse the power of the soul, but it cannot create its own lasting power.

The soul brings to our consciousness the knowledge of the Divine, suggesting it from time to time in our memory or conscience or intuition as the Divine tries to break through to us. "My soul is a continually self-organizing process, a channel between me and the ground state of reality. All of me and all of my experience has a soulful, a sacred, dimension," writes Danah Zohar (Zohar 1997, p. 121).

Our consciousness may consider this knowledge but lose it in the processes of segmentation, analysis, and articulation. With the ego in control, the notion of the Divine just does not compute. We cannot reason our way to God—the God "of whom reason knows nothing," as Dietrich Bonhoeffer expressed it (Bonhoeffer 1955, p. 153).

ENERGY OF THE ACORN

The soul is movement, energy, purpose. James Hillman, in his power-ful book *The Soul's Code*, says he is writing about "calling, about fate, about character, about innate image. Together they make up the 'acorn theory,' which holds that each person bears a uniqueness that asks to be lived and that is already present before it can be lived" (Hillman 1996, p. 6).

The soul is not static; it is headed somewhere. It is *being* and it is *becoming*. Paradoxically, we cannot be aware of the soul if we are overly concerned with *doing*. Doing is the work of the ego. This is a paradox the typical business leader cannot appreciate. Joseph Jaworski writes, "Over time, I began to feel that the organizing principle of the universe is 'relatedness,' and that this is more fundamental than 'thingness.' It kept occurring to me that this new understanding is what's missing in how we think about leadership. We're always talking about what leaders *do*—about leadership style and function—but we put very little emphasis on the *being* aspect of leadership" (Jaworski 1996, p. 57).

We may tend to think of *being* as a state of neutrality, one without power or motion, a condition of something that is acted upon—the result of something. But that is far from the case. That would better describe a weak ego. Hillman warns, "Today's main paradigm for un-derstanding a human life, the interplay of genetics and environment, omits something essential—the particularity you feel to be you. By accepting the idea that I am the effect of a subtle buffeting between heredity and societal forces, I reduce myself to a result" (Hillman 1996, p. 6).

The closest analogy we can make for Truth or Reality is *energy*. The soul is an element of that greater energy. Gary Zukav says, "Your soul is not a passive or a theoretical entity that occupies a space in the vicinity of your chest. It is a positive, purposeful force at the core of your being" (Zukav 1989, p. 31). Locked temporarily in our mind and body, we may overlook the soul, but it is there burning brightly. It is part of that Creation that was put into motion and cannot be stopped by the ego.

POWER OF CONNECTEDNESS

The soul's energy is inexhaustible because a soul does not stand alone. Each is a part of the energy of the entire dynamic, evolving universe. As the quantum physicist would say, we are all part of a network of relationships or, as the Christian believes, the body is made up of many parts, each of value to the whole.

When we permit the soul to soar, we are amazed at the connections that show up for us. When we commit to something and focus on it, things that relate to it come our way. People appear from nowhere with ideas or resources. Relevant information flows across our desk or shows up in our e-mail. Some people call these coincidences "synchronicity." Carl Jung coined this term for "coincidences" that are "connected so meaningfully that their 'chance' concurrence would represent a degree of improbability that would have to be expressed by an astronomical figure" (Jung 1983, p. 339). Explaining these occurrences, Joseph Jaworski says, "A powerful force exists beyond ourselves and our conscious will, a force that helps us along the way, nurturing our quest and transformation" (Jaworski 1996, p. xi). The Christian refers to them as the workings of God or of the Holy Spirit.

Ordinary little events—as well as big ones—can add up to breakthroughs in power and capability for us if we are in tune with the oneness of which we are a part. When this power flows through us we are *empowered*. We are in a state of being where we see all sorts of possibilities. We ally with forces far beyond the power of our ego. We contribute to the whole rather than allowing our ego to detract from that wholeness.

Is it any wonder, then, that people who are living in their spiritual dimension can do amazing things? After all, says Frank Larkin, "Spirituality is the ultimate motivator!" (If that's the case, it may not be long before we see spirituality abused as consultants try to sell it, or even religion, to improve the bottom line! And the cause of our problems will still go unattended.)

In the business organization, we may try to harness people with administrative procedures and financial chains, but the energy we capture is a small fraction of the power that would come from souls fully engaged with the power that links them together. We may get them to resign to certain change, but the effort they apply to it is nothing compared to the energy that would come from the heart of the universe if their souls were allowed to unleash it.

We may try to harness people with administrative procedures and financial chains, but the energy we capture is a small fraction of the power that would come from souls fully engaged. . . .

Rising to unprecedented heights of performance by operating at a deep level departs from the traditional seeking of power. It comes by giving up power, by recognizing the power in others—the power of the community. It requires the mentality of the "suffering servant" who will endure pain and suffering to pursue his or her vision and values, Zohar told me. In our interview, she said, "Christ himself was a servant leader. He didn't just serve the poor. He didn't just serve the lonely, the cut off. He served, in fact, his God, by which I mean his deep vision, his deep sense of value. Through serving that God, he then served the poor, the disinherited, and so on."

Her words could also describe Christian executives who operate at the level of the soul, soaring above the cares of the ego. Because they are bent on engaging with other souls, they are not overly concerned about saving their own souls. Their sense of connectedness flows out into the world, drawing it together. Their principles and values are cast by the call to nurture the interconnected system of life.

FIVE

Christian Paradoxes

etting in touch with their souls and engaging with others: that sums up the behavior of Christ-centered leaders. They are growing in their own faith and living it out in ways that stimulate other people to get in touch with their own deepest beliefs.

Christ-centered leaders are doers. Before interviewing any business leaders for this book, I verified with others that these executives really walk the talk. You can get them to talk about what they are doing, but seldom, if ever, do they take credit for the good things going on around them. They believe God or Christ or the Holy Spirit is doing the work. They view themselves merely as vehicles—a role for which they are thankful. They feel challenged to work to glorify God through the manner in which they conduct their business and in the excellence of results—product, service, financial performance. They strive to make their daily life a witnessing or reflection of God's love. They see their organizations as vehicles for using their gifts from God. They do not try to make their business into a church, but they do treat it as a ministry or a platform for practicing their faith and praising God. Business growth, when it comes, is an outcome of that.

I am not aware that any of the Christian managers I interviewed had anything but a strong biblical base that served as the foundation for their beliefs. This does not mean they are all biblical scholars. They work at learning "the Word" through private, often daily, reading and in Bible study groups at church, at work, or in groups of business persons around town. I found none that take every passage of the Bible literally. They regard it as the Truth, but truth revealed often through analogy. My findings match with those of Laura Nash, who did not find the Christian executive "seekers" she interviewed to be fundamentalists. That is, they are not people "who take biblical passages more or less at face value" (Nash 1994, p. xii).

GOD'S POINT OF VIEW

If, as a growing number of us agree, we need a fundamental transformation in the heart of our business organizations, Christ-centered leaders offer an example of what *transformation* means. We can apply to them the passage from Colossians 3:9: "You have taken off your old self with its practices and have put on the new self, which is being renewed in knowledge in the image of its Creator."

> **C**hrist-centered leaders are doers. They feel challenged to work to glorify God.

In our search for models of leadership, we have too often skimmed off lessons from various figures ranging from Attila the Hun to Jesus Christ. Attila was only a man. It's little wonder that he's easy to copy, and, because he was a great conqueror, it's not surprising that many managers have done so. To understand the behavior of those who walk in the company of Christ, however, we have to understand where they are coming from. They know Christ is more than man. He is divine as well, and His path is not easy to follow.

Some authors and consultants who have been drawing on Christ as a model of management or leadership in recent years completely overlook the central truth that's at work inside Christ's followers. The leaders don't copy Him; Christ works through them. He transforms them. Christ did not come to teach us management techniques to help us better ourselves in secular matters. Instead, He taught us to lose ourselves as we serve others and transform the world.

Trying to emulate selected things Christ said or did that relate to business is like trying to win the Rose Bowl by simply putting on a football uniform. Christ-centered executives do the reverse—they relate their business behavior to Christ's teachings. They begin with a *relationship* with Christ. Their courage and optimism come from knowing that He is in control. From that comes the behavior that others see as both Christlike and successful in business terms.

Many of their values or behaviors are those that others can and do arrive at, but the end toward which they work is unique. They are not employing certain values in pursuit of goals for their egos. They see themselves instead as stewards of the world. If we would want to copy them, we have to start not with their values, but with the worldview that grounds those values. That's what gives these leaders direction, commitment, and power. At the same time, their adherence to their particular worldview may give hope to persons of other beliefs that they can immerse themselves in secular affairs without surrendering their spirituality.

In this time of talk about paradigm shifts, what could be more mind-bending than the way these men and women strive to look at the world from God's point of view rather than their own, and serve God rather than themselves? What could be more revolutionary than companies run as vehicles for God's work rather than for man's? This is what happens when spirituality is the *response to* a higher being's wishes rather than a mere *consideration of the possibility of* a higher being.

As you get to know them, you see that these leaders have a view of life that addresses many of the challenges or questions we have discussed earlier, such as:

- How do we get in touch with our spiritual dimension or soul?
- How do we come to embrace the right values?
- Is religion really changing people's lives?
- How do we become other-centered?
- Is there an inevitable conflict between the worldviews of science and religion?

Before we can answer that last question, we have to understand just what the scientific thinking process and the content of science are.

The scientific method of hypothesis, experimentation, and verification is quite appropriate for dealing with the material world. The conflict with religion comes when we (not especially the scientists themselves) assume that this method of learning is the only means to knowledge or wisdom. We have been guilty of misusing science by insisting that everything has to be proven. There is no way of proving God. We can't reproduce, at will, experiments to prove God's existence. But those who follow Christ's path believe if we commit to opening ourselves to the possibility—if we have faith—God will do the proving.

There is no way of proving God. But if we commit to opening ourselves to the possibility— if we have faith—God will do the proving.

As for the content of science, the old Newtonian view, which for centuries has helped us understand what is taking place on Earth and in outer space, conveys the concept of separate bodies. While this does not contradict the Bible, it has led us to make too much of individuality, and thus we have had an apparent science/Bible conflict. The new quantum science, with its lessons about connectedness, seems more in harmony with the central message of the Bible and of Christ, however. It offers no justification for thinking that science renders Christianity obsolete.

Before the current rise in popularity of modern physics, Teilhard de Chardin wrote,

> Towards the end of the nineteenth century, the Christian view of the world might have seemed to certain eyes limited and out-of-date because at the base of its theories it maintained intransigently:
>
> 1. Faith in a God, personal centre of the universe.
> 2. Faith in the primacy of man in nature.
> 3. Faith in a certain totalization of all men in the bosom of a single spiritual organism.
>
> Is it not remarkable that by precisely these three characteristics, which seemed to mark it as a decayed and out-of-date doctrine, but which we have just rediscovered, . . . Christianity now tends to present itself to reason as the most progressive religion? (Chardin 1966, p. 232)

THE PARADOXES
OF BEING CHRISTIAN

Christ-centered people seem to be walking contradictions. And they are—if we look at them from the usual, dualistic viewpoint of most people, because many of the basic truths of Christianity challenge our "normal" thinking. As we said in chapter 4, the soul's paradox is its existence in both the spiritual and secular realms. These leaders have no problem seeing that, often, two sides of an issue are right. In later chapters we will explore some of the paradoxes that characterize their beliefs. Among them:

- Being concerned for others *and* being effective in business
- Recognizing Christ as God and human
- Loving your neighbor as yourself
- Knowing that we have fallen from God's grace but God has redeemed us
- Living out deep obligations and enjoying unbounded freedom to be what God created us to be
- Standing for unchanging principles while driving change
- Being in the world but not *of* it
- Acting in the present and serving the eternal
- Seeking individual solutions for monumental problems
- Being peaceful yet highly energetic and forceful
- Honoring the individual and the group
- Taking time for reflection to prepare for action

We could list many more such paradoxes. The point is, those who embrace the Christian worldview are able to live with paradox because they are aware of deeper truths that lift them above human-made distinctions and divisions. While many of us look for simple answers in our faith, these people are willing to live with complexity.

CHRISTIANS IN THE NEW AGE

The Christian worldview was not a good fit with the worldview established in the Industrial Age. Paradoxically, the Christian view does harmonize well with the emerging paradigm (some aspects of which may be called "New Age") on several key issues:

- The search for meaning
- A transcendent ground for all existence (God)
- A self that is part of a greater whole
- The search for unity
- Disenchantment with materialism
- Favoring cooperation over competition
- Concern for oneness of mind and body
- Concern for the planet (Although Christians, as well as others, participated in exploitation of the planet in the past, they know humans were charged in the beginning with being stewards of it.)

It may be surprising to some of us that the "new" or emerging paradigm is, in many ways, the old paradigm. Long before modern science, even before old science, God instructed us in the truths of the world. Long before our minds began their feeble attempts to explain, our hearts *knew*. God waits patiently as we humans sift through one science after another!

> Those who embrace the Christian worldview are able to live with paradox because they are aware of deeper truths that lift them above human-made distinctions and divisions.

Unfortunately, Christianity is not widely regarded as being very "progressive" or "with it." Some forms of Christianity, in effect, served our business organizations by separating our spiritual and work lives. In doing so, they failed both the individual and the organization. In recent years, some people turned to Eastern religions or New Age thinking. Some of the attractions of Eastern or Native American belief systems are their mysteries and paradoxes as well as their disciplines for living those faiths. For many Christians, faith has been made too simple and not especially demanding, thereby losing all the mystery and power of a God who will not be bounded by our puny views.

The Christian voice is seldom heard in the late-1990s surge of conferences on business and spirituality. Despite the preponderance of people who regard themselves as Christians, it is puzzling to find that Christianity is not well represented in literature designed to help manage or lead them. Today, if you look in the management section of your bookstore, you'll find that it seems quite okay, however, to draw upon other religions or philosophies as sources of wisdom.

In the early 1980s, as a business writer covering Quality of Worklife and Quality Circle development, I encountered one ex-seminarian after another consulting in that field. Something about their background made them right in their mindset, faith, and education for dealing with the new "people issues" that were emerging in business. Then came an unusually high percentage of Mormon writer/consultants in the field—such as Steven Covey and Margaret Wheatley. And the study of Buddhism and Zen began appearing in management literature. So I could not help wondering, "Where were mainline Christians in the workplace?"

Some aspects of Christianity do not fit the easy flow of much of today's spirituality thinking. Perhaps the most serious division is where we place God. New Agers invite us to search within ourselves for God. Or they assert that we are God or, at least, one with God. A central belief of Christians, however, is that we have been separated from God. God is *out there*, but, through Christ's death for our sin, we are able to become reconciled with God, to draw closer. Separation and reconciliation is the central story of the Bible. In the Old Testament, we see God's repeated attempts to bring us back into relationship. In the New Testament, we see Christ dying for our sins—the ultimate effort at reconciliation.

If we seek God, we find God has been waiting for us. God is present in the world, making a difference, wanting us to make a difference. God wants us to be involved in the world. Sometimes, however, we choose to draw inward, to search for meaning within ourselves. This, too, is the story of the Bible—our continually falling from grace and worshiping either ourselves or the things we make.

A second departure from Christianity in some of the New Age thinking is the focus on self. Much of it offers us techniques to serve our physical and psychic quest to get ahead, to be Number 1, to win. Some New Age techniques may be simply self-help efforts; others are downright antisocial. Yet, even followers of the Christian faith, over its long history and in its many forms, have wavered between social consciousness and self-centered activity. The thrust of Christian churches has swung back and forth over the centuries, from preaching guilt and self-denial to promoting joy and self-fulfillment, from fostering a spirit of community to seeking salvation for oneself. In each age, some Christians have focused on feeling good about themselves, but not especially feeling good about others or doing good for others.

Selfishness has, then, reared its ugly head inside as well as outside the Christian community, but people who are Christ-centered reject egocentric spirituality. Christ, not their egos, occupies the center of their consciousness. They are aware of evil in the world, of sin—their own and others'. Yet they are thrilled by the possibilities for the individual to do good, and they respond enthusiastically to the command to do good for others.

We can credit New Age thinking with challenging our modern culture's celebration of unsustainable and unreal concepts of rugged individualism and competition. While that may threaten nominal Christians who want to maintain our present culture and worldview, it does not threaten those who truly follow Christ in being stewards of the world. New Age thinking has opened the door to dialogue about spirituality; this allows Christians to step forth and show that the loving God who created us and others who are brothers and sisters in the Creation is the central manifestation of their spirituality.

A POWERFUL MIX

Time and time again, most of us have heard the charge: "You can't be a Christian and be successful in business. Business and religion don't mix." Well, I have met more than one business leader who disproves that notion.

I had been hearing about John Beckett, an Ohio businessman, for years before I met him. To many people inside as well as outside the company, he is the model of a Christian businessman. As I toured one of the R. W. Beckett plants with him one day, I was impressed not only with the loving environment but also with the effectiveness of the workforce and the way it had incorporated so many new management techniques. I realized then that, while being a follower of Christ does not give a person new techniques for managing or leading, it does prepare the heart and mind for employing them.

Gary Oatey, president and CEO of Oatey Company, a 550-person manufacturing and distribution firm, believes that working to follow Christian teachings and the gospel "orients your thinking in a way that allows you to implement those management practices in a way that is noticeable." By that, he means, people see that you are coming from a deep regard for them.

Being a Christian won't make you a good leader; it won't ensure you can use all the latest management techniques effectively and be a financial success. On the other hand, you cannot fully utilize these techniques without employing a loving approach to people. This is why management so often impedes performance rather than improves it, even when it tries new productivity or quality improvement techniques. Look at the endless attempts by business to manage change and improve quality and then imagine how great it would have been if these tools had been in the hands of companies operating by biblical principles! These principles would lead us to be concerned with achieving, not controlling.

> Such values as honesty, openness, and respecting others lead to better decision making.

It is quite natural for leaders driven by their Christian faith to nurture in themselves and in others what are now seen as the attributes that make an organization effective. Such values as honesty, openness, and respecting others lead to better decision making. They are the hidden foundation on which many of the new management techniques must depend if they are to work.

If a company operates at the soul level, there is no inherent reason that it should not succeed in business. "We are a very solid company," Carole Hamm points out. "We are a debt-free company. We think that production is important." She is convinced, if people are working on developing their spiritual dimension, "they can't help but produce a good bottom line. It doesn't happen in the reverse."

It is understandable, then, why some Christian-led companies have produced amazing financial results. That shouldn't be surprising, says Don Kline, vice president of member services for the Fellowship of Companies for Christ International, an organization that serves Christian executives and company owners. "After all, God set the rules of the marketplace long ago," he says.

I make no attempt to correlate the depth of a person's spirituality with business success. There are, however, many cases of companies succeeding financially as they follow Christian principles. ServiceMaster, for example, a company with $6 billion in sales, has improved its earnings per share by 20 percent in each of the past twenty years, chairman Bill Pollard tells me. R. W. Beckett Company was a relatively small venture that John Beckett inherited from his father in the 1960s; it has grown to a $100-million-a-year operation that employs more than 500 people.

These leaders succeed in business because their nontraditional approach to leadership matches what people need for personal growth and what organizations need for economic growth:

- They are other-directed; they do not serve themselves.
- They are people-builders, not people-users.
- They open people to new possibilities rather than seeing themselves as unchangeable.
- They invite inquiry and self-discipline, not quick solutions.
- They reveal their inner values without bulldozing others into changing their beliefs.

In business today, we need leaders with character who know what they believe and who can be trusted. These Christian leaders build trust because people around them can see that they have the ability to *blend* the spiritual and the material, their faith and their work. They don't segment "business ethics" from any other sort of ethics. They believe that the purpose for their business lies in the spiritual realm and that they must reflect this through excellence in all that they do.

Can you be a Christian and a business success? Yes. But it depends on how you define *success*. If you mean a success in life first and success in business a possible second, yes. If you mean go all out in business and use faith as a crutch or aid, the answer is no. Frank Larkin points out that the Christian approach is not just a better way to run a business but a better way to live a life. "These people just happen to be CEOs or senior managers."

ON THE FRONTIER

Spirituality and religion are the next frontier for management, and the way these Christians are living out their faith makes them pioneers in an uncharted area. They are operating in a mode of love, justice, and respect for human worth. They do so not because it's good business, although their actions often produce good business results. They are proving that Christianity is not worn out—not something to be abandoned. What has broken down is our willingness to apply its central teachings, not the soundness of the teachings or their relevance to business activities.

> **C**hristian leaders build trust because people around them can see that they have the ability to *blend* the spiritual and the material, their faith and their work.

These Christians' faith allows them to be windows through which they invite God to work where they are. This brings both peace and power. At Seaberg Industries, chairman George Seaberg estimates that about two-thirds of the eighty employees are Christians. One day, as we walked together through the plant where workers were busily but cheerfully designing, cutting, bending, and welding parts for agricultural equipment, George paused to say quietly, "Every employee is on my prayer list every day." That is a power that cannot be captured in management techniques.

PART II

Right
Relationship

SIX

A Personal God

S everal years ago, I hosted at my home an all-day meeting for the supervisors of one of the departments that reported to me. After a bit of socializing, the eight of us sat in chairs around the family room. Silence . . . It seemed to me that we were waiting for an opening prayer. But we didn't engage in that; we moved into the business of the day. After the meeting, Ray, the department head, and I were privately reviewing the day. "You know, at the beginning, I felt we were going to open with prayer," he said. "I did, too," I replied, grinning. Maybe prayer would not have been inappropriate. Although I did not know the religious beliefs of the persons attending, I felt confident that a prayer would not have offended them. We were already on a high spiritual plane; through our months of working together, we were connected in some deep way. If one of us had spoken a prayer, it surely would have touched a commonality of feelings and hopes.

At a leadership seminar in Scottsdale, Arizona, in 1994, about twenty executives were sitting in a session led by Jim Kouzes, chairman of the Tom Peters Group. When he asked each of us to name a person in history we most admired, one person named Jesus. Someone remarked, "Yes, certainly, he was one of the greatest persons who ever lived." The nominator came back with *"Lives!"*—stressing the present tense. From there, the session climbed onto a high spiritual plane, largely but not entirely Christian.

As the sun began to paint the clouds into the dawn of an already hot July day in 1997 in Longboat Key, Florida, I sat on the beach recalling what I had observed in the previous two days. I had been a guest in a meeting of the officers, regional managers, and company-owner members of the Fellowship of Companies for Christ. In time, a prayer began to compose itself in my mind. It went something like this:

> I've been in many meetings with groups of business executives and noted the power of influence they have on other people's lives. The people at this meeting are skilled. They are experienced. They have the power of position. But they have placed themselves in Your hands, Lord. They reveal You in their lives. In this group, I see Your power at work.
>
> Give them the strength to hold their faces to You in this world of distractions. In the beauty of Nature, it is relatively easy to be reminded of You—Your Creation, Your continued presence. But in the world of humans and manmade things it is all too easy to forget. May Your constancy be met with constancy in their hearts.

"SPIRITUAL BEINGS HAVING A HUMAN EXPERIENCE"

Each of the three meetings described reflects the deep relationships that people can and do have with one another in "the business world." A group of people working together and respecting one another can rise to the spiritual realm as they nurture deep connections to one another. Sometimes, even in a group of strangers meeting for a brief time, someone will remind others of their spirituality, and a dam of feelings and faith seems to burst. A group of busy businesspeople who share their Christian faith reflect a power greater than any one of them or all of them together.

We can see the Spirit breaking through as people connect soul to soul. This is not abnormal. It reveals what we humans really are. "We are not human beings having a spiritual experience. We are spiritual beings having a human experience," Teilhard de Chardin reminded us. (Cashman 1998, p. 68)

People have always found something to worship—money, power, Nature, or a greater mystery. For Christians, the great Mystery is God as revealed through Christ. When Paul visited Athens, he roamed the city, studying its life, and became distressed at seeing all the idols the Athenians had erected. As he stood before the Areopagus, the body that ruled over religion and morals, he said, "As I walked around and looked carefully at your objects of worship, I even found an altar with this inscription: *To an unknown god.* Now what you worship as something unknown I am going to proclaim to you" (Acts 17:23). The Christ of whom he would tell them would lead to a God they could know—a God beyond rational comprehension, yet a God they could experience.

A PERSONAL RELATIONSHIP WITH GOD

To understand Christ-centered leaders, it is essential to appreciate that they do not merely allow that God may exist, nor do they merely acknowledge that He does exist. They *experience* a personal *relationship* with God. This is the cornerstone of their faith, which connects them to God in a direct, very real way. They are responding to a personal, involved God who wants us to love Him and all of His Creation.

> **By putting their relationship with God first, some Christian leaders are able to open themselves to opportunities they could never create for themselves.**

"God is first and foremost interested in a personal and abiding relationship with me, not in what I will do on His behalf," believes Alan Ross, president of the Fellowship of Companies for Christ International. "It is me He seeks first. If I seek Him, I will find Him. And when I find Him I can have an abiding relationship with Him." By putting their relationship with

God first, some Christian leaders are able to open themselves to opportunities they could never create for themselves. "God is more interested in you having a deep relationship with Him than He is in your performance for Him," Ross says. "Once that relationship is established, He will be able to use you in ways you never imagined" (Ross 1998, p. 2).

The Christian leaders who are the subject of this book operate with this relationship to God at the center of their lives. Few of them regard themselves as *religious;* they are not caught up in the dogma or ritual of religion, although some may embrace such things to express and strengthen their relationship with God. They recognize that they are bound in a human–God relationship and countless person-to-person relationships. Because they are in touch with their souls, they are markedly different from the many millions of managers whose souls are covered with scar tissue created by tearing the spiritual relationship out of their lives and by isolating themselves in the material world.

Business management involves learning the importance of relationships, but it does not know how to build them. The new science suggests to us that we are all connected, that all parts of the universe are bound together in relationship, yet it cannot explain the source of those connections and does not help us understand how we can participate in the incredible connecting power. The Christian basis for relationships or connections has several aspects:

The power that holds the world together is love. Where there is absence of love, there is separation and strife. True relationships are grounded in a connectedness at the soul level, where we find the energy that creates dynamic, growing, thriving unions. Without this energy, the ego is forced to cope with a chaotic process of giving and taking, of making and breaking promises. While the soul comes from a world of loving connections, the ego lives in the world that it creates—one based on separation and leading to alienation. When we deny our souls, we are in poor relationships with others, and we find it difficult to relate our work lives to the rest of our lives. We merely follow our ego as it grasps for ephemeral things and flimsy connections.

The source of love is God. "We love because He first loved us . . ." (1 John 4:19). "Love comes from God. . . . God is love" (1 John 4:7–8). In other words, love is the very essence of God. The Christian experiences the involvement and guidance of a loving God who has been seeking humankind through all of history. What we are called to do is return God's original and ongoing love for us.

Christ taught us how to love. Christ was not a man who decided to be ethical and loving; He was (is) God, the essence of whom is love. His life, His words, His acts, and especially His death reveal an unparalleled depth of love. He leads us far beyond "following the golden rule" with which many nonbelievers content themselves. Christ summed up His central message of love in the two great commandments: "Love the Lord your God with all your heart and with all your soul and with all your mind and with all your strength," and "Love your neighbor as yourself" (Mark 12:30–31). Thus, He invites us to a higher order of being.

> True relationships are grounded in a connectedness at the soul level, where we find the energy that creates dynamic, growing, thriving unions.

Christ shows us how to use our natural ability to love. His commandments do not force us to do something that we are incapable of doing. Why would He ask us to do the impossible? Loving is what we were created to do. We are not commanded to love in the sense that we must work at overcoming an inability to love. We are commanded in that we are invited to follow what's wired in, what we were designed for.

The true Christian loves others in partnership with Christ. Christ is the embodiment of a supreme, loving relationship, not the random act of some abstract power of the universe. Try as we might to be like Christ, we can only walk with Him and allow Him to work with us or through us. Together we engage in living and loving in a way that makes our relationships stronger, deeper, and more lasting.

Beyond that, there is the possibility for a still greater depth of love. Some Christian leaders say they feel that God has "filled" them with love. For them, love is more than emotion. It is more than an act of will to love others. It is the result of an act of God. That's profound yet understandable; when we let God into our lives, we let love in, because God is love.

"If we love one another, God lives in us and his love is made complete in us" (1 John 4:12). "Whoever lives in love lives in God, and God in him" (1 John 4:16). Thus, we complete the circle. As part of this swirling energy, we are carriers of God's love—in everything we do.

ANTIDOTE TO ME-ISM

The beliefs of the Christian executives I have studied do not constitute a sterile spirituality. In their actions, these leaders demonstrate a deep love for God and for others. For them, the "power" or "force" or "ground state" that others refer to is a power that has a face. A distinguishing feature of their faith is the belief that God is active in the world. Their response is one of action as well, because they believe we are all invited to help continue the evolution of this active God's Creation, each to be stewards of certain aspects of it.

In order to understand the personal and business success of Christ-centered people, we have to appreciate their conviction that we have all been created by a loving God—that each of us is created in God's image and, therefore, each of us is of inestimable value. Because of this, they break with management's common lack of compassion and civility. Their employees do not walk around "with terror on their faces." Christ-centered leaders can take the position of Daniel Hanson, who says we should seek opportunity to "create pockets of wellness in this sick system."

This does not mean these leaders are soft on people. They hold themselves and others to high standards of right and wrong, of fairness and honesty. Contrary to what some may think, it takes guts to be a Christian. But, says George Seaberg, chairman and CEO of Seaberg Industries, "There are a lot of gutless managers out there." As Carole Hamm of Country Cupboard Inn says so simply, "This is difficult work."

Their spirituality is not self-serving; they do not view the world in terms of what it can do for them. Because their purpose in life is to allow God to work through them to minister to others, these leaders enable other people to find purpose and meaning in their work and their family lives. They institutionalize love, not indifference, which allows people to give their best to the organization.

Serving God and serving people leaves little time for being concerned about being oneself. These leaders reflect a humility as they accord the interests of others the same priority, if not a higher one, as their own. They follow Paul's words in Philippians 2:4: "Each of you should look not only to your own interests, but also to the interests of others."

Believers of any faith can be accused of resorting to religion as a means of finding comfort, of serving the self by filling some deep personal need. There is only a small bit of truth in that for these true believers and followers, however. As C. S. Lewis pointed out, "The Christian religion is, in the long run, a thing of unspeakable comfort. But it does not begin in comfort. . . . Comfort is the one thing you cannot get by looking for it" (Lewis 1943, p. 39).

Contrary to what we might assume, not everyone who converts to Christianity today is indulging in me-ism. While the self-indulgent Baby Boomers are today middle-aged and constitute a large portion of the new joiners of the Christian churches, many are turning outward. In fact, Donald E. Miller, who studied several hundred members of "new paradigm churches," which appeal to that generation, learned that their conversion generally leads to less—not more—emphasis on the self (Miller, 1997).

INCLUDING EVERYONE

Christians, like adherents of most religions, are often accused of being insular, of distancing themselves from nonbelievers. But this is not true of Christ-centered leaders. They have enough position power to be an influence on most or all of the people in their organization and on the people with whom the organization does business. They could, if they wanted, choose with whom they associate, whom they would favor, for whom they would show concern. Instead, they show genuine concern for others, actively reaching out to them, and quietly praying for them.

The executives I have studied range from owners of companies doing a few million dollars in sales per year to chief executive officers of companies in the several-billion-dollar ranks. A few of them are not Number 1 in the company but head large divisions. Perhaps the larger the organization, the less latitude they have for doing things their way, but in all cases, they reveal a focus on *relationships* and open their arms to all people. As Bill Pollard told me,

> I don't have the privilege in ServiceMaster of defining my faith to exclude people. In all of my other involvement with Christian organizations, they take great pride in defining who they are and, in the process, exclude people. Whether it's membership in a church or a college with a statement of faith or whatever—the process of saying who they are means they have embraced a definition which, by its very nature, excludes some people.
>
> I don't have that privilege or opportunity, or maybe problem, in the marketplace because the customers I serve, the people I work with, represent the world. I'm reminded that they represent the world that God so loved that He gave His only begotten Son.
>
> My faith says I need to love the people who don't agree with me, I need to work with people who don't agree with me. I need to so live my faith that they will embrace the same faith. In that sense, my faith is inclusive.

That doesn't mean that it doesn't stand for something, he told me. For those who have different beliefs, he requests, "Accept my principles if not my starting point."

These executives and company owners range from those who have been Christians all their lives to those who are recent converts. All of the executives with whom I talked regard themselves as being on a path, not as having *arrived*. They welcome association with members of any faith who are searching and growing. They aren't out to win spiritual debates.

Carole Hamm says she is not concerned what religion her coworkers are so long as they are working on finding and revealing their true spiritual selves. The real issue, she believes, is "each person's personal faith, their inner journey, and the character they are developing. That faith cannot be forced, for it is the natural flow of who we are. It is our innermost being, demonstrated to the outside world."

The chaos of thinking and lifestyles in our world today makes for a rich environment in which Christians can grow in influence. Carole believes strongly that, as a leader in a company, the depth of her faith is important both to her and to those people around her. She asks how a leader could deal with all the complexity and chaos facing him or her "without first having a real depth of personal

All of the executives with whom I talked regard themselves as being on a path, not as having *arrived*. They aren't out to win spiritual debates.

faith—that thing that you hold on to when everything else seems to be going haywire, when the system seems so backward, and the problems that society is bringing you are really sometimes more than you think you can personally cope with." She thinks, "Sometimes in the workplace we try to know all. I think [it's better] when you can say to yourself as a leader, 'I don't have all the answers. Where am I going to seek some guidance and some wisdom?'"

Bill Pollard and Carole Hamm typify those Christian leaders who reveal a faith that leads to inclusion, not exclusion. They work with Christians of any denomination or no denomination, with non-Christians and nonbelievers. They are not overly concerned about the church as an institution. When you talk with them about their faith, they do not lead off by telling what denomination they are. They are more concerned with principles. Although they are uncompromising in living by certain principles, they work together with people who share those same principles but differ in style, ritual, and practices. They don't let dogma stand in the way of their reaching out to others. Tony Ciepiel, president of Realty One, observes, "The God of the Bible is so practical. Whether you're Christian or not, the principles work." This is not to say these executives are willing to compromise or water down their faith. To repeat Bill Pollard, "Accept my principles if not my starting point."

Christianity "has generated patterns of thought in life that are really quite universal in their implications," Max Stackhouse, at Princeton Theological Seminary, pointed out to me. "And there are parts of the other world religions that can come close to those same ethical principles. Christians interacting with non-Christians to strengthen those ethical principles that we have in common is one of the ways by which we can work together. In the final analysis, I believe, Christianity provides the best foundational set of concepts for a whole interpretation of humanity; we don't have to force everyone to believe as we do on this point, but we can make it safe for other people to discover."

The ability of Christ-centered leaders to work with others demonstrates a faith that can be lived out without being divisive in the business place. This same inclusive thinking applies to their view of "the business world" as an integral part of God's Creation—one in which they should be proactive. Because they are focused outward rather than on themselves, they have the resources to serve all their stakeholders—employees, suppliers, customers, and the communities around them. They appreciate each person's uniqueness, and, from that, it seems to flow quite naturally that they nurture environments that support what business needs today—bringing people together to community, collaboration, commitment, and creativity.

> **We would get to the root of our productivity and quality problems as well as the toxicity of corporate environments if we were more concerned about the *virtuous organization*.**

In their own lives and in what they expect of others, they demonstrate a respect for self-reliance and people's reliance on one another. This translates into the belief that we should step out in direct contact with others, not rely on government or some other third party to do our "loving" for us. For this reason, they are, more often than not, politically conservative. Laura Nash's research supports this finding. She says evangelicals in general are politically conservative—"noted for their emphasis on self-discipline, hard work, thrift, and delayed gratification" (Nash 1994, p. 16). Theologically, I found the group to comprise both conservatives and liberals. They come from mainline churches and from nontraditional churches. It would be difficult and erroneous to try to fit them into the usual categories or stereotypes.

THE VIRTUOUS ORGANIZATION

Living out the commandments to love can enable us to build relationships that are far deeper than what we find on an organization chart or even in networks of people getting things done because the connections are based on goodness to one another. There are those who insist that when they use the terms "spirituality" and "business" together they are not talking about *goodness*. But how we can build healthy relationships without living by values that constitute goodness toward one another? How can we be part of the fabric of the Creation if we deny the source of love that binds it together? Although the rising amount of management interest in teamwork, commitment, and empowerment is encouraging, it is equally discouraging to hear the insistence that we stay away from the very core of what makes all those things possible. The useless spinning of management techniques and the endless programs serve the consulting industry, but they don't get us to the heart of the matter.

As people network electronically, we have heard a lot of talk about "the virtual organization." It's exciting to think of all the possibilities of working together even if we aren't physically together. Isn't it likely that we would get to the root of our productivity and quality problems as well as the toxicity of corporate environments if we were more concerned about the *virtuous organization*? Concentrating on technique and technology is pointless unless we begin with the search for goodness. By not recognizing who we really are and loving as we really can, we are doomed to fall far short of our potential—individually and corporately.

SANCTIFIED, MAYBE; SEPARATE, NO

The Christ-centered executives I studied are highly mindful of maximizing the opportunity for themselves and others to do far greater things than we normally expect even in the meanest and leanest organizations. They work hard at getting *results* in human as well as financial terms.

They don't use the power of their faith to do business. They use their business to live out their faith. They just happen to be in business—or they are *called* to be in business—so that's where they follow Christ's commandments and serve as stewards in their part of the world. We will see in subsequent chapters how they express love in their work and their work relationships.

They are convinced they are created in God's image and, for that reason, they feel obligated to do what they do for the glory of God. If they look bad, then God looks bad. We might say they are *sanctified;* the word means "set apart" or "holy." Yet they do not see themselves as set apart; they are very much involved in the world that they love. They do not see themselves as holy; they are more likely to consider themselves as undeserving recipients of gifts.

Again and again, they will state that "we are all sinners." Now, is this just some mysterious church talk? No. Well, if we try not to do wrong or bring harm to others, why then are we sinners? The sin of which we are all guilty is that of separation from God. Relying on our human emotions and rational thinking, we live in a secular world, blinded to any world in which there might be a God.

When we speak of Christ's saving us, redeeming us, or reconciling us to God, we should realize that He opened us to transformation. We might say, Christ's resurrection opened the way to our own resurrection. Christ did not die as a sacrifice to a vengeful God, but to put an end to violence and domination that separates us from God and prevents us from being what a loving God wants us to be. (Wink 1998, p. 92) He came not to just save us as individuals but to enable us to transform the world.

These leaders express less concern with their own salvation than they do with glorifying God. They work hard at following Christ and allowing Him to walk with them. They are not seeking power to be more successful in conventional terms. They do not try to assure themselves worldly comforts first and then follow Christ; they follow Him first. The more they are filled with Christ, the more they do good things, not to win reward or recognition or even salvation in the here-after. They act out of love—a goodness that does not involve expecta-tion of a reward, although it often reaps the greatest of rewards. They get their lives right so their God-given gifts can be at work in the world. They know that sanctification, if that's what they have, is con-ferred by God, not earned.

RECONCILIATION AND FREEDOM

A central Christian belief holds that, although humankind alienated itself from God, their God sent a Son to die for their sins—to open the door to reconciliation. No matter how dark one's track record, each has been freed from his or her wrongdoings and, with a clean slate, is once again able to love. The Christ-centered leaders I studied frequently ex-press thankfulness that they have been freed by a loving God.

Christ not only brought forgiveness; He also brought the fabulous gift of freedom. The relationship that God offers certainly has its obligations—its commandments—but it is freeing because believers don't feel they have to prove themselves. Reconciled to God, they are free to be what they were intended to be—to love themselves and oth-ers. As Thomas Merton put it, "Sin is our refusal to be what we were created to be—son of God, images of God. Ultimately sin, while seeming to be an assertion of freedom, is a flight from the freedom and the responsibility of divine son-ship" (Merton 1964, p. 4).

Freedom to be "what we were created to be"! That's freedom from the constraints we put on ourselves and on one another when we are lost in ego-driven concerns. It's a freedom *to*, something more positive than a freedom *from*. It's the freedom to participate in the power of the universe. In business we have made a profession of con-straints and separation, but Christ-centered leaders believe their pur-pose in life is to *reconcile*—to bring the world together. It lifts them, then, not to a state of self-serving ecstasy, but to a joyful fullness.

SEVEN

How Christ
Comes to Them

Why does God let us do bad things?

Because He wants us to make up our own minds.

Even to do bad things, right under His nose?

He doesn't want us to do bad things, but to know good from bad and be good of our own free choice.

Why?

Because He loves us and wants us to love Him, but if He just made *us be good, we couldn't really love Him enough. You can't love to do what you are* made *to do, and you couldn't love God if He* made *You.*

But if God can do anything, *why can't He do that?*

Because He doesn't want *to. . . .*

Why doesn't *He want to? . . . It would be so much easier for Him.*

God—doesn't—believe—in—the—easy—way . . . Not for us, not for anything or anybody, not even for Himself. God wants us to come to *Him, to* find *Him, the best we can.*

—James Agee, A Death in the Family, p. 49

The ways to finding God are many. The Christian business executives I have studied vary in the how and when they "discovered," "acknowledged," or "turned over" their lives to God. They are not all cut from the same cloth.

APOLOGIES AND COMMITMENT

Some say they only recently "came to the Lord." They apologize for not knowing all they need to know about the Bible or how this relationship works, where it will lead, or how to express it. But they offer no apology for what they do know about Christ's being the Lord of their lives.

Some have been longtime, perhaps lifelong, Christians. Of those, some will confess they were churchgoers or even "Christians" much of their lives; however, something along the way caused them to go deeper in their relationship with God. They often distinguish between their childhood introduction to Christ or even adult church attendance and their coming to the Lord. For some, it has been a matter of coming to Christ, drifting away, and coming back again.

Some committed to Christ and then became successful in business. Others were business successes first but found something lacking in their lives; success in business had not meant success in life. Bob Arciero, member of a men's group at Saints Peter and Paul Cathedral in Providence, says that many of these men are in their fifties and sixties, successful in their professions or occupations. At some point most of them realized, however, that something was missing. They found they needed a relationship with each other and with Christ, he says.

FEW LIGHTNING BOLTS

For those who have had a conversion in their lives, it sometimes came in a flash, but that's not a prerequisite. More likely, conversion was not the event of high emotionalism we might expect. They didn't burn brightly like a Roman candle and then fizzle out in their faith.

David Musacchia says he found the Lord at age twenty-eight. "It was no great spiritual awakening. It's a process; I'm always growing." Although he had been proceeding in the growth of his faith for several years, when he attended his first Tres Dias retreat for Christian men, the intense experience caused him to realize he still had a long way to go.

Conversion for most of the Christian executives I interviewed took the form of a quiet rising above the emotions and a lessening of concern for the self. It offered an inner peace yet an outward drive to change their lives and live more purposefully. In all cases, they feel their conversion was the beginning of a long process, one that is still going on. It begins as an encounter with God that leads to a commitment that puts them on a path; it doesn't place them at a destination. It's where they begin their faith journey, which they see as never ending. The relationship *develops*—it doesn't simply occur. It is a dynamic thing that takes time and a great deal of effort.

Conversion for most of the Christian executives I interviewed took the form of a quiet rising above the emotions and a lessening of concern for the self.

As they walk in the path, they tend to focus less on themselves and more on the people around them. Donald Miller's study of members of "new paradigm" churches shows that their conversions have generally led to less focus on the self, contrary to the impression that conversion always leads to becoming wrapped up in oneself and feeling an exclusive relationship with God. (Miller, 1997)

Christ-centered executives employ a variety of worship styles and hold varying beliefs on the fine points of their faith. There is no stereotype. They span all the Christian denominations, and some are in nondenominational churches. They eagerly participate in nondenominational gatherings of Christians and willingly engage in work or discussion with persons of any spiritual path.

FROM FAILURE AND FROM SUCCESS

Often, but not always, a person undergoes a conversion after hitting bottom and realizing the need to turn his or her life around. There are numerous cases of alcoholics, drug abusers, adulterers, and criminals who have converted and renewed their lives.

Far more of us have had a mixture of good and bad in our lives. We enjoy the good, perhaps feel guilty about it, and regret the bad.

John Shumate, the real estate developer, recalls a radical change that sorted out the good and bad in his life.

John saw himself as both a success and a failure.

I was making lots of money, building and developing. I had the Ferrari, the big Mercedes, the BMW, a big boat, a Rolex watch, an adulterous lifestyle. Sometimes for me to spend $15,000 a month on clothing was nothing. All that meant nothing except I was dead. None of these things could fill the void inside my life. I was a man who had everything a man would want in the world except for an inner peace that only Christ Jesus could provide.

I assumed it was *religion* that I needed in order to stop doing the bad things I was doing—to get my life back on track, go to a church and be religious, but it was really quite contrary to all that."

JESUS ENTERS

Like many of us, John assumed there was a biblical world and a secular world, and that the two could be kept apart.

When I asked the Lord into my heart, life really changed. I did that on the living room floor. It was a supernatural move of God in my life one day. God was always trying to get to me, wanting me to turn my life over to Him. I don't believe God predestined that day; I believe that He *foreknew* the day I was going to come to Him. I don't believe we are like robots and He had everything set up. I think He is continuously wanting us to turn our lives over to him. I think He wanted me to turn my life over to him years before that so I wouldn't go through all the trouble I went through.

I feel very inadequate because it's all Jesus who did anything, and there's a lot of stuff that I'm still dealing with in my personal life—fasting, seeking His face more, spending more time with Him. I preach relationship between people and Christ all the time. At the same time, Jesus wants to have the same relationship with me. And so God told me this once: "John, you're perfect in my eyes." I wondered how so? How could that be with all the wrong things I had been doing? He basically said, "I know that. I really don't want you to do those things, but that's not why I called you perfect. Did you not receive my Son into your heart? Did I not totally forgive all your sins? Did I not put a robe of righteousness on you? Well, John, I look at you as perfect. There's nothing you did to deserve it."

A born-again Christian is perfect in God's eyes, even though in our flesh He's still molding us. God reaches different people in different ways. God wants to use all of us.

In his own case, the financial power John has acquired places him in a position to be able to witness to other leading businessmen in the community.

Like John Shumate, Tony Amato was also a business success. The owner of ten mattress stores at an early age, he had a healthy family and a good life. But something was missing, he knew. He had done some heavy drinking and engaged in a little recreational drug use. At age twenty-seven, he began searching for healing from panic attacks and from a haunting guilt. He consulted a psychiatrist who recommended Zen and other techniques. All the while, he had Christian friends who were praying for him.

Tony was a longtime Catholic, but, he says, "I had a fear of being a 'Christian.'" Intending no offense to the Catholic faith, he means he was a nominal Christian but not one walking with Christ. He had seen too many coworkers who used Christianity "as a crutch." They read the Bible yet lied to customers in order to improve their income—even when they intended to use it "to further God's kingdom."

One day, after attending a prayer breakfast, he went out for coffee with a friend who then challenged him: "Tony you're on the fence in walking with the Lord." Tony can smile now when he confesses, "It's easy to be on both sides—to do what's convenient." Then he turns serious: "Yet, I couldn't turn away. God's been too good to me. It doesn't get any better than this."

So, he says, "I received the Lord as ruler of my life. My whole life changed. But I was really nervous about it. I had a fear of change, of being obligated." A really difficult time came when he went home to tell his wife about his new commitment. He found her and their weeks-old baby lying on the bed. He lay down to tell her what he had done, but she said she didn't want to hear about it! "She hadn't married a Christian, a person who prayed and studied the Bible," he says painfully.

Yet, at the moment he was talking with his wife, he "felt the Holy Spirit take over my body." During the four years since that event, Tony has repeatedly asked himself, "What do I have to live up to? God knows I'm going to screw up. I still have that guilt. I'm suddenly totally conscious of everything I do—like a *higher consciousness.* I'm now thinking before every action. I still screw up, but I'm catching myself sooner and sooner." In his search for a better understanding of how to live his new life, Tony attends both Catholic and Presbyterian church worship services, Bible study sessions, and meetings of the Fellowship of Companies for Christ International. He is active in an inner-city project for housing the homeless, where his prior acquaintance with alcohol and drugs equipped him for dealing with the recovering addicts who are trying to get their lives straight.

"THERE'S MORE TO THIS THAN ME"

You do not have to be a reformed alcoholic or drug abuser or even have a lot of bad content in your life to become a Christian. Some followers were doing well without a close relationship with God, but they asked themselves if they were doing the right things. Tim Conlon, president of the billion-dollar Berg Electronics Corporation, is a man who has enjoyed a string of successes on the fast track through the business world. When I asked him about the history of his relationship with Christ, he said,

> I have been Catholic all of my life. I have only been Christian maybe the last ten years. I remember when I went back and made a real sincere confession. I went from probably age twenty to about thirty as an atheist-agnostic and then started sort of a slow progression back. I would have to say it was the combination of the prayers of my mother, the example of my father, and then certain life events that caused me to assess where I was in life and ask what was my purpose for being here—the birth of my first child, the death of my father-in-law—the kind of things that strike you as "There's more to this than me."

Shortly after that, I developed my own mission statement. I had been told by a senior executive that I had what it took. I guess his affirmation of what my ego had been telling me kind of set me on the course of "I know I'm going to make it." And I needed to decide how I wanted to "make it" and what I wanted to do with making it. This was all during about a six-year period. I went through making my way back to my faith, off and on, and assessing what I wanted to do—what my mission was. The mission I came up with was—and it's still my mission—to provide long-term secure employment for as many people as possible. Now that's not jobs for life for everybody. There are occasions where you can't maintain your workforce—like when one of your big customers doesn't do as well as you had expected. You may also fail in making the right decisions. To me that's the most painful of all.

For Tim, building the relationship with God goes on. When I first talked with him about his faith, he said, "The first thing I want to make clear is that, by no stretch of the imagination, am I perfect. Am I living the message? I don't know. I try to go to mass everyday. I tell my kids and I tell people who comment on it that, 'I don't go to mass every day because I'm holy. I go to mass every day because I'm not.'"

OTHERS IN THEIR LIVES

The spiritual development process is inevitably triggered by or helped along by the people these followers of Christ find around them in their church, small groups, or family. John Shumate attributes his breakthrough, at least partly, to friends. "It must have been their prayer and then their spending some time to tell me so that really did it for me." Tony Amato, as we saw, felt the prayers of friends and was confronted by one who took the time to point out that he needed to get off the fence. Tim Conlon points to the prayers of his mother and the example of his father for leading him to and bringing him through the process of building a relationship with God.

Some, like Bob Boehm, president of Boehm Pressed Steel, have found support for their spiritual development in the workplace. He says the departure of key people from his company seemed, at the time, to be creating a bad situation. When his Number 2 employee left, he hired a new person who happened to be a Christian. After many years of using the same outside accountant, he went to a new one who is a Christian. Looking back on these changes, he feels blessed that he now has people inside his firm as well as several outsiders who are helping him come closer to God.

> "I don't go to mass every day because I'm holy. I go to mass every day because I'm not."

Pam Carlson, CEO of ROC Carbon Company, says a turning point in her life came twenty-three years ago. Her first husband had died of cancer when he was thirty-one. At twenty-seven, Pam was left with a three-month-old baby and a two-year-old child. She was in rebellion, she says, and she was determined not to give her life over to a god who had torn her family apart. She later married a man who was "equally in rebellion." She wanted a oneness in her family and to live by Christian values, but her life wasn't working out that way. A neighbor began praying for her and talking with her. In time, Pam said, "God, if you really are real, I want you to show yourself to me. If you are real, you can do something about this situation because there is nothing else I can do."

She cleaned up her language but reserved two words that she would continue using because "I didn't want anybody to know that I am different. 'Continue to do your work, God, but I'm going to be like this.' And He took me like I was and started working on the inside. After about six weeks, I noticed I wasn't saying those words like I used to. I realized He must be doing something in me so I really turned my life over to Him." Pam quit smoking and, overnight, she felt like she had never smoked before. She hasn't smoked since, and she says she can now point to that incident as proof that He is real.

In none of these cases did the friends or family members tell the individual what to do, or try to sell something he or she should believe in. They did it through prayer and example as they lived their own loving relationship with God.

GOD'S DOING

John, Tony, Tim, Bob, and Pam, like hundreds of other people, regard the "coincidence" of being influenced by people around them as God's putting specific people in their paths. God is not only seeking them out but helping them connect. The experience of each of them embodies a common message: God wants us "to come to Him, to find Him the best way we can," but He is there first, seeking us and waiting for us. There's nothing we do that's so bad that He will not seek us.

> **John, Tony, Tim, Bob, and Pam, like hundreds of others, regard the "coincidence" of being influenced by people around them as God's putting specific people in their paths.**

On the other hand, there is nothing we can do that's so *good* that we will be sure to find Him. These Christians believe their faith is the result of God's eventually coming to them once they are open to the relationship. They do not expect miracles, but they generally find "a supernatural move of God"—in their own transformation. They are in awe of what God has chosen to do in their lives.

"It is not our way to Him but His way to us that has to be prepared," Dietrich Bonhoeffer advised. "Christ is coming, of His own will, by His own strength, and out of His own love" (Bonhoeffer 1955, p. 140). As much as we might hope and prepare, the coming to faith is an act of God, not of the individual. Or, as Bonhoeffer expresses it: "Christian life is the dawning of the ultimate in me" (p. 141).

Jimmy Carter, who was a businessman for many years before becoming president of the United States, recalls the distinction made by theologian "Karl Barth, who said that religion is our search for God, and that this always results in our finding a god that is most convenient for our own purposes. He distinguishes this from faith, which results from God's seeking us through Christ" (Jimmy Carter 1996, p. 220).

Carole Hamm says, "I still sometimes am awestruck at *how Christ comes to us.* I didn't know that I went searching. Maybe there was a part of me that was very thirsty and hungry. I had received an education of Christianity as a young child. But, for years, I had put my spiritual growth on hold. We were very successful in our business. My husband and I were busy rearing a family, building a future together—and that was a piece of our life that just never got addressed. We were good people, doing good work, we ran an ethical company, and were providing some good things for the community. Then about five years ago, my husband had a heart attack at the age of forty-four." That "stark reality" changed things for her. "But it has been a five-year journey of personal growth. I began to deepen my own Christian walk and have the kind of faith that I still continue to groom and grow and process."

Another event led Carole even deeper in her faith—one triggered by a total stranger. She tells of her first visit to the Servant Leadership School in Washington D.C. "I was fearful of the city and, in order to protect myself, I went out and purchased a can of mace. As I shared my upcoming trip with a coworker, he stopped me dead in my tracks with his comment: 'So, in the name of Jesus Christ, I mace you?' Oh, how the truth hurt. I went home that night and threw out the can of mace. The following day, I drove to the city, remembering how I had been taught to avoid eye contact with people on the streets. But, as I walked to the school, I allowed my eyes to meet those of a man sitting in front of Christ House. Tears came to my eyes and I felt a compassion for this stranger. My fears turned to love. My thoughts about him, as well as my thoughts about the poor, changed. He has no idea what he gave to me that day. It was a *new consciousness* that he stirred within me."

EIGHT

New Selves

C arole Hamm refers to a "new consciousness." David Musacchia speaks of a "higher consciousness." When we look deep into the lives of a leader who is centered on Christ, we find that he or she has undergone or is undergoing a fundamental shift to a worldview that is quite different from the one that prevails in our business culture.

Life-changing shifts in how we view the world don't come easily, as countless people have learned. In recent years, as part of the quest for productivity and quality improvement, business managers have tried "change-management" programs. Consulting firms have set up change-management divisions to serve them. The bolder explorers even go so far as to use the big T-word—*transformation*—but they often mean transformation of someone else, not themselves.

We do need a transformation in business, as we saw in chapter 3, but we seldom find a way to undergo one in our own lives, much less enable others to do it. Transforming ourselves is like trying to fly by putting our hands under our thighs and lifting ourselves out of our chairs. Undergoing a transformation requires more than wanting one. Embracing a new paradigm requires more than dissatisfaction with the present one. Both require a vision of, if not an experience of, something that works better. Christians with whom I talked may or may not have wanted a change, but something better presented itself, nevertheless. Many of them describe the change as both pleasant and discomforting, as they threw off the worldview that may keep others from achieving significant change. That is not to say that these Christians know where the revelation and transformation will lead. They proceed on faith.

TRANSFORMED BY GOD

Some, like Tony Amato, believe the Holy Spirit has taken over or, at least, has become a very real presence in their lives. That is why they are willing to change their behavior. The willingness to do so seems to come without their trying, yet they must work hard to put intent into action. Again and again, as we explore the transformations of those who walk in Christ's company, we find that they are convinced the change came about, not by their own efforts, but by God's. These executives go through a transformation when Christ enters into their lives. They experience Christ living in them. As a result, they find they are obeying Paul's charge: "Do not conform any longer to the pattern of this world, but be transformed by the renewing of your mind" (Romans 12:2).

As they enter this new life, they notice changes in themselves and what they see around them:

New Language. Randy Vesco, a principal in the management firm Vesco and Duffy Associates, recalls that after he committed his life to Christ several years ago, he began encountering a new language. "I started attending meetings. I was hearing new words like *witnessing, testimony, calling*." Tom Ford, vice president, A. W. Fenton Company, has observed that newcomers to the faith are often concerned that they lack certain experience even though they may have lived moral lives and have not gone through any great failures that have to be righted. Many of them admit they are less familiar with the Bible than others with whom they are now associating, and they sometimes feel uncertain about just how to relate to the beliefs and behaviors to which they are being introduced.

New Behavior. Having Christ within them leads to changed beliefs that, in turn, leads to changed behavior. With the Spirit within them they generally attain an inner peace—not a set of controls—that rules their emotions, calling up positive ones to displace the negative ones. It seems strange to the individuals themselves that they have the ability to overcome the usual fears that stood in the way of changing their behavior. They learn to give up control, take on obligations and responsibilities, and grow into deeper relationships. This does not come easily. As they look at their new selves, they wonder how they can avoid "screwing up" in living up to the accompanying new commitment, but they plunge ahead.

New Benchmarks. They find themselves judging their behavior by higher standards, not by what their peers are doing. This means not just doing right rather than wrong but striving for excellence rather than "good enough." They don't see themselves as doing things better than others, but as becoming different. Their entire natures have been altered radically. Yet they may be haunted by concern, "not that others will hate us, but that we will learn to hate worldly things and have to give up material comforts," says one Christian executive. As Randy Vesco explains it, "We each have spiritual and secular turf we try to protect."

New Perspective. "Christians desire to do the right thing out of love and obedience to God and love for our neighbors, not because we are afraid of unpleasant consequences or because we may somehow benefit from it," writes Dick DeVos of Amway (DeVos 1997, p. 60).

Being in the process of transformation, they work at trying to see the world from God's point of view—to know what God wants for them and for the world. As we are told in Romans 12:2, "Then you will be able to test and approve what God's will is—his good, pleasing, and perfect will."

Even their view of God has undergone a change! To a large degree, we tend to think of God as the maker of the great machine that
was put here to serve us. As theologian Paul Tillich wrote,
"Enlightenment theologians . . . always portrayed God as a wonderful
technician who made the best possible machine for the glory and well-
being of man. Everything . . . had a purpose for the human race"
(Tillich 1967, p. 350).

Surrendering to Christ as Lord does not mean that a Christian can
look to God to improve the odds of getting what he or she wants.
Instead, looking at the world from God's point of view changes the individual's wants. Talk with one after another of these Christian executives, and you will hear expressions of confidence that a wise and
loving God will provide the right things. Although they may be masters of facts and numbers, they place their lives in the hands of something they know but cannot verify. That's transformation!

In a series of audiotapes called "Leading a Company for Christ" prepared for the Fellowship of Companies for Christ International, Bruce
Wilkinson, one of the founders of the group, explains why even would-
be Christians fail when they try to force behavioral changes: "We put
Christ in a stained glass building. We try to work on behavior without
changing our beliefs." Alan Ross of FCCI points out, "We have been
teaching people to behave like Christians without the power of Christ."

With God leading the transformation process, the Christian generally rises above *improving* the self. He or she expresses it in terms of
being *different*, not just better at the same old things, as God works
within. The dramatic change in perspective and expectations that happens is illustrated by some of the items on a card called "The
Philosophy—Better or Different," used by FCCI members for discussion (see table, p. 94).

GETTING THE SELF OUT OF THE WAY

In observing and studying Christian executives, I found that they
work hard at getting their selves out of the way so God can enter and
work through them. They rise above selfish interests that battle with

World's Perspective	Biblical Perspective
Self-centered	Christ-centered
Self-improvement emphasis	Changed/transformed heart
Better by degree: more moral, more ethical, fairer	Different
Work on one's ability to love	Spirit produces love

the universe. This is very much in keeping with the New Testament, where *self* is mentioned only eight times, five of which are in the following three passages:

> Romans 6:6: For we know that our old *self* was crucified with him so that the body of sin might be done away with, that we should no longer be slaves to sin. . . .
>
> Ephesians 4:22–24: You were taught, with regard to your former way of life, to put off your old *self*, which is being corrupted by its deceitful desires; and to put on the new *self*, created to be like God in true righteousness and holiness.
>
> Colossians 3:9–10: Do not lie to each other, since you have taken off your old *self* with its practices and have put on the new *self*, which is being renewed in knowledge in the image of its Creator.

The self needs radical repositioning, not mere improvement. The Christian takes on a new life in which the self is not supreme. "Therefore, if anyone is in Christ, he is a new creation; the old has gone, the new has come" (2 Corinthians 5:17). This then, is the ultimate antidote to affliction of me-ism on which our business culture has been so heavily based.

In business, we attempt to elevate individualism to a level that defies what science teaches about how the world works and what the Scriptures teach about how it should work. Science and Scripture reveal our interdependence with one another and with some greater power. They do provide for individuation—the uniqueness of each individual within the community—but this does not justify our regarding business as a place of combat, where someone has to lose.

When we ignore our interdependence and need for community, we defeat all of us.

In recent years, some of us have begun to challenge outdated notions of individualism. That, says Frank Larkin, is because "It's experienced as an 'I gotta get mine first.' That's not individuality at the soul level. That's individuality at the social level. That's what we've been conditioned to believe. Individuality is critical to Christianity, but at the soul level." It is there that we find the most powerful motivational agent. Christianity, he says, "is not about limiting myself but about expanding myself and doing so much more."

Frank believes that Christianity is not a set of rules about what we cannot do but a challenge to rise to what we were born to do. "Christianity is very proactive; it is about striking forward. It is the most proactive theology that has ever been introduced to the world. Don't study Christianity if you don't intend to do anything," he warns. "What you have to understand is Christ is the ultimate means to engage my soul, to activate it, to live a fulfilling life. We're not all going to go through the same Christian path and end up at the same point because each of us is made in the image of God—but, like parts of a mosaic, each of us is an element of God."

> Christian executives work hard at getting their selves out of the way so God can enter and work through them.

Those who walk in the company of Christ are confident as they stride forward even though they don't see all the way to the end of the path. Pam Carlson believes much of the walking depends on being submissive to God and whatever He offers. When she began attending sessions of an FCCI program called the Masters Institute, she realized, "In order to go deeper with God, I must have a consistent time with the Lord in His word and in prayer, both listening and talking with Him. How would I ever do that? By simply asking the Lord to give me a heart for His Word. I did that, and something wonderful happened! I had a heart for His Word. I wanted to read the Word. I wanted to converse with God. There was a renewal in my relationship with my

Creator. And all it took was a heart action—one that asked God to do the work and expected Him to do it."

> **Those who walk in the company of Christ are confident as they stride forward even though they don't see all the way to the end of the path.**

In a later session of that same program, Pam went through an evaluation exercise by peers, subordinates, and others to point out her strengths and weaknesses as a leader. It was not an easy experience for her because, she says, she likes approval. But she came away with a list of shortcomings, saying, "I have no idea how to tackle that, but I am going to give it to You and I want You to work in my life and make me the kind of leader I need to be." Pam says, "I could tell almost immediately the kind of difference that He was making in my life. I felt more like a leader. I acted more like a leader just by yielding to Him."

"My faith has everything to do with my optimism," explains Dick DeVos. "For one thing, it is easier to take a positive view of life when we believe that the world was created and didn't just happen. If we believe that people were made special, with a purpose, and are not accidents of nature, and if we believe that there is a God watching over the world He made, then we can take comfort that ultimately things are going to turn out for the best, even though the results may not always occur when or how we want them to" (DeVos 1997, p. 110).

PRINCIPLES AND VALUES

Biblical principles, if truly followed, would ease or eliminate many of our problems. In business, however, we are not used to discussing the principles or values we will follow. Numerous experts do say that a business organization should operate from a base of values, but too many of them claim that no particular values are required—that it is necessary simply to clarify whatever values drive an organization and make them known in a values statement. This is not only ethics nonsense, the exercise serves little business purpose because it fails to engage the people in our organizations at their deepest level and win their full commitment. Not all corporate values we might choose would be in harmony with the principles or laws that preserve and advance the universe.

Principles are those truths that allow the creation to stay in unity. They were set in place by the ground force that created and sustains the universe—God. While we may not fully comprehend the truth, principles show "as far as we can discern it, how we think God wants us to live," says Max Stackhouse at Princeton Theological Seminary. They instruct us as to what we should value in our lives and how we should behave in order to serve the unity of the universe.

Humankind discerned certain principles long ago. A core of principles has appeared in one religion after another. They relate to respect, dignity, fairness, honesty, and justice. The new science model of the physical universe would call these principles the laws that hold the fabric of the universe together. In effect, they describe the force—love—that holds all together.

For Christ-centered persons, principles are demonstrated in the life, words, death, and resurrection of Christ. A relationship with Christ leads them to principles that become the core of their being—something more powerful than the mere guidance that might be derived from a handbook or a model.

If we live only in the world of the ego, however, there are no such principles, and there is too little room for love. The rules of the game, then, have to do only with struggle and survival. Principles, in contrast, foster the oneness and connectedness of each aspect of the universe, preserving both the individual and the collective whole. For the Christian, faith leads to an understanding of these principles, which become translated into what we value; values then shape behavior; and feedback on our behavior strengthens our faith. And the cycle goes 'round.

Principles are eternal, not something we devise for a given situation. Unfortunately, in modern times, we have turned from eternal truths to personal opinions and wants, and we get lost in the present. Without principles to live by, we become disoriented. We attempt to devise our own "principles," but principles are not things that we decide on or invent; we discover them. They begin with God's needs, not our ego's needs. Guided by them, we can drive meaningful change into the world; without them we are tossed about by every change that comes our way.

The values that really bring people together in value-creating communities and drive a business to excellence are those that serve God and people as well as the business entity. Bernie Nagle and I found that the altrupreneurs we described in our book *Leveraging People and Profit* are driven by some very specific, other-centered, community-building values. These include:

- Caring, concern, compassion, respect for others
- Community, interdependence, teamwork
- Honesty, openness, trust, constancy of purpose
- Empowerment, integrity, joy in their work, learning
- Commitment, creativity, initiative, resourcefulness, responsibility
- Excellence, improvement, service.

(Nagle and Pascarella 1998, p. 50)

Who would object to the embodiment of these values in their business? Workers and customers want the business organizations with whom they are associated to adhere to such values.

A NEW VIEW OF THE COMPANY

Since the Christian's transformation enables a different view of self and of the world, the Christian executive sees his or her company in a different light, and makes sure that it attends to the human issues that are now presenting management with its greatest challenges.

We might say these leaders see themselves working "in the company of Christ" in that they walk with Christ and work in a company owned by Christ. Obviously, a person like Bill Pollard, who chairs a company of thousands of stockholders and thousands of employees, cannot label his company as belonging to Christ. The company does state, however, that it is in the service of God, and Bill and many of his key managers are Christians in the service of God. Although the company is not owned by God in legal/financial terms, it is in the service of God.

Even in a family-owned company like R. W. Beckett, John Beckett believes, the idea of a "Christian company" would be theologically incorrect. "Christ transforms the *individual*, not the corporation," John says. Yet he admits that, at one point in time, "I released the company to God. I committed our company to God."

While a corporation is a legal entity—artificially separated from its management and owners—we cannot truly separate our personal lives from our corporate lives. Those who see themselves leading companies for Christ see beyond legalities to more fundamental truths. They believe that everything is ultimately owned by God. The company may not be owned by

Righteous companies, **not power centers—** that is how many Christian executives view their organizations. Because they worship God, they put people ahead of the structure.

Christ in the law's eyes, but a chief executive or owner can commit it to being Christ-focused. They regard themselves and even the stockholders merely as stewards of what God has put in their hands. They view the physical and financial assets as being entrusted to them or "the company" by God. And, certainly, they believe, the employees entrusted to them are God's people. That is why some of them will not draw the line and make the requirement for employment exclusively Christian. They, like Bill Pollard, see themselves as serving all God's people.

Is Berg Electronics a "company of Christ"? I asked Tim Conlon. "If my chairman and my board were to read that kind of phraseology, they might take exception to it," he said.

> Yet, while there are imperfections, I think that we are a pretty good company. I think we treat people with respect and dignity. When relationships don't work out, we make sure that the person is given some kind of package where they go away with some financial continuity. I don't think I've ever let anyone go with less than a six months'—and usually it's a year—severance package. That isn't necessarily altruistic. The way the next person you want to hire measures you is on the basis of what he hears, and what he hears is what the last person you fired has to say. I think we are a pretty righteous company.

Righteous companies, not power centers—that is how many Christian executives view their organizations. Because they worship God, not the organization, they put people ahead of the structure. They shape the organization so that it honors God, rather than allowing it to become a Frankenstein monster that takes over its creator.

Dan Hanson of Land O'Lakes repeatedly expresses concern about the organization's becoming so preeminent that it actually rules our lives:

> We need to make sure it doesn't become so real we let it dictate to us our work and our relationships and our relationships to God. I love the biological model (which regards the organization as an organism) in the sense of the various roles and pieces coming together, so long as that whole doesn't become so reified that it becomes overpowering. I think that is what has happened, and then it becomes a matter of control. The higher you get, the less control you have in a lot of ways, however. Now you're locked into a certain lifestyle and materialism, and you've lost touch with those things in life that are really important.

NINE

Living with Paradoxes

"**M**ost Christians today identify the sacred solely with their personal and individual life, so that their faith has less and less to do with the culture 'out there,'" say Brian J. Walsh and J. Richard Middleton in *The Transforming Vision* (1984, p. 100).

Time and again, Christians have heard the message about being the salt of the earth, about being in the world and being an influence on the culture around them rather than accepting the world as it is. Christ's own prayer to God was "not that you take them out of the world but that you protect them from the evil one. They are not of the world, even as I am not of it" (John 17:16). They are to be engaged in the world but not totally shaped by it.

Some Christians do not, however, try to change the culture to fit their view of the sacred. In fact, they too often hear sermons that suggest they get out of the secular or business world, adds Dick Leggatt of the Ohio Roundtable. They are left, then, with two separate worlds—an evil secular one, from which they must isolate themselves, and a spiritual one, to which they must retreat.

Christ-centered leaders, however, do engage in the secular world, relying on their faith to guide their daily actions. In their leadership positions, they work to change the culture around them. They are not torn between God and the world. By putting God's concerns first, they can see material things in perspective and enjoy the beauty of the world without becoming slaves to it. They see their role as one of reconciliation. God created a good world. We fell. God is trying to reconcile with us. These leaders try to reconcile humankind with God, and much of their effort is directed to reconciling people to one another.

This does not always translate into their taking up national causes, although some do. They do not look for grand solutions. They work, first, at the needs close at hand. They engage people one on one. They attend to the needs of an employee, a family member, a poor individual on the street. As leaders, they tend to getting their own companies in line. That's why the FCCI's motto states, "Changing our world through Christ, one company at a time."

TRUTH IN PARADOX

Operating with the old, biblical view of the world causes the paradoxical behavior and beliefs that characterize leaders who are truly walking with Christ (see chapter 5). When I mentioned some of these paradoxes to Carole Hamm, she replied, "As a Christian you have more options. You're a little more open to this discerning; where you used to think that a decision was cut and dried, you see that there are more sides to look at. I like to think that the hope lies in the future of the whole struggle. Without that struggle, I'm not quite sure we would further ourselves. So I welcome that struggle. There were times when I would have run from it."

More options? Doesn't Christianity present some universal truths on which there can be no negotiating? Yes, but on the other hand, one of these principles has to do with being open and forgiving. Some of the Christian leaders to whom I posed such questions revealed that they welcome spiritual dialogue. They are willing to learn from and to inform others in an ongoing search for truth and balance. "There would be some concern on my part if we didn't have some balance," said Carole Hamm. We all do not have to be "running the same course," as she puts it.

Persons who have integrity see the worth of others. They are courageous enough to state what they believe and stand ready for dialogue. They tell why they are doing what they are doing. Integrity, says Stephen Carter in a book by that name, "requires three steps: 1. *discerning* what is right and what is wrong; 2. *acting* on what you have discerned, even at personal cost; and 3. *saying openly* that you are acting on your understanding of right from wrong" (Stephen Carter 1996, p. 7).

INTEGRITY PREVAILS

Living with Christianity's paradoxes does not lead to schizophrenia. The executives I have studied take paradox in stride because their worldviews permit them to rise above simplistic thinking. They find their overarching identity in being followers of Christ. For them, embracing paradoxes rather than denying them brings their work into the perspective of a meaningful and purposeful whole life.

> **P**ersons who have integrity see the worth of others. They are courageous enough to state what they believe and stand ready for dialogue.

God's work for Christians comes in many forms. Some are called to be of great influence on their organizations, to change the "system." They are chosen to be concerned with the big picture, to wrestle with big goals, and engage in strategic action. Yet, I do not find that their heavy corporate workload necessarily takes away from them the personal warmth that one should expect of Christians. Paradoxically, some who are not perceived as "people persons" are people-oriented at heart. They may be seen by some as lacking personal warmth, but this does not mean they don't love others or are not dedicating their lives to serving others.

Gordon Heffern, retired chairman of Society Corporation and Society National Bank, has long been a prominent dedicated Christian in the Cleveland area. Shawana Johnson, in her work on an Executive

Doctorate of Management at Case Western Reserve University, did extensive research on Gordon that reveals his paradoxical nature. Perhaps it would be more accurate to say "his paradoxical image." In interviews with members of his family, fellow corporate officers, and people who reported to him, positive descriptions such as *consistent, generous, compassionate, caring* were expressed frequently. On the other hand, there were a few mentions of being *intimidating* or *distant* or *making others uncomfortable.*

There were still other descriptors—such as *strong-willed, goal-oriented, demanding,* and "He attributes his success to God"—that may explain his mixed image. Gordon is truly centered on God. He knows what he believes. He strives to do what he sees as right. The strength of his convictions may strike some people as "coming on too strong." The fact that he is intent on serving God's goals may leave him lacking in charisma. While he has been an effective networker in business terms, he is not known as a socializer. Yet, hundreds of lives have been touched by his warmth.

One interviewee in Shawana Johnson's study said, "A bank executive was having a difficult time with alcohol and lost his job and home because of it. Gordon brought him in to live with his family and supported him in overcoming his alcoholism. I can't tell you how many times Gordon used his own personal funds to help individuals who had financial problems."

In his dealings with subordinates, Gordon was noted for getting to know people well and being "a great mentor." He also insisted that other managers in the company be mentors by advising subordinates and giving them opportunities for development. "Gordon really looked at people, not just what was apparent to the human eye. He looked at them to see who they really were. He looked through to their potential," says another interviewee.

Obviously, an officer in a large company can't know all employees well. But when he was president of Goodyear Bank in Akron, Gordon heard that one of the employees had been diagnosed with cancer and had been given a 10 percent chance of survival. That person recalls, "Unbeknownst to me, Gordon formed a prayer chain in the Akron area and hundreds of people were praying for me daily in the community and at work. Now, Gordon didn't know me that well, but he reached out and touched my life in a way no other person has. I am alive today because Gordon Heffern started that prayer chain."

Whatever the rough edges of a person's image may be, integrity prevails. After years of studying business managers, however, I have become convinced that the primary reason for their failure to maximize an organization's performance is their *lack* of integrity. Very few of them are dishonest or immoral. By lack of integrity, I mean they fail to bring the secular and spiritual together and get in touch with their souls, which span the two realms. Far too many of them suffer an inability to know or even care to know who they truly are. When they talk about "the big picture," they mean business strategy, not the Really Big Picture.

> **Christ-centered leaders do not compartmentalize the spiritual aspects and the secular aspects of their lives. By living in the two worlds simultaneously, they can live meaningful lives.**

Some sense that they need to find some sort of *balance* in their work lives and their spiritual lives. They may try to offset the emptiness in their work roles with compensating activities in their personal lives. But balancing empty work lives with over-correction in our private lives still leaves a divided self.

Douglas LaBier of the Center for Adult Development calls "the struggle for work-life 'balance,' by far, the most frequently voiced complaint of career professionals today. But the fact is that work-life balance cannot be achieved. The reason is simple: our culture puts human development in the service of economic development, which makes 'balance' impossible. Life serves economic development and business success, rather than the other way around" (La Bier 1998, p. 15).

Most, if not all, of the Christ-centered business leaders I studied seem to attain a *blending* that is more integrating than futile attempts at balancing. They do not compartmentalize the spiritual aspects of their lives into certain blocks of time and the secular aspects into others. By living in the two worlds simultaneously, they can live meaningful lives. They are driven by the same values on the job as off the job. That is the mark of integrity.

They live out the advice we find in the best of leadership literature. Some examples:

- Warren Bennis, in *On Becoming a Leader:* "The process of becoming a leader is much the same as the process of becoming an integrated human being" (Bennis 1989, p. 4).
- Peter Vaill, in *Managing as a Performing Art:* "Not only does the new executive role call for individuality, it calls for the *whole person.* Less and less does it make sense to think of these positions as delimited functions that can be described in traditional 'duties and responsibilities' terms. Today's executive is learning that everything he or she has ever done counts in the job" (Vaill 1989, p. 19).
- Max De Pree, in *Leadership Is an Art:* " Our value system and worldview should be as closely integrated into our work lives as they are integrated into our lives with our families, our churches, and our other activities and groups" (De Pree 1987, p. 24)

Both the leader and the led find self-fulfillment by being whole persons and a part of the greater whole. Self-fulfillment—a popular topic these days—is not a selfish accomplishment when it is genuine. Self-fulfillment is attained not for our own sakes, or on our own terms. It is a matter of becoming what God intends us to be, and that involves being other-centered.

MULTIPLE ROLES

Most of us are haunted by the fear that we can't possibly integrate our lives because we have so many roles to fill. The push and shove of one role versus another makes us wonder, "How do I find time to deal with all my roles? How do I set priorities?"

To begin with, we don't select all our roles for ourselves. Yes, we choose to accept a job or a promotion, we choose to marry, we choose to join a group. But many of our roles are bestowed on us. Each of us is someone's child. We become parents. We live next door to neighbors. We find ourselves "volunteered" to handle a project. Regardless of who chooses our many roles, they don't fit into a nice pattern. They vie for our time and attention. Sometimes they conflict.

Each of us is in an enormous network of relationships, says Max Stackhouse. "It is likely that nothing less than an understanding of and a commitment to covenantal mutuality under God can bring moral and spiritual coherence to what is otherwise experienced as a seething chaotic mass of dominations and arbitrariness. The only way to negotiate our way through the mazes is to recognize that each of us is made in the image of God and on that basis we are called to be persons of integrity in the midst of a pluralism of vocations" (Stackhouse 1997, p. 155).

Serving God should not be on our list of roles because it is the touchstone against which we evaluate each of our roles. It puts our roles—our relationships—into a meaningful context. "Without an integrating center of identity, without a sense of being called and empowered by God to fulfill one's gifts and serve God, the neighbor, and the community, these activities become only a whirl, a drudgery of socially imposed activities with no sense of purpose or vision" (Stackhouse 1997, p. 156).

There are a number of questions we can ask ourselves to help us analyze our roles:

1. What are some of the key roles I fill?
2. Which do I do well? Where do I fall short? Which would I rather ignore?
3. Which roles conflict with others?
4. Which are in harmony, reinforcing one another?
5. In which roles, if any, do I feel I am working with God?
6. How do I feel about each role? Excited? Committed? Determined? Resigned? Overwhelmed?
7. From God's point of view, which roles are most important?
8. How would God have me fill each role?
9. How does God work with and through me in each of my roles?

Christian leaders' worldviews help them to answer questions about their roles, give them the commitment to fill them, and allow them to permit God to work with and through them. Being followers of Christ is their overarching purpose. Being a business executive is just one role through which they live that out. Somehow, they say, this view enables them to find time and energy for meeting the critical obligations of their roles. As a result, when people refer to them they are not likely to say, "He does such and such *and* he is a Christian." They are more likely to understand, "He does such and such *because* he is a Christian."

David Musacchia says, "A lot of people prioritize God, family, work, and so on. That's somewhat pagan thinking. God should be the head of all. Everything should glorify Him." Rather than ranking God along with all our other roles, we should put Him first with the others relating to Him.

CAPTIVES OF ORGANIZATIONAL ROLES

The role of a leader is paradoxical in itself. It calls for a blending of the two modes: thought and action. As a marketing executive, Michael Prewitt knows that a professional has to "be smart, have the answers, be on top of your game." On the other hand, as a seminarian, he is learning the importance of listening and searching. The hard reality: A customer, for instance, thinks, "Don't tell me about your vulnerabilities, tell me about your expertise." When a business question comes up, "You've got to have a quick answer—something out of your bag of tricks that says 'I know what to do here' as opposed to 'This situation is going to require God's grace and I've got to listen as hard as I can' and not have an answer before I get in there."

Daniel Hanson warns (at the close of chapter 8) that the organization can easily rule our lives if we allow it to tell us how to think and act. It can define our work role to the point of trampling our effectiveness in filling any of our other roles. Even when it presents inviting and even exciting opportunities, it simply feeds our ego while starving the soul.

"The person, split off from his or her own capacity to reflect and find meaning, becomes captive to the role defined by the workplace.

The antidote to this state of affairs is to find a role that includes the whole person," Alan Briskin advises us (Briskin 1996, p. 195). The productive way to think of an organizational role is "as a psychological stance, an idea that we hold in our mind, rather than something written on a piece of paper" (p. 196).

"The challenges we face in the workplace of today can be seductive and intimidating," Briskin warns. "On the one hand, we can be swept away by the promise but not the reality of empowerment. We are led to believe we are in charge of our destiny, but the realities of the organization often prove otherwise" (Briskin 1996, pp. 197–98).

Talk with managers who have lost their corporate roles through downsizing or restructuring, and you won't have much difficulty sorting out those who had defined significant roles for themselves from those who had let the company define roles for them. Those with integrity—with a purpose defining their lives—seemed to be able to accept their job loss more readily than those without it. If they were serving a high purpose in their work, not just filling a job, they were, perhaps unknowingly, creating options for seeking another position or organization or even a new career through which they can continue to serve that purpose.

FINDING OUR 'WHY'

He mused like a man only half-awake on how it had all come about, the long train of trivial accidents, affirmed one by one, that made a man's life what it happened to become.

—John Gardner, *Nickel Mountain*

We frequently struggle to manage our collection of roles without knowing what they all add up to. We feel the need for something to move toward, rather than just letting life happen and allowing ourselves to be victims of circumstances, as John Gardner's character did. We ask one of life's fundamental questions: "Why am I here?"

But how do we arrive at the why? Often, we begin by listing our gifts or talents, but that doesn't point to the one best place where we can apply them. Or we start with our roles and add them up, but the pieces do not give us direction. We find ourselves confronted with a divergence between our gifts and what we are in a position to do with them. The gifts and roles don't always match.

Richard Leider, author of *The Power of Purpose,* suggests what amounts to a totally different approach—starting with the why itself, defining the purpose of our life. "It is not what deeds we do that give us a sense of purpose, but knowing why we do them" (Leider 1985, p. 24). Unfortunately, in our busy lives, we worry about what's and how's but neglect to ask why. Geoffrey Bellman, in *Your Signature Path,* points out the never-ending spiral this triggers: "Our current personal, work, and community malaise is fed by the absence of whys in our lives" (Bellman 1996, p. 85).

> **We do not need to invent a "why" in our lives. It's already there. Purpose is the soul's expression of itself.**

We do not need to invent a "why" in our lives. It's already there. Purpose is the soul's expression of itself. Some people express it clearly and openly, others are searching for it, and still others have no awareness that there might be a purpose to life. We all ask why questions. Whether it is a deep philosophical inquiry ("What's the purpose of life?") or a more down-to-earth question ("Why am I doing this work?"), people constantly express or search for purpose. It is a basic human need that satisfies the search for self-identity and for unity in some larger self. (Pascarella and Frohman 1989, p. 27)

Richard Nelson Bolles, author of the *What Color Is Your Parachute?* series of books, suggests working at three purposes or missions. The first is to seek out through frequent communication, "the One from whom your Mission is derived. The Missioner before the Mission, is the rule. Your Mission here is to know God, and enjoy Him forever, and to see His hand in all His works." The second: "Do what you can, moment by moment, day by day, step by step, to make this world a better place, following the leading and guidance of God's Spirit within you and around you." The third: "Exercise that Talent which you particularly came to Earth to use—your greatest gift, which you most delight to use, in the places or settings which God has caused to appeal to you the most, and for those purposes which God most needs to have done in the world" (Bolles 1989, pp. 348–49).

Leaders who are clearly aware of their God-given purpose are driven to fulfill this purpose, not to add up their roles and talents to see where that might lead them. They allow God to lead their lives; they don't allow their lives simply to happen. As we said in chapter 3: Rapid, concurrent changes look like chaos to the person who wants to maintain control and stability, but present opportunities for the person who plunges into change and growth with *purpose*. Christ gives these people a higher level of purpose that transcends what they should avoid or what limits them and moves them into proactive lives centered on love.

THE POWER OF PURPOSE

When we think of mission or purpose, we generally think of a direction or destination. But purpose provides something else equally as important. It releases in us the power of determination to reach that end. Purpose enables us to deal with multiple roles without losing sight of why we are in each relationship. It gives meaning to today's action as we work toward the eternal.

In recent years, many companies have engaged in writing purpose statements or mission statements. Yet, very few contain any reference to the spiritual dimension—to eternal truths, and, by omitting these, they fail to tap the power of the spirit. Many of them tend to construct a purpose for the organization that does not relate to the souls of the individuals in it. No matter how determined an individual may be about pursuing his or her "why," management practices dictate against releasing the power of the soul because they promote control. But the power of the soul cannot be controlled from outside. It demands a special kind of leadership to bring it forth.

> **Purpose enables us to deal with multiple roles without losing sight of why we are in each relationship.**

People with a deep sense of purpose meet a fundamental requirement for truly successful leadership. They are willing to take risks for what they believe, they are not afraid to seek the help of others, and they have the ability to inspire others to join in their quest. Paradoxically, their organizations gain power as they relinquish control.

The effective leader is concerned not with just his own purpose but that of each of the persons whom he or she leads. He knows each person has a purpose that goes far beyond merely doing the job the organization hands her. "We're not here just to fill a slot," Frank Larkin reminds us. "It behooves us to look around and say 'My God, I wonder what that person's purpose is. They don't seem happy, therefore, how could they be fulfilling that purpose?' Could you imagine the repercussions of this person being unable, for whatever reason, not to experience the fulfillment of their purpose—not only for them personally but for the world? Imagine the anguish of God seeing all the minds and souls that have perished without ever being engaged."

PART III

The Power of Servanthood

TEN

Called to the Right Place

Regardless of what they had in mind as they worked their way to their present leadership positions, Christ-centered business leaders make use of the opportunity to live out their faith on the job. "My main mission in life is to know the will of God and to do it. I see my role as a Christian and translate it into practical day-to-day expression," John Beckett told the world in an ABC television interview in 1997. How different from the hundreds of executive interviews in which the CEOs refer to maximizing profit or generating record returns for investors!

A HIGH CALLING

Christian leaders like John Beckett optimize profits and earn good returns, but they have a higher calling. They do not merely try to *balance* their worldly comforts and business successes with their following Christ; they follow first and let that shape their leadership roles. They see their roles as filled with obligation and opportunity to serve.

Following Christ offers a way of life that is deeply purposeful and engages the true self—the soul. God gives all of us talents and experiences. It's up to us whether to use them for our own purposes or to use them as openings for God to work through us. There is much that these executives, with their talents and contacts and, sometimes, considerable financial resources, can do. Many whom I have met engage not only in big projects but reach out one on one to aid people around them.

"I believe that we are called by God to utilize the skills He gave us to perform certain kinds of work. When we perform our work with integrity, it becomes a form of ministry. My faith teaches me that all work should be done for the glory of God," says Dick DeVos (DeVos 1997, p. 134).

Carole Hamm confesses, "It would be easy for small business owners to sell out as times get more and more chaotic. But there's real Christian work that we're called to. It behooves us to stay there. I think that's where we're supposed to be." She didn't always feel that way, however. She is part of a business that was founded by her father, and she originally was there simply out of heritage. Not until her spirituality began deepening did she "see it as a personal ministry."

When I asked Pam Carlson if she felt a sense of calling to be CEO of ROC Carbon Company, she had already told me she had been a schoolteacher and at one time wanted to be the mother of twelve. She had no aspirations of running a company. Shortly before her father's death, she began to work at the company he had founded. In time, the man who was operating as CEO for a ten-year period saw potential in Pam that she didn't know she had. Looking back, she says, "I feel like it's a calling—that's really what God wants me to do. And it's not a calling because I feel like I know how to do this. I feel like it's a calling because that's what He wants me to be as a member of the family. After my father died, my mom was advised to sell the company. Something seemed to tell her not to. She thought she was saving it for my brother." It turned out that Pam's brother was not qualified and not especially interested in running the company. Pam doesn't regard these developments as God's giving the company to her for her own sake. She has dedicated the company to God, and, even if the company were sold to one of the many firms that have expressed interest in buying it, she would want to be sure that the same values and focus would be maintained.

RELIGIOUS ENOUGH?

Some Christian leaders say they have nagging feelings that they should be pursuing a more "religious" career. Like Dan Hanson, they sometimes feel they should be spending all their time at God's work. Early in his life, Dan was a pre-seminary student. He went into business, however, and became more successful than he ever dreamed. Now the head of a large division of Land O'Lakes, happily married, a father, and a part-time teacher in a business school, you might think his thoughts of seminary are far behind him. Yet there have been times when he has considered leaving the corporate world for mission work because "life didn't have the meaning it should."

Dan has had two near-death experiences. One was at the age of twenty-five; he was in a car accident, and he was told he wouldn't live. At age forty-five, he overcame thyroid cancer. He says he got the message: "You need to be around longer. Part of me believes there's another chapter yet. In the meantime, there's important work for me where I am."

Michael Prewitt, also, is a successful businessman. In 1979 he founded a marketing, design, and communications firm that now employs forty persons. This fifty-three-year-old company president is enrolled in Princeton Theological Seminary, with two semesters to go in a three-year program that will have taken him six years to complete.

"I have a couple of goals in my life at this point, one of which is to serve the church. Another is to write. I have been a writer all my life. I finally feel now that I have been disciplined enough and also have a goal in mind for my writing, which is very clearly involved with my Christian faith, my discipleship, and my feelings about the church.

"I started into seminary not really very intentional about being ordained, but I am under care now to be ordained. That's still a very open question for me." He is asking himself whether he can serve the church best by being ordained and serving in a parish or by going back into the business world. "I have financial responsibilities. I also have great love for the work I do, which is going well. How do I balance all that? I'm very seriously listening to God and listening to my family and listening to the church in terms of people I meet and things I could do for the church in communications and marketing.

"Many people have said to me, 'Your ministry is your company.' I'm not overt at all about naming the Name or saying that we have a greater purpose than supplying the product we supply or making a profit or serving our clients. That's not my way of witnessing." But one of the things that has changed for Michael is his ability to witness by being a listener, to be available to people in need. The heavy load of school and business work is making it difficult for him to do that at this time, however.

Michael is writing a book on marketing aimed at making church leaders aware of "some of the tools that the secular corporate world is using routinely now." He recognizes there is a danger in applying new marketing concepts to the church and reaching beyond traditional ways of proclaiming the gospel. "We need to stand under the power of the Holy Spirit and be very careful about using these human techniques and human devices, and yet we can't run away from them and say the only faithful way to talk is the way the monks talked in the twelfth century."

While it might seem that being a missionary, a monk, or a theologian is more "Christian" than being in business, helping others connect the secular and spiritual worlds is an especially powerful way to serve God. Although the work situation may present an overwhelming rush of problems and distractions, some Christians are shaping the culture around them. They do God's work in the secular world and witness to others by explaining why they are doing it.

Teilhard de Chardin, writing to a friend who was prospering in business, said,

> How, you ask, can the success of a commercial enterprise bring with it moral progress? And I answer, in this way, that since everything in the world follows the road to unification, the spiritual success of the universe is bound up with the correct functioning of every zone of that

universe and particularly with the release of every possible energy in it. Because your enterprise is going well, a little more health is being spread in the human mass, and in consequence a little more liberty to act, to think and to love. . . . Because you are doing the best you can (though you may sometimes fail) you are forming your own self within the world, and you are helping the world to form itself around you. (de Chardin, *Divine Milieu* 1960, p. 36)

Any of us may puzzle over what to do in life, especially if we are looking for a high calling and seeking to dedicate ourselves to God's work. We may ask why we are where we are rather than somewhere else. We may be overly concerned about finding the one career, the one job, or the one task that God wants for us. We become restless, dissatisfied, or disappointed. We may have such a preoccupation with the right occupation that we miss our true calling—to do what God wants done wherever we are.

We can be *available* to do God's work anywhere by recognizing the opportunities and resources God puts before us. We need not be concerned about finding just the right skill to offer or finding what's most needed in the world. As Alan Ross of FCCI says (see chapter 6), our primary concern should be our relationship with God, not our performance; when that relationship is right, God will use us in ways we never would imagine.

Like many of these Christian leaders, when we find what seems to be a calling, we may not feel that it's what

> Helping others connect the secular and spiritual worlds is an especially powerful way to serve God.

we would have selected for ourselves. Moses did not ask to be leader of the Jews. Paul did not seek to preach to the Gentiles. Yet, could either have selected a role that would have been more influential?

Leaders who diligently follow Christ offer a valuable lesson about finding a meaningful calling. They do not regard work as a secular thing to endure while shelving their faith. They do not get so caught up in the demands of work that they miss the many opportunities to act in love toward others. They do not languish in their work, thinking it not as worthy as other things they should be doing as Christians. They look at the needs around them and find opportunities for filling a higher purpose. They continually ask themselves, "Which customer, subordinate, peer, or stockholder needs our loving attention?"

Contrary to what we might assume, business can be a high calling. Bruce Wilkinson tells FCCI members that business can be a place to be a "priest" to others. "There are two expressions of a Christian's involvement in the marketplace that apply directly to establishing God's purpose there," reads an FCCI discussion card. "Tent-making: Essentially, working to provide an income to meet the expenses of our daily living in order to perform a particular ministry as a vocation. Platform ministry: Essentially, using a business as the key place from which ministry will be launched as a channel for 'priesting' or reaching people for God."

> **We can be *available* to do God's work anywhere by recognizing the opportunities and resources God puts before us.**

"My work is my ministry," says Mirko Vukovich, president of Colorado Real Estate and Investment Company, a firm that manages twenty-five manufactured home communities with a total of 5,000 residents. "I work on merging my personal objectives, which are Christ-centered, and business objectives, which are profit-centered. I won't do things that in any way would be a detriment to the Lord's glory. By the same token I have to make sure that all of the things that we get involved in have some sort of a business profit in them.

"That's the challenge of Christian business today," he says. "We have to be able to minister to the believer and nonbeliever. *In fact, we're called to.* I really need to have a company that is a good environment for my employees be they believers or nonbelievers. You don't have to be a Christian to be comfortable here, but you do have to be hard-working and truth-telling. There are behaviors and attitudes that we won't accept. There's always that challenge of how you do your business. You can't run it the way you run your home. It has to be a little more objective and sterile, if you will. Yet, I want to make sure that everything we do is built on Christian principles."

WORK IS A NECESSARY GOOD

Work has always been our calling. We may have the mistaken idea that humans were put in the Garden of Eden to lounge, eat, and sleep. But we learn in Genesis 2:15, "The Lord God took the man and put him in the Garden of Eden to work it and take care of it." We were given not only responsibility for the beasts but for ourselves and the complex relationships of a living planet. Work is not a choice; it is our nature. When we are the leaders of others, we fail if we do not enable others to take part in work and fulfill their natures.

"Work is a necessary evil," we have heard many times. But no advice could be more wrong. *Work is a necessary good!* It has always been God's will that humanity work as a co-creator of the world, but we chose a course that turned a gift into a curse. We are part of the Creation's unfolding—a creation that God saw as good but that we have come to see as evil, as something lowly, because we have lost the connection with God.

"We human beings are in and of nature, we help to make reality happen, we are free agents with a responsibility for co-creation. More than that, quantum science shows us that we are, in our essential physical and spiritual makeup, extensions, 'excitations,' of the underlying ground state of Being," says Danah Zohar (Zohar 1997, p. 153). "Quantum physics recognizes that we live in a participative universe in which living beings are cocreative insiders" (p. 88).

> "**W**ork is a necessary evil," we have heard many times. But no advice could be more wrong. *Work is a necessary good.*

We forgot why we were working and for whom. We forgot we were once insiders. After eating from the tree of knowledge, we broke our loving relationship with God. So we were condemned to "painful toil," earning a livelihood "by the sweat of your brow." We lost sight of work's having a purpose beyond earning a living.

Yet we sense that there is some spiritual dimension to what we do here on Earth. For all of history, we suspected that work is more than a matter of just performing tasks. It is part of who we are—or at least who we should be. For Christians, its purpose is to glorify God by living a life that reflects God.

Work occupies a big portion of our daily lives. There is a danger that the demands of the job will overtake all other aspects of our lives. Because work represents a big chunk of time and is "out there" where we can isolate it, we may easily divorce it from our faith. We can easily dismiss work as reflecting only materialistic interests. The challenge to Christians is not to balance their work and their spiritual lives but to bring their spirituality into their work. Christ-centered businesspersons make that connection. "Each day, I ask what I can do for the Lord," says George Seaberg. Leaders like George see their work as:

1. An opportunity to contribute, to test their talents, to build community;
2. An opportunity to allow God to work through them, whatever their talents;
3. An opportunity to direct their work outward to others;
4. An opportunity to enable others to engage in God's work.

Nearly all of the adults I have known have gone to work first to meet economic needs. But many of them eventually discover needs other than financial to be met or greater opportunities to explore. They work for self-fulfillment. They work for recognition. They find they enjoy developing and exercising certain talents. They embrace a cause to which they can dedicate themselves.

This is especially true of these Christian walkers who have attained corporate leadership positions. In many cases, they would work even if they had no financial need to do so, because they see their work as a ministry. One day, as I interviewed two Christian business owners, I asked them what they would do if they won the lottery and no longer had any financial reason for working. David Musacchia, who is in the industrial supplies and services business, answered, "I work because I'm obligated to support my three daughters and wife. If I suddenly had all the money I needed, I might back off a little in my work. I might take one-week or two-week vacations, which I can't now. But I would consider it an insult to my character to quit. I would still service my customers."

Bill Gibson, who heads an insurance and financial services company, said, "Would I keep working if I didn't have to financially? Yes. I don't know what else I would do in addition to or what different focus I would have. But we aren't meant to sit around. I have an obligation to our clientele. We do our best for those who trust us. Maybe I would broaden the services we offer them. I might give every employee a bonus."

Some might expect Christians to be unconcerned about work—to lie back in confidence that God will provide. While these Christian leaders do believe that God will provide the fruits from their work, they don't expect fruits without work. More important, their work is centered on doing God's will and harvesting fruit *for others.*

GOOD WORKS FLOW FROM LOVE

There is a danger that work can be distorted into a mechanism for proving our value or elevating our status vis à vis one another. It can be too self-oriented—quite the opposite from what God intended it to be. The Christian who remembers that God loves us knows that we don't need to prove our worth and that we can't offset our sins through our daily work or special good works.

A classic debate among Christians has to do with whether salvation comes through faith in God's grace or through the doing of good works. Numerous passages in the New Testament speak of salvation through God's grace, not through

> **C**hristian leaders' work is centered on doing God's will and harvesting fruit *for others.*

anything we do to earn it. They teach that forgiveness of our sins is a gift from God. "For it is by grace you have been saved, through faith—and this not from yourselves, it is the gift of God—not by works, so that no one can boast" (Ephesians 2:8–9).

The next verse in Ephesians, however, points up the role of work or good works in our lives. "For we are God's workmanship, created in Christ Jesus to do good works, which God prepared in advance for us to do." We do have a job to do. We were given an assignment at the outset and we are further commanded by Christ to action— to love.

James gives the best-known call to Christian action: "What good is it, my brothers, if a man claims to have faith but has no deeds?" (James 2:14) "Faith by itself, if it is not accompanied by action, is dead" (James 2:17). "I will show you my faith by what I do" (James 2:18).

We might ask, "If God chooses to save or not save us, what's the point of doing good works?" But God intended that we love others, that we serve as stewards of the Creation. We are commanded to do good things! Doing good things reflects the love of God and God's love for us. They are the reflection of our faith in God. Seeing the outburst of love from a woman who washed his feet with perfume, for example, Jesus confirmed she had been forgiven (Luke 7:47). Her action was an expression of her love. It was obvious to Jesus that her sins had already been taken away.

Paul, likewise, told the Jews, "The only thing that counts is faith expressing itself through love" (Galatians 5:6). Faith manifests itself in action. Abraham was considered one of the most righteous men who ever lived. Following God's command, he offered to sacrifice his son Isaac on the altar. "You see that his faith and his actions were working together, and his faith was made complete by what he did" (James 2:22).

The Christian executives I studied seem more concerned with love than salvation. The way they live their lives on and off the job clearly expresses their faith and love. They welcome the many possibilities for doing good works through the business activities inside the company and outside through service to the company's many stakeholders. In addition, some of them engage in doing good works in the community or even on a national level. They do good, not out of guilt or as an attempt to win salvation. They are not compensating for things they have done or not done in their lives. They love without restriction.

Many of the things they do for others could be attributed only to love of others, not selfish concern.

BEING A BLESSING

Lest we become too caught up in what a Christian does, we should note that many Christian leaders speak in terms not of doing, but of *being*. As they take account of themselves, they hope that they will be known not for specific things they do but for *what* they are. They want to reveal their souls, which reflect the image of God.

Some serve as outstanding witnesses to God just by what they *are*, even when they are unable to *do*. In this regard, I'm reminded again and again of Frank Walter. An All American athlete in high school and a star quarterback at Virginia Military Institute in the 1950s, Frank went on to be an engineer, an educator, and an entrepreneur. He created Bay State Polymer Distribution, a successful distributorship of thermoplastic polyurethane. Active in his church and his community and the loving father of six children, he was known for his concern for others and his ear for their problems. His wife Mary Ann says of him, Frank "truly enjoyed his work. He saw it as a way of helping people with their business needs rather than just selling them something."

But this active life occurred before I met him. I got to know only a man with a rare disease that was slowly destroying his nervous system. Little by little, over several years, he slowly lost much of the use of his hands, his arms, and his legs. From time to time, he suffered from double vision. When his kidneys shut down, several of his friends volunteered to drive him to dialysis treatments—a twenty-five-mile trip across town, three times a week, to a hospital where specialists understood his rare disease. We started by helping him, but, as the months and then years passed, we realized *he* was helping *us*. His spirit and faith were inspirational to each of us. He thrilled to the beauty of each day. "I love life!" he told me one day, his voice raspy from the gaping hole in his throat put there to prevent his choking should he fail to swallow properly. He led me to see the progress of daffodils making their bright appearance each spring. "I love being an early riser!" he said one dark Wednesday morning as we drove to Bible study; he pointed out the lights of a plane approaching the airport more than ten miles away, calling my attention to the unusually good visibility.

Many people came to see more clearly because of Frank. His undaunted faith and love of God, his *being*, not his doing, was a blessing to those who knew him. His physical condition was not one that any of us would choose. But it was in his weakest state that he found his calling. It was there that others saw his strength, his courage, his love for others, and his faith in God.

Frank left his family and friends two gifts: the reminder that life is a wonderful gift; the example that it is through what we see, what we believe, and how much we love that we reveal we are made in the image of God.

ELEVEN

In Service as Stewards

Not only must humanity be involved in the world, we are charged with overseeing the Creation. It is our job to lead the world that God created, help sustain it, and enable it to progress according to God's will. We should remind ourselves that we were not thrown into the world without purpose or equipment. We were given gifts and opportunities. "What do you have that you did not receive?" (1 Corinthians 4:7) We *received* everything; we created nothing ourselves. And with these gifts come obligations:

- Skills and talents; we are obligated to make use of them.
- The place we're in; we are obligated to cultivate the world there.
- The people around us; we are obligated to help them become what God wants of them.

No talent is so limited that we should feel ashamed to share it with the world. No amount of talent is so poor that the world doesn't need it. All talents are too precious to be wasted by not using them or by using them for meaningless purposes.

THE GIFT OF RESPONSIBILITY

In the parable of the talents, a master who was leaving for a journey entrusted his money to his servants to manage during his absence. To one, he gave five talents; to another, two; and to a third, one. On his return, he asked for reports on their stewardship of his wealth. The one with five talents had earned five more. The master said to him, "You have been faithful with a few things. I will put you in charge of many things." The servant with two talents entrusted to him had earned two more. He, too, was told he would receive more responsibility. The man with one talent had buried it. The master, angered by this laziness and wickedness, said, "Take the talent from him and give it to the one who has the ten talents. For everyone who has will be given more, and he will have an abundance. Whoever does not have, even what he has will be taken from him" (Matthew 25:14–29).

We should remind ourselves that we were not thrown into the world without purpose or equipment. We were given gifts and opportunities.

Often, people take that last sentence out of context, to accuse Christ of saying the rich get richer and the poor get poorer. They overlook the fact that none of this money belonged to the servants; they were working for the master, not themselves. What these men gained was *responsibility* for managing more—for the master. The servant who failed to manage his master's money well, however, had the possibility of further opportunity taken away from him.

"As a Christian, I acknowledge that what I have—whether a loved one, a talent or a gift, or property—are gifts from God," says Dick DeVos. "As quickly as they are given, they can be taken away. For me, submission to our Creator is fundamental to breaking down the tendency toward self-centeredness and the misguided sense of self-importance we humans so often struggle with" (DeVos 1997, p. 74).

Our stewardship role in God's creation is a gift in itself, but the things over which we are to be stewards are not gifts; they are entrusted to us to manage for Someone else. People in close relation-ship with God see quite clearly that they are nothing in themselves other than what God has given them. They know their purpose; they have the answer to the "why" in their lives. Even their compa-nies are given to them for stewardship, not ownership.

They swim upstream against today's prevailing mindset. Robert Wuthnow described that mindset several years ago, when he wrote that "much of the middle class seems to have forgotten even the most basic claims that religion used to make on the material world. Asked if their religious beliefs had influenced their choice of a ca-reer, most of the people I have interviewed in recent years— Christian and non-Christians alike—said no. Asked if they thought of their work as a calling, most said no. Asked if they understood the concept of stewardship, most said no. Asked how religion did influence their work lives or thoughts about money, most said the two were completely separate" (Wuthnow, 1993, p. 200).

The person focused on God doesn't lack this spiritual founda-tion for life and work. For some of the Christ-centered leaders I studied, their faith *determined* their careers. Others were well into a career before they allowed their faith to direct their lives; they now let it shape their thinking and direct their actions. Virtually all of them feel compelled not only to use their talents, but to use them for God's purposes. Their faith does not merely temper their human behavior but acts as a force for directing their behavior to a higher purpose. As one executive told me, "Christianity is not just to give us moral parameters or just to feel good. It shows us that we are partners in God's unfolding work."

In a country where we have unparalleled opportunity for exer-cising our talents, how many of us do so? How many are too lazy? How many of us think of directing our talents toward "God's un-folding work"? As I was writing the previous paragraph, I took time out to make a trip to the drug store. There in the mall parking lot I found signs of laziness or misdirected abilities: dozens of abandoned shopping carts. It takes minor talent to return a cart to the store, so this wasn't a sign of lack of talent. Judging from the way shoppers scurried in and out of the parking lot, it couldn't have been a matter of laziness; more likely, it was a matter of priorities. What priorities? Why, it was Super Bowl Sunday!

Dick DeVos says, "Stewardship is making good use of time, resources, and God-given talents. In keeping with my Christian perspective, I define a steward as 'one who is entrusted with the management of property, finances, or other affairs *not his own.*' This understanding is very much in line with the notion that what we have is entrusted to us—not as owners, but as stewards" (DeVos 1997, p. 174).

It is, perhaps, easiest to see an executive's stewardship role as the management of the stockholders' investment in his or her company. But it's neither the executive's company nor the stockholders'. Even company "owners" do not own "their" companies. Bruce Wilkinson, a founder of and teacher for FCCI, reminds executives and owners they should approach their roles with a perception of stewardship, not ownership. "It's not your company. It's Christ's. What would be the goals He'd like to achieve? What priorities would He have?" Perhaps even harder to recognize is that a company leader is the steward of "gifts" other than money. More than one executive pointed out to me that the greatest responsibility they feel is as stewards of the employees who have been put in their charge.

Executives not only have to manage many gifts, but they are stewards for many masters other than the stockholders. Customers, suppliers, the local community, the industry, and the world—all have expectations of what the company does and how it does it. With so much entrusted to them and so many masters taking account of their performance, it is easy to see why so many corporate leaders take a defensive position. In contrast, working in relationship with Christ puts one on the offensive for the service of all.

THE NATURE OF A SERVANT

Outside the ServiceMaster headquarters building stands an eleven-foot-high statue of Jesus washing a disciple's feet. From what I can determine, this statue stands for *service* rather than a particular faith. On the "service wall" behind the statue are engraved the names of twenty-five-year veterans of the company.

For Christians and many others, Christ stands out in history as the ultimate servant. Paul instructs us to take that same servant stance. "Your attitude should be the same as that of Christ Jesus: Who being in very nature God, did not consider equality with God something to be grasped, but made himself nothing, taking the very nature of a servant, being made in human likeness. And being found in appearance as man, he humbled himself and became obedient to death—even death on the cross" (Philippians 2:5–8).

Paul himself became a servant and regarded doing so as a gift, not a choice of his own. "I became a servant by the gift of God's grace given me through the working of his power. Although I am less than the least of all God's people, this grace was given me: to preach to the Gentile . . ." (Ephesians 3:7–8).

Executives' busy schedules don't always permit them to be as involved with others as much as they'd like. Yet, they devote a considerable amount of time to high-level ventures where they can use their position power and contacts to do God's work. Equally important, they frequently do the little things that demonstrate their love. They are not too busy to greet workers or strangers. They are not too busy to be courteous. They are not too busy to return phone calls. In my research, I was amazed again and again at the number of executives who personally responded to my phone messages and how many called me to conduct an interview on the phone or to meet face to face once we had agreed on a time.

These coworkers with Christ are not overly concerned with their personal status. They heed Christ's words: "For he who is least among you all—he is the greatest" (Luke 9:48). We can understand, then, examples of humble service, such as John Beckett's going to the home of an employee who was suffering severe back pain to pray for her even when he didn't want to. This was an employee who had been stirring up discontent among her fellow workers. When John heard she was immobilized with back pain, he thought, "Well, she finally got hers!" Then, he says, he felt a nudge by the Holy Spirit to go to her house and pray for her. Grudgingly, he went there. When he said he would like to pray for her, he didn't expect the positive response he got. Immediately after his brief prayer, she said her back felt warm. Then she stood and said her back was better! The next day, says John, she returned to work and never again spoke a word of discontent.

THE HUMBLE LEADER

It is important to distinguish service done out of love from service done as compensation for something missing in our lives or as self-inflicted penance. Sometimes people engage in volunteer efforts and do genuinely good work to supplement the meaningless work they perform in their occupations or professions. Others do it as compensation for wrongdoing. These people are living in two worlds, trying to balance the wrongs in one with the rights in the other.

Business leaders who are focused on Christ integrate their worlds. We can see they do good works on the job. Outside the job, their Christian behavior may or may not include a heavy load of social activity. Regardless how much they do inside or outside their company leadership roles, they are humble about what they have done. It is nothing compared to their deep feeling of gratitude for Christ's having died for their sins and permitting them to be reconciled with God. They also see the endless challenge before them in meeting people's needs. They recognize that other people are God's workmanship, and that these people, too, want to be in service. These factors create in Christ-centered leaders a strong commitment to service; in turn they win the commitment of their followers to service.

Leaders who are truly engaging their souls in their work want that same engagement for the people who report to them. They are deeply concerned with the spiritual welfare of others. They want their employees to become self-reliant, self-fulfilled, and service-oriented. Usually, we design many of the goals and incentives in our organizations to appeal to what people want for themselves. The Christian "walker" designs the goals and incentives to encourage members of the organization to express what they want to do *for others* and, thereby, enable them to see worthiness in their work and their organization.

The concept of "Servant Leadership" has been coming into wider and wider use in business since the 1970s. We are slowly moving away from seeing ourselves as managers and workers and heading toward regarding ourselves as servant leaders and stewards—a relationship in which everyone is responsible for the organization. Those at the "top" are simply in a position to serve more others than anyone else.

> The Christian "walker" designs the goals and incentives to encourage members of the organization to express what they want to do *for others.*

Servant Leadership, written by Robert K. Greenleaf and published in 1977, was a collection of forward-looking essays, lectures, and articles written in the '50s, '60s, and '70s. He observed then: "A fresh critical look is being taken at the issues of power and authority, and people are beginning to learn, however haltingly, to relate to one another in less coercive and more creatively supporting ways. A new moral principle is emerging which holds that the only authority deserving one's allegiance is that which is freely and knowingly granted by the led to the leader in response to, and in proportion to, the clearly evident servant stature of the leader" (Greenleaf 1977, pp. 9–10).

Larry Spears, executive director of the Greenleaf Center for Servant Leadership, tells me: "There are many associated with us who have a specifically Christian perspective. There are maybe many more who are doing so from a more broadly spiritual perspective—who may or may not consider themselves Christians. They see in servant leadership a means of bringing spirit and spirituality into the workplace."

SPIRITUAL BASE FOR EXCELLENCE

To servant leaders, "the business of business no longer restricts itself to manipulating things and nature and people for profit," says

Danah Zohar. "Rather, business becomes a spiritual vocation in the largest sense of that word. I believe it is only from such a basis of spiritual servant leadership that really deep transformation can come about in the corporate world" (Zohar 1997, p. 154). "Servant leaders must know what they ultimately serve. They must, with a sense of humility and gratitude, have a sense of the Source from which all values emerge" (p. 153).

One of the biggest transformations or changes in value that business has undertaken since the birth of scientific management in the early 1900s has been the recent Quality Movement. There have been many cases of outstanding success in improving a company's quality of product and service. At the same time, there have been many failures, and perhaps many more cases of companies' making improvements that fell far short of what they could have been.

For the most part, management has adopted quality programs without having instilled the necessary spiritual base. Many of these programs have been directed at employees without the necessary change in management's worldview having been effected. God made the world and saw that it was good; workers too often did their jobs and saw that it was junk. Pins, pizza parties, purpose statements, and propaganda have been offered to raise worker interest in quality, when often it has been management's interest that needs lifting.

Because of its competitive, self-oriented mindset, management often aimed "quality" programs at building corporate pride when, perhaps, they should have been seeking to generate humility. They sought to instill a spirit of winning when they should have been trying to direct the organization's concern to service.

Some Christian executives I studied have implemented the quality techniques, but they approach them with a worldview that begins with love and service. Time and again, they will tell you they are working to glorify God in all they do. If the techniques serve that purpose, they will use them and use them well. With or without the techniques, their relationship with God translates directly into a quest for excellence in all that they do—what their company docs, how it does it, and its profitability. As Paul instructs us, "Whatever you do, work at it with all your heart, as working for the Lord, not for men . . ." (Colossians 3:23). In addition, some will point out, they are dedicated to excellence because other Christians are looking to them as models for behavior.

Yes, these business leaders are concerned about profit, but only as a means of sustaining the company, not as an end it itself. They need to survive in secular affairs so they can be an influence there. This requires not only being strong in their faith but being highly competent in tending to business considerations—another Christian paradox which they master well.

THE POWER OF GOD WITHIN

Top corporate executives and company owners have power that most of us don't have. Their skills, experience, and position give them the opportunity to have significant influence on the lives of others. We hear and see many cases of abuse of this power, when it is used for selfish ends and thereby becomes unloving, unfair, and unjust. Flip Wilson, a popular comedian of the '60s and '70s, frequently did sketches that inevitably led, at some point, to his predictable line, "The Devil made me do it!" Christian executives could say, "God made me do it!" They seem to have the power to do not only what they want to do, but sometimes to do things they had not intended to do or could not have done through their own abilities alone.

For leaders who operate with a Christian starting point, power becomes something far greater than what they might have sought for themselves. Furthermore, it grows exponentially. If we look at the accomplishments of Christian executives on or off the job, we might attribute their unusual power to one of three things:

> For the most part, management has adopted quality programs with-out having instilled the necessary spiritual base.

1. *They are really turned on by their relationship with God.* Even the most skeptical observer can see that this seems to be true as these leaders display excitement, joy, and reverence.

2. *God is working with them; He's on their side.* They would put it differently: They are working with God in an effort to be what God wants them to be.

3. *God is working through them.* This is the way most of them explain their manner of proceeding in the world's work. "All along, I have had a certain sense that something needs to be spoken through me," Daniel Hanson said in our conversation on the matter of God working with or through him. Bill Pollard told me, "Oh yeah, I sense that from time to time. Sure. That's part of my faith, that I believe the Spirit of God works in and through me. But it's not always that easy to identify. Have I had a great idea or is it that the Spirit of God gave me that idea? There are probably as many times when I have been upset about the way I have acted or conducted myself and asked, 'Boy, why hasn't the Spirit of God worked more effectively in that situation?' So, there are as many failures as there are successes."

Dorothy Marcic defines spiritual power as "the capacity to influence others, not by controlling them as in political power, but through love, by example, as a result of kindness, consideration, humor, and wisdom—or the power of truth. Those who have it do not feel arrogant and self-satisfied, but rather gain a greater humility, realizing that the true source of the power comes from a Higher Power, not from themselves" (Marcic 1997, p. 49).

John Shumate, the Columbus, Ohio, real estate developer, sees this power as God's blessing his business.

It has just been awesome. He told us to start a Christian radio station in Columbus for the youth; we built a radio station. It came on the air March 1996—a full power FM station, nonprofit, worth millions. God gave it to us for hardly anything. We broadcast throughout central Ohio. Music for the youth—rock—all Christian. We also give them the word of God. It's the only one like it in the United States, they say. God is doing some awesome things with it. Just my wife and I—oh, the Lord did it. He told us to build it; we built it.

There was no FCC license available in Columbus. Our attorneys in Washington said, "No way," but God supernaturally hid a frequency that no one even knew about and saved it for ten years for us. And He told me to buy the building. We bought an existing radio station that did not have a license. God did exactly what He said He would do. He did something that I could not do. It was out of my control.

GOING WITH THE FLOW

Control does not seem to be in the vocabulary of the executives I studied. If anything, they go with the flow; they yield to opportunity and assistance that is presented to them by the power that links the universe.

Because they have wholeheartedly committed to God, people, information, and other resources show up for them from both expected and unexpected places. They seem to ride the waves of synchronicity (see chapter 4), taking advantage of the connectedness of the universe. Their talents and experience are often just what's needed to serve God's wants in a particular way at a particular time, they feel. Sometimes, even their weaknesses or past wrongdoings give them the ability to relate to others in a way that permits them to serve.

"When you open the channel, you are connected to a source of unlimited energy," believes Frank Larkin. We receive this energy through grace—as a gift, he says. Paul describes the incredible power coming from God, "who is able to do immeasurably more than all we ask or imagine, according to his power that is at work within us" (Ephesians 3:20).

> "When you open the channel, you are connected to a source of unlimited energy."

As I met with twenty or more men and women at an FCCI weekend seminar, I had a mental picture of open windows through which power was flowing. These Christian executives and company owners seem to serve as the openings through which God works. Whatever their talents, skills, and position power, they make themselves available for God's power to flow through them. Their human spirit and the Holy Spirit work together. An important part of permitting this power to work, some point out, is that others have to be able to *see* God at work; they cannot claim this power as their own.

Many companies are looking for ways to tap the people's "spirit" in order to get better performance, but it seems that they may be thinking in terms of hustle or enthusiasm without recognizing how close they are to the human spirit that is linked, in turn, to The Spirit. They are not fully tapping into the power of love. Those who walk in Christ's company, on the other hand, are in the vanguard of love-driven, servant leadership. Although they don't consider themselves revolutionaries, these leaders are linked to the power that can transform the world for the better.

PART IV

In Covenant with Others

TWELVE

People as Whole Persons

nyone who suspects you are a Christian may rightfully ask, "If you are in touch with God, show me you have put aside your self-interests. If you are in touch with a God of love, show me how you love. If you are on the right path, show me how to find it."

Christ-centered executives show their faith primarily through their relationships with others—employees, customers, suppliers, the community, and their families. There are many stakeholders in their companies, they know, but God is Number 1. God enables these executives to have a perspective that allows them to enjoy the worth of each of the other stakeholders.

These executives are drawn to lead at a deep level, out of respect or love for the individual. They are not "good to" their employees just to bend them to the corporate will; they don't serve their customers just as a means of serving themselves. The leaders' integrity and honesty enables them to build strong relationships with others, even with those whom they don't lead. By acting as complete persons and regarding others as such, they are far more effective than those managers who have only distant relationships with people they see as faceless.

For Christ-centered leaders, the relationship with God expresses itself outwardly. "I think what affects us on the inside obviously also affects us on the outside in the lives of the people that we touch," says Carole Hamm. When her commitment to Christ reached a certain point, "I started seeing a difference in how I related to people. They had always been very important to me, but there was a deeper sense of caring and concern for who they were, first as individuals, and who they were as the persons that they brought to work. I began to see changes in the lives of people around me. When I, as a leader in this seven-day-a-week business, say it's okay for my husband and me to be in church on Sunday, for example, I begin to see the same kind of privileges are needed by the staff."

THE POWER OF RELATIONSHIPS

Leaders like Carole, who are in a deep relationship with God, move outward to build relationships with people that are based on a deep respect for others. Too often, when we speak of *respect*, we think of it in a negative way—what we will *not* do to a person. But respect can be positive. These leaders appreciate the good or the Godliness in other persons, and they care about them. They go well beyond appreciation or feelings of sympathy; they act with compassion. Their caring is made apparent through their actions more than their words.

Closeness and caring in the business setting are not matters of intimacy or romance, but of being concerned for other people's welfare and taking steps to ensure it. It involves genuinely sharing the other person's joy and hurting. The Christian relationship is more than refraining from hurting others; it involves hurting *for* others.

A contractual relationship establishes a minimum of what we will do for others, but the Christian relationship leads to maximum effort because it is powered by love. In time, this love is reciprocated as it spreads throughout a community. "Caring is contagious," says Daniel Hanson. There are three other reasons to care for each other, he points out. "Caring is good for us. In fact, it is natural to the human species." Caring "generates a power of its own. This power can be a source of energy for the individual as well as the organization." And caring relationships at work "make work more fun" (Hanson 1997, pp. 56–57).

COVENANT VERSUS CONTRACT

Executives who work for Christ believe it is important to keep their promises. They build their relationships as covenants, not idle promises or mere contracts. A covenant is a living thing; a contract is dead, static. A covenant opens potential; a contract limits damage. A covenant is relational; a contract is impersonal. Because they are open-ended and highly committed to their relationships, these leaders are always moving toward excellence; they do not need programs to remind them of the need for excellence or quality.

> A contractual relationship is a minimum of what we will do for others, but the Christian relationship leads to maximum effort because it is powered by love.

At Applied Industrial Technologies, a company that supplies over a billion dollars' worth of supplies to industrial firms around the world, "promise keeping" is one of the seven core values by which employees guide themselves. Adherence to this value promotes covenantal relationships internally as well as externally. After meetings of the company's officers, each of them makes covenants about what they will do as follow-up. The promises are related to both professional and personal issues. Chairman, CEO, and president John Dannemiller says the company's covenants extend to all its constituencies: customers, associates who devote their lives to the company, shareholders who are entitled to a decent return on their investment, suppliers who count on the company to move their products, and the community in which the company can "show God's love through human hearts and hands."

The word *covenant* appears hundreds of times throughout the Scriptures. God initiated covenants of love that were made with heart and soul. These covenants were intended to be everlasting, forever, for the generations to come. Each of them was a living deal, not a short-term contract with a specified time limit. The concept of covenant is more in keeping with the concept of oneness with God at the center, unlike a contract, which is entered into by separate parties. A covenant is a pledge to one or more of God's people with God in on the deal.

God made a covenant with Noah to spare him, his family, and the animals he brought aboard his ark—a covenant for generations to come (Genesis 6:9). God made a covenant with Abraham, making him the father of many nations. "I will establish my covenant as an everlasting covenant between me and you and your descendants after you for the generations to come, to be your God and the God of your descendants after you" (Genesis 17:7). Over time, God made other covenants with leaders such as Isaac, Jacob, Moses, and David.

Time after time, however, God's people have broken those covenants and turned away. Yet God offered still another covenant through Christ, one He wrote on His people's hearts rather than on stone, as were the Ten Commandments. "I will make a new covenant," said God, "because they did not remain faithful to my covenant" (Hebrews 8:8–9). "I will put my laws in their minds and write them on their hearts" (Hebrews 8:10). Christ established that new covenant by atoning for our separation from God. "This is my blood of the covenant, which is poured out for many for the forgiveness of sins," He said (Matthew 26:28; Mark 14:24).

This is the nature of the covenantal relationships that Christ-centered leaders build. They serve for the long term. They value long-term employee service; they see no end to serving each of their customers; and they serve their stockholders for the long haul. They do not get lost in the immediate or the urgent. For them, fairness and justice in the process of doing is as important as the results of what they are doing.

THE BODY HAS MANY PARTS

We frequently hear workers accuse their leaders of not walking the talk. Employees don't perceive their leaders as doing what they say they believe, doing what they say they will do, or dealing honestly with all persons. Those who walk in Christ's company honor all their relationships, regardless of ranking in the corporate hierarchy or in the world outside.

John Beckett is the same person whether he's dealing with a senator or an assembly-line worker, says Dick Leggatt, who has had a long-term working relationship with John. I suspected that the day John and I met and toured the Beckett Company's plant and offices. I saw the ease with which employees came up to ask him about his recent trip to the Promise Keepers' "Stand in the Gap" rally in Washington or the Christian book he was writing (*Loving Monday*, 1998). Over the years, I have accompanied many executives who walk through their plants and talk with others. For some, it comes naturally; for others, it seems a bit contrived. But for employees to take the initiative in a conversation—that's something else! I saw that difference the moment I met John, in fact. I had been waiting in the reception room for a secretary or assistant to greet me and take me to him. John himself came through the door and, from then on, conducted himself as though he had nothing to do that day but spend time with me.

> Those who walk in Christ's company honor all their relationships, regardless of ranking in the corporate hierarchy or in the world outside.

Christian walkers show their concern and love without restriction. They may disagree with people, but that does not lessen their regard for them. They know that people want to be valued. They do not draw the line around only Christians or a certain type of

Christian. The walkers' covenant is with everyone, even those they don't particularly like. "If you love only those who love you, what reward will you get?" Christ asked (Matthew 5:46).

Perhaps it is their awareness of humankind's sinful nature that allows these leaders to accept anyone, despite their particular sinfulness. As Dick DeVos expresses it, "Those of us who believe we have been forgiven through the sacrifice of Jesus Christ must also forgive others. God forgives our faults, and so should we forgive the faults of others" (DeVos 1997, pp. 205–6). "Because Jesus sacrificed himself to gain our forgiveness, through faith and confession we are forgiven—mistakes are not held against us for eternity. We are not weighed down forever and can go forward with a clean slate—without our mistakes accumulating" (p. 111).

Christ-centered leaders do not seem to express care for others in order to get a reward. Instead, they seem to think of the people around them as part of the oneness of God's Creation. This oneness is expressed by the biblical analogy of each of being a part of one body. "Just as each of us has one body with many members, and these members do not all have the same function, so in Christ we who are many form one body, and each member belongs to all the others. We have different gifts, according to the grace given us" (Romans 12:4–6). We could liken this "body" to the interconnected universe described in modern scientific terms. We humans are tiny bits of the world and are seemingly insignificant, yet each of us has a part to play in the whole.

Michael Prewitt believes that one of the great values we can derive from business is its potential contribution to social cohesiveness. The hard reality of business makes it a demanding place in which to establish covenants. Yet, when covenants are effective, it is through business organizations that the common good can be served so well. As Michael says, "There's something very fundamental of the practice of business that you could call a 'covenant.' Business is very definitely a part of contributing to the common good by creating that cohesiveness."

He illustrated his point by describing his relationship with one of his workers whom "I really don't like. She's sour but good at what she does." When she asked for permission to telecommute so she could deal with a child care situation, he realized, "It wasn't about whether I like her or not. It wasn't about whether I would do this woman a favor. There's a covenant here—'I'm going to give you my energy—as much as I can give you. It doesn't matter whether you like me or I like you. I'm going to do something for you and you're going to do something for me that bonds us together in a way that's beyond how I feel about you on a given day.'"

"At ServiceMaster, we have chosen to build our objectives on the conclusion that we live in God's world, and that every individual has been created in God's image with dignity and worth. It is where we begin as we try to determine the right way to run our business," Bill Pollard writes. "In a pluralistic society, not everyone will agree with our starting points. But few would disagree with the great potential for good as a firm acknowledges that it is right to promote the dignity and worth of every person and the value of serving others" (Pollard 1996, p. 52).

When I consider the way some Christian executives live in covenants, I am struck by how diligently they pursue the instructions on being a Christian that Paul lays out in Romans 12:9–21:

> Love must be sincere.
> Hate what is evil;
> cling to what is good.
> Be devoted to one another in brotherly love.
> Honor one another above yourselves.
> Never be lacking in zeal, but keep your spiritual fervor, serving the
>   Lord.
> Be joyful in hope,
> patient in affliction,
> faithful in prayer.
> Share with God's people who are in need.
> Practice hospitality.
> Bless those who persecute you;
> bless and do not curse.
> Rejoice with those who rejoice;
> mourn with those who mourn.
> Live in harmony with one another.

Do not be proud, but be willing to associate with people of low
   position.
Do not be conceited.
Do not repay anyone evil for evil.
Be careful to do what is right in the eyes of everybody.
If it is possible, as far as it depends on you, live in peace with
   everyone.
Do not take revenge, my friends, but leave room for God's wrath. . . .
Do not be overcome by evil,
   but overcome evil with good.

BETTER DECISION MAKING

When leaders don't truly understand people, they raise the odds of
making bad decisions. They misjudge how the people who must
implement their decisions will respond, and they fail to anticipate
how those affected by the resultant actions will react. Yet, people
don't show up on the radar screens of many so-called leaders.
Others are quite people-conscious, but they regard people as something to be cared for; they take a paternalistic approach to leading
their organizations.

Some, on the other hand, see people as whole persons and
treat them as unique, valuable beings who are capable of self-
management. They are, therefore, more demanding in their relationships, encouraging others to grow toward their potential. To
them, serving others does not mean being paternalistic. It means
treating others as equals.

Christ-centered leaders have a clear reason for doing this. They
believe others are made in the image of God and are therefore worthy of their caring. They believe, too, that some people need caring
for, and that all of us need something to care *about*. They may well
do things for others, but they are especially dedicated to enabling
their followers to do things for themselves and for others, in turn.

Managers who deal in averages or majorities fail to see individual differences—differences in needs and abilities that can make a
difference in an organization's effectiveness. To understand a person, it is essential to understand not only what he or she appears to

be but what he or she insists on struggling to be and what God wants him or her to be. The Christian leaders I studied create organizations that allow room for individuals to explore and express that spirituality. Their covenants allow for expansion; they do not put people in boxes.

Effective organizations are built of whole persons serving whole persons. That means leaders must share in the stewardship of the persons working with them—of seeing that they grow. "Leadership in the firm has a responsibility to the ethical, professional, and personal development of every individual in the organization," believes Bill Pollard. In doing so, leaders can make God's presence seen in their organizations.

Max De Pree, former chairman of Herman Miller, says, "The first sign of what I call God's presence is a wholehearted acceptance of human authenticity. Second, because we are authentic, we are entitled to certain rights as insiders: the right to belong, the right to ownership, the right to opportunity, the right to a covenantal relationship, the right to inclusive organizations. Third, leaders in groups with a clear moral purpose make themselves vulnerable. . . . A clear moral purpose removes the ego from the game. Fourth, groups with a clear moral purpose to their actions take very seriously realistic and equitable distribution of re-

> **Managers who deal in averages or majorities fail to see individual differences—differences in needs and abilities that can make a difference in an organization's effectiveness.**

sults. The fifth sign of God's presence I'd like to suggest is personal restraint . . . the belief that personal gain falls far down on the list of important achievements in one's life" (De Pree 1997, pp. 180–84).

In striking contrast to the usual image of corporate management, leaders whose relationships begin with a relationship with Christ are restrained and reveal a high degree of humility. They even allow themselves to be vulnerable—to express their concerns, their failings, their fears. Since they enjoy the security of knowing that God loves them, they don't need to look perfect or win every game. They don't see the purpose of their business activity as piling up winnings for themselves; they are willing to restrain their own wants and encourage others to make a contribution to the organization and share in the fruits of the success they create.

ACCOUNTABILITY AND RECOGNITION

In addition to fairness, openness, and love, which form the basis for covenantal relationships, an organization needs discipline and accountability. Each party committed to a covenant has a responsibility to the other and is accountable for doing what he or she promised. In business, accountability has traditionally been up the line; we are accountable to the boss or the owner. Today we are more likely to be accountable downward as well. And across— among our peers and our team members. Even in the early '80s, it was evident that the typical chain of command and management by control was not working well. "Rather than a chain of command, today's successful corporation fashions a chain of mutuality" (Pascarella 1984, p. 147).

Although mainline churches have hierarchies of authority, Christ had little time for His disciples' concern about rank. "If anyone wants to be first, he must be the very last, and the servant of all," he told them (Mark 9:35). Rather than scrambling to get to the top of the organization, then, we should see everyone holding himself accountable for serving, whether at the bottom, the middle, or the top.

Holding others accountable takes time and effort. It's all too easy to let poor performance slip or to disregard misunderstandings. One manager complained to me about his boss: "I wish she wouldn't try to soothe me. I wish we would work together to solve the problems we are having." The Christian manager, on the other hand, is usually known as being tough but fair.

Responsible leadership is seeing greatness in people and letting them know it, and it includes letting them know when they are not living up to their potential for greatness. People want to know how they are doing, where they are going wrong, and what they are doing that's good. Straight feedback is a way of honoring people, affirming who they are, and showing appreciation for their contributions. They don't want meaningless pats on the back. They want to be dealt with honestly and openly. It is more Christlike to be brutally honest than to be just plain brutal by failing to treat other people as complete persons with opinions and needs. It is better to search for the truth together and strive for the higher ground. Covenants are forged in the heat of caring dialogue.

EYE CONTACT

It is easier to avoid confrontation than to engage people. It is easier to avoid looking at strangers who pass us by than to look them in the eye and show respect for them. But we diminish both ourselves and the other person when we take the easy route. As we saw in chapter 7, when Carole Hamm encountered a poor man on the street and decided to look him in the eye, she saw not "the poor" but a poor *person*. She was transformed. She saw more clearly.

George Seaberg of Seaberg Industries tells the story of how getting to know a stranger hitchhiking along the road led to his hiring of a person who has become a long-term, key employee. George went into business in late 1973. In the following March, his then-small manufacturing company occupied leased space in back of an auto body shop. After a few months, he found he needed an office for design work, billing, and making phone calls to customers. So he walled off an office of cinder block with a false ceiling, working on it night after night.

> **R**esponsible leadership is seeing greatness in people and letting them know it, and . . . letting them know when they are not living up to their potential for greatness.

By late summer, he was finishing the job just as flies started coming in, as they do in Rock Island, Illinois, at that time of year. George recalls, "I had just completed the office. I had put in the glass the night before. There must have been two hundred flies trapped in the space the next morning." So he drove to the hardware store four blocks away to buy flypaper.

Backing up, he explains,

The day before I was going to Peoria (about a hundred miles away), and that's the time of year when there are a lot of people out hitchhiking. I used to pick them up. As I entered onto I-74, there was a guy staring at me with the most forlorn look. I felt so bad I almost stopped and went back to pick him up, but I didn't. Later I told the Lord, "Lord, I'll pick up anybody. The next hitchhiker, I see I'll pick up." I went to Peoria and back but didn't see one other hitchhiker. Not one!

So the next day, on the way back from the hardware store, there was this guy hitchhiking—a scrungy looking guy, with a "down" look on his face, his hair in a pony tail, a beard. He looked a mess, but I told the Lord I'd pick the next one up. It was only two blocks from my office, but I picked him up anyway.

Craig Kinzer was very polite, and George told him he was looking for someone to work for him. "Would you like to come to work?" he asked. "I got his phone number. Then I left him off after just two blocks!" Craig, who was hitchhiking home five miles beyond where George picked him up, resumed hitchhiking. "A week or two later, he came to work for us. Only God could put that together," George says. "He was my seventh or eighth employee. I had in mind for him to do welding. I found out later he had been a gifted student in one of the top high schools in the country. He was homecoming king, a wrestler, played football, and went into mechanical engineering at Iowa State. After two years of study, he got married and dropped out of college.

"He had built homes. He was bright. He learned on the job— learned very well. He's the kind of person that, if you can direct him at the kind of thing he likes, he'll do well—many things. He has written poetry and stories for his kids. He builds furniture. He's the computer specialist here. He's got a lawyer's mind. He remembers stuff that I forget." Craig passed his welding days long ago. He's now vice president of manufacturing. And, George adds, "He's like a little brother to me."

THIRTEEN

Employment Covenant

The old employment contract is dead. Downsizing has left millions of people unemployed and millions more overworked. Many people say their work isn't fun anymore, and the corporate life is something to be escaped as soon as possible. The promises of empowerment, employee participation, and humanistic management are being broken by those investors and managers who look only at today's bottom line.

With the death of traditional loyalty to the company, there must be some new sort of implied contract if business organizations are going to be successful. As workers become more mobile and organizations become more flexible, both parties have to find a reason and a way to make promises to each other, even if on a temporary basis. Revolving relationships, if they are to be effective, will have to be built on solid promises to uphold principles by which to operate and goals toward which to work.

Even in today's chaotic business environment, leaders who are Christ-centered operate with a long-term covenant that takes the limits off their employees' performance and establishes principles for behavior that sustain the organization as well as the individual. These covenants go well beyond any labor contract, which is merely a legal package of limitations. Because the leaders' covenants are open-ended, their companies can maximize employees' opportunities to be real people and can help them raise themselves to levels of performance the employees may not have thought possible. The internal relationships the leaders nurture not only serve the people inside the organization but contribute to the organization's ability to fulfill its business mission.

In these companies, we do not see workers treated as functionaries. They are more like members of a family. Quite often, their families are also regarded as part of the company family. When George Seaberg hired a friend to become his first employee, his wife cautioned him, "You're not hiring an employee; you're hiring a family."

> **C**hrist-centered leaders operate with a long-term covenant that takes the limits off their employees' performance.

Workers are concerned not only with the work they do but also with their crucial roles as providers for their families. In turn, the relationships within their families have an effect on their work performance. Recognizing these realities, Christian management pays close attention to family needs and opens the way for workers to be members of healthy families. Management sees the worker–company relationship as an important ingredient of both corporate success and individual success. When George Seaberg speaks of growing the company, he describes the importance of attaining a certain size in order to be more competitive and thereby ensure jobs for his workforce.

Tim Conlon, as we saw in chapter 7, has a mission to "provide long-term secure employment for as many people as possible." This does not lead him to make any guarantees, but he is dedicated to doing his best to preserve jobs under whatever circumstances present themselves. Several executives told me that their appreciation of the human worth of their employees forces them to take the long-term view, study technological and market trends in order to anticipate problems and opportunities, and find ways to avoid laying people off.

LEADERS AS REAL PEOPLE

In the companies of Christ, the leader, too, is a very real person—perhaps head of the family or very much a part of a family. Unlike many business executives who are perceived merely as caricatures rather than living, breathing human beings, these Christian executives reveal their humanness. Their relationships are genuine and long-lasting.

Nearly two decades ago, I described the *real* person who would be the successful leader of the future. He or she would:

- Deal with all aspects of the business in ways that reflect appreciation for people as whole persons;
- Find ways to enable the worker to invest more talent into the job and derive meaning and personal growth from it;
- Appreciate the human relationships within an organization and between the organization and the outside world;
- Take an optimistic view of people, building on cooperation rather than on conflict;
- Reveal himself as a human being with fears, wants, and the need for growth. (Pascarella 1981, p. 15)

The Christian executives I have studied in the past two years fit this bill right down the line. What they see in people and demonstrate to them enables them to build the trust that forms the core of an effective organization.

Even in the best of companies, we can notice the absence of trust and genuineness. Sometimes, the relationships we think we have in a company are just surface relationships. One executive who has moved among several companies during his career remarks about how little he has heard from friends he worked with in the past. "I find a sort of 'amnesia' among coworkers from all eras of my career. Some people simply do not build 'relationships'—only 'networks.' Big difference!"

We see posturing by management in front of workers, by managers among other managers, and by workers to impress their managers. But genuinely Christian-led companies display an uncommon openness and naturalness. Their leaders are real people doing real things for real people. Chick-Fil-A is known for hiring clean-cut kids and awarding scholarships, for example, but it does such things out of principle—not just as a play to impress or motivate workers.

Carole Hamm displayed this openness and genuineness when I asked her what her title was. She replied that the subject never interested her. "We look at ourselves as owners who provide counsel to a management team that we have helped and encouraged to take on—I'm not sure I like the word *empowered*—responsibilities. We are not as involved in day-to-day operations as we once were. There was a day when we were very hands-on management, but we've realized that they [the management team] need us in a support role these days because there is just more to deal with. We find ourselves providing some aid in attitude, training, counseling. I don't know how you wrap that up in a title."

CONTINUITY AS A STRATEGIC ADVANTAGE

If management is autocratic, it can control out a great deal of people's bad behavior, but it cannot control *in* the infinite number of details that make for quality work. Better business decisions come through love, concern, and respect, which open the door to communications and creativity and encourage people to work together to seek win-win solutions.

Tim Conlon explains what he calls the "comfort level" at Berg Electronics. "I have what I describe as a conversational style. I'm not hierarchical. Things don't have to come to me through my direct reports, and I don't necessarily contact the organization through my direct reports. I will dip right down through the organization and go directly to the person I think is responsible for a customer or a product line or a project, and I will ask a question and have that person report directly back to me with an answer." That method of operating might get middle managers out of joint in a conventional organization. Conlon admits, "It used to do that here, but we've been at this for five years now and people know it's my style and it's the culture of the company."

Because of the comfort level, "We don't have a lot of turnover," Conlon says. "Very few people leave this company voluntarily. That stability provides us with a strategic advantage in that there's a continuity; you're not retraining your workforce all the time. You're not having to have that period of inefficiency where people don't exactly understand how things work in the company."

Operating in a Christian way actually does work, Gary Oatey agrees. "People respond favorably to being treated well. They stay late, if necessary, and take care of customers. Honoring God—there's a return on the investment for that. The more we partner with people the more it pays in the long run." A man to whom Oatey sold one of its affiliated companies asked, "How do you find these good people?" "Investment, training, development within the culture," Gary answered. "We have competitors who have all the same equipment and materials. Why do we have the largest market share? It's the people."

> **M**anagement can control out a great deal of people's bad behavior, but it cannot control *in* the infinite number of details that make for quality work.

DRAWING NO LINES

The people in companies headed by Christians comprise both Christians and non-Christians. In a family-owned company, you may find that the management staff are all Christians. Such is the case at Shumate Development and at Colorado Real Estate and Investment Company.

In larger companies, especially publicly held ones, however, you will begin to see a mixture of Christians and non-Christians in the workforce; the upper echelons may or may not have a preponderance of Christian executives. At ServiceMaster, Bill Pollard's predecessors at the top were Christians, as is his present Number 2 officer. But, says Pollard, his faith is personal and cannot be mandated to others. He sees his challenge as demonstrating his faith in the way he treats others, "including those who do not agree with me or my faith."

When these executives are hiring people, they look for the right character or morality first, and skills second. Bill Pollard says he once was on the board of directors of a company that was selecting a new CEO. They explored how each candidate determined right and wrong and what their reference points were. If they viewed God as their source, it might come out in that discussion. If they had another source, what was it? "We ask that internally, too. If you don't want to embrace God, the God I believe in has given you the choice to reject Him. But if you're going to reject Him, what is your source of making the right decisions in treating people, in running a business?"

We may debate about whether Christians should be tolerant of others' views or see their faith as the only true one. But, in business at least, it is tolerance that opens the door to loving non-Christians. At Seaberg Industries, about two-thirds of the eighty employees are Christians, George Seaberg estimates, yet all of them are on his prayer list every day. The Christian executives I interviewed believe that when their faith stands in the way of their loving people, they are not being Christlike. Furthermore, they are less likely to be effective in either business or evangelizing if they are exclusive in their treatment of people. "It's also discriminatory," Tony Ciepiel of Realty One points out. "And you're held at a higher standard when you're in authority—even higher if you're a Christian. People won't let you get away with it."

EMPOWERMENT THROUGH CARING

The converse of the old employment contract—the one in which we felt the organization would take care of us no matter what—need not be a chaotic everyone-for-himself environment. To succeed, organizations will have to be based more on self-reliance that's blended with mutual caring on an individual-to-individual basis. It is the only way we can continually raise performance without increasing stress. Leaders of the companies of Christ are not people-users who force people to attain corporate goals or their own personal goals. Coming from a worldview that holds others as spiritual beings, they allow people to empower themselves to do things that are good for them as individuals and for the organization. Rather than trying to reprogram people, these leaders help them to develop themselves and take care of one another. That's true empowerment.

Despite all the talk about it, empowerment has really not become popular in management practice, because it is a very personal thing. It has to do with giving something to someone else—giving a person the room to exercise his or her responsibility. Empowerment does not lend itself to being a management technique or fad; it requires long-term personal investment on the part of the person being empowered and the leader making it happen. The company can provide the environment and resources, but the leader has to provide respect, trust, and caring.

Helping people develop themselves could be misinterpreted as paternalistic, but paternalism limits people. It says, in effect, "If you work for me, I'll take care of you. You're not too bright; I'm going to tell you what to do. Your work is boring; I'm going to pay you well." The Christian approach is actually more demanding. It means: "If you work for me, you're going to have to learn. You're going to have to meet the standards that we've agreed upon. We're going to have to sit down and solve any problems together. I'm going to tell you when you do well, and I'm going to tell you when you screw up. You and I may have some misunderstandings, but we will work on them together."

Tony Ciepiel says, "Just because you're the boss, doesn't mean people will do what you tell them to. Leadership is about being a servant and motivating people to do what's best personally and for the company. The only way is to have their trust. If you do that, you won't have people stressed."

Tony recalls his first day on the job as chief financial officer at a firm on which he had frequently called in his previous job. One of the employees, whom he already knew, not realizing that Tony was now working for the company, told him she was bored, unhappy, and ready to quit. He said, "Well, I have bad news and good news. The bad news is I'm your new boss. The good news is I'm committed to you. I'll help you. If you want to leave, I'll help you find a job. I'll help you get where you want to be." In the fifteen years during which they have worked together, he has guided her into becoming a CPA and taking on more responsibilities. She has also followed him to his present company.

PEOPLE AS PERSONS

One of the ways these leaders show their love for other people in the company is by getting to know them as individuals. They ennoble them, help them discover their uniqueness, and build their self-esteem by showing that they love each of them without qualification—even when they don't particularly like them! They permit employees to grow by creating jobs that provide challenges and giving frequent feedback on how well the employees are meeting those challenges. They provide information, resources, training, and the freedom to learn and grow. They help them put their work into a broader context and envision what they are working toward. They enable their employees to be whole persons.

As much as possible, they accommodate the work situation to individuals' personal needs and family situations, so the employees can deliver the best possible results at work. The executives know they can't solve people's personal problems for them, but they encourage them to face those problems and seek the help they need.

They look for the leadership qualities in others. I witnessed John Beckett's leading a quarterly meeting of salaried personnel. Manager after manager would, during his or her report, credit one person or another with some accomplishment or assistance. All was done in a relaxed manner, sprinkled with humor and an occasional reference to Scriptures. But the business results they were reporting were impressive. As John wrapped up the meeting, he reported on several observations he had made in recent weeks and presented them as "things that you might consider in your planning activities." He offered insights for consideration; he did not set goals or issue orders.

John is the chief executive officer and has about ten persons reporting directly to him. That team operates as the chief operating officer, he says. They have broad powers for spending and investment. His primary role: to provide overall direction, select key personnel, stay in touch with what's going on in the world, and set boundaries (which people want, he believes).

I have met many managers who make a game of the financial numbers and devise games and parties so people will have fun progressing toward numerical goals. The Christian executives I studied and their followers have their eyes on the numbers, and nearly all of them will make some reference to the need for having fun at work. It's important to note, though, the fun they generate comes primarily from the work itself—the real (not the numerical) results—and the process of working together in a caring community. They are upbeat because they feel good about themselves and about the people with whom they work. Because of that, people may work hard, but the community spirit allows them to do so with less stress than people doing the same amount of work in a less positive environment.

Creating a caring environment is not the easy way to manage. It takes constant effort. Caring relationships at work can be troublesome, Daniel Hanson warns. They bring with them claims and responsibilities. They can be unpredictable, chaotic, and emotional. Caring leads to growth, but that growth sometimes has to come through conflict and peacemaking, he says.

In today's less structured organizations, each of us has to learn to be both a team player and to manage our own careers and lives. Teambuilding programs have been very popular in recent years. Often, however, they have disappointed management and the people on whom they have been imposed. They may or may not lead to solid relationships because the main thrust of management practice has not allowed the time or the place for genuine, caring relationships that support teamwork. On the other hand, people sometimes develop informal, unofficial communities in which they care for one another and care about their work. Top management, rather than nurturing these communities, has often quashed them or cut them up in the name of restructuring, reengineering, or resizing.

Caring relationships at work can be troublesome, Daniel Hanson warns. They bring with them claims and responsibilities. They can be unpredictable, chaotic, and emotional.

Building caring relationships is not a matter of determining which techniques to implement or which practices to avoid. It begins in the heart and will, and then cascades outward in caring for other persons. One of the fundamental values on which Beckett Corporation operates is "profound respect for the individual." John Beckett explains, "We want our work and work relationships to be dignified, challenging, rewarding, and enjoyable. We make the well-being and continuous individual growth of our employees high priorities" (Beckett 1998, p. 89).

HIGH STANDARDS

Christian leaders are likely to demand a great deal from their employees because they see them as having unlimited potential. They don't like to see people operating at less than capacity—not because they want more productivity from them but because they want people to use their gifts and to demand more from themselves.

"How big is the gap between your potential and current reality?" asks the employee book on core values at Applied Industrial Technologies. Another of the company's seven core values (in addition to Promise Keeping, described in chapter 12) is Personal Mastery. The company encourages employees to prepare themselves for careers regardless of who their future employer might be. Personal Mastery is wrapped in a collection of values that uphold the importance of the whole person. These values are more than words posted on the corporate walls. They are part of an intensive education process that all employees undergo. In fact, a walk through AIT's new corporate headquarters might give you the impression that you are visiting a school. Room after room is dedicated to education in both technical skills and people skills. The core values pulse through virtually all the spoken and written communications.

The leaders I studied exemplify the company's values and high standards in their own performance. Tony Ciepiel says, "I do believe in working hard. Work hard, play hard, seek God—all with a lot of energy. An executive in today's work environment has to work a minimum of fifty intense hours a week. Which then creates pressure to balance your life. If you believe everything is spiritual—work, family, fun—then it's a challenge."

"I wouldn't describe myself as being the favorite person throughout the company, because I'm tough. I demand performance," Tim Conlon admits. "Sometimes in order to land a particular order, for example, it takes extraordinary effort, and I demand that."

Setting the bar high applies to the moral standards that leaders set, too. How do they drive these standards throughout the company? "You can create priorities," Tony Ciepiel explains. "One reason I came to this company was I knew the owner had integrity. He told me always to err on the side of conservatism, to protect the company name and reputation. If that's important to me, it's important to people who work for me. Honor your commitments. Be willing to apologize for doing something wrong. Admit your mistakes." Word travels fast.

When the leader has high moral standards and lives by them, the word gets around and behaviors come into alignment with them. That does not mean that people who share high standards and high goals will not have disagreements. In fact, they may be even more likely to disagree than those who don't particularly care about what's going on. The Christian approach is to accept disagreement as part of becoming whole persons and doing what it takes to build working relationships. The leader is tolerant of people's differences, although he or she may be intolerant of any *indifference*.

In the dysfunctional organization, people talk to impress, control, complain, and find weaknesses. Officially, they may try to cover up any hint of disagreement. In the healthy organization, people talk and listen in order to share ideas, build strengths, and find opportunities to turn differences into consensus on the most desirable course of action. Dan Hanson believes differences are opportunities to learn and grow unless we have a win/lose view of conflict and see them as threats. Consensus comes more easily when people are value-driven and results-oriented rather than concerned about status or self-preservation; they come to agreement to live with a decision even if it is not 100 percent of what they want, so they can get on with doing what has to be done.

STEPPING IN

Being a Christian "has hurt me and it has helped me" in dealing with employees, says Tony Amato. "You can be held hostage by employees who hurt the company." Other leaders agree: Being a Christian does label them as someone with high morals but possibly as someone who can be a soft touch. Therefore, these leaders have to stand firm on their employees' behavior as well as their own.

> The Christian approach is to accept disagreement as part of becoming whole persons and doing what it takes to build working relationships.

Tony says, "If people see an employee who lies, cheats, and steals, they know the guy at the top does, too, because he would stop it otherwise. If the owner has moral integrity, a person without it can't work for him. And if the owner doesn't have it, a person with it can't work for him."

Christian top executives encounter all sorts of issues when they live and lead by high ethical standards:

- One company owner's sister married one of his key managers. When that manager was later considering a divorce, he asked if he would still have a job if he went through with it. The owner told him Yes, that what he thought of him didn't matter, but that he had to "get right with God." To ensure he wouldn't be biased in dealing with the manager, the owner made arrangements for him to report to another officer in the organization.

- A CEO, in his travels, realized that some of his company's independent sales representatives were not reflecting the company's character, its values, or its commitment to the customers. "They don't properly represent us," he said to his management team, suggesting that some changes needed to be made.

- Mirko Vukovich became involved with a conflict between an employee with "an attitude problem" and a controller who was not good at dealing with conflict. The employee wanted to sue the company. Her husband came to Mirko and told him she was feeling guilty and miserable, asking if all the parties could get together and resolve the problem. They, plus an outside friend, got together and worked on the problem. "We had not handled everything perfectly ourselves," Mirko admits. "In fact the controller quit right after that, saying she wasn't cut out for this." She had even been a bridesmaid in the employee's wedding, but then came the big blow up. It took about two years to work through the conflict before the two women eventually became friends again. "There was a lot of growth and learning on everyone's part," says Mirko.

Despite their openness, Christian leaders are likely to set tough standards and take disciplinary action, if necessary, when it comes to matters of sexuality, alcohol, and drugs. These are areas of "intolerance" for some of them. Among the executives I interviewed, I found they draw clear lines on what they believe is moral.

"Discipline is love. We won't tolerate fighting, stealing, or wearing shirts with printing on them that's in poor taste," says George Seaberg. When it comes to alcohol or drug problems, his employees have to accept company-paid assistance or resign. Whether discipline is called for or not, however, these executives display love in their dealings with the problem persons. They speak in friendship as well as in authority. Referring to colleagues about a worker who was a crack user, one company owner said, "We have to get him help," but others in the company were less patient and understanding. "Get rid of him," they said. In this case, the worker remained employed there until he eventually decided to leave on his own.

Tony Ciepiel says, "I've stepped in as a *friend* even when no company infraction or legal infraction was involved. (I have stepped in as *president* if it was an infraction.)" Tony once stepped in as a friend when one of his employees was having an affair; he told the employee, "I think you need to consider. . . ." That was several years ago, but he still gets cards from the former employee and his wife. "I have also been involved in cases where the person was falsely accused," he says.

Frequently, these leaders step in to break the very rules they live by when it's more human to do so than not to. One of the persons interviewed in Shawana Johnson's study of Gordon Heffern said, "Although Gordon was a disciplinarian, he also knew that you have to break the rules when you need to—when the right thing is to not apply the rules." While a leader's breaking the rules can lead to chaos, it can lead to admiration and respect when done by someone with a track record of being firm but compassionate.

Some of the executives with whom I talked said about their own behavior that they are concerned not only about behaving properly but allowing no room for misperceptions. Perceptions as well as actual abuses of the employment covenant can occur when the CEO's family members are employees of the company. Many of the leaders of smaller, family-owned firms have sons or daughters in the workforce or the management ranks. Some take great care to avoid any favoritism or grounds for anyone's suspecting it. Gary Oatey describes how that issue is handled at his company. He is the third generation of family to head the company. The fourth generation—nine youths ranging in ages from fourteen to twenty-two—is coming along. A long-standing company rule states that any family member has to have five years' experience working somewhere else before coming to Oatey company. They have to model the right behavior and leadership qualities. If none emerges in the years ahead, Gary feels they would have to sell the company or go public and put it in the hands of professional managers. "There are too many jobs and families at risk," he explains.

CHRISTIAN GATHERINGS

In a growing number of companies we find groups of workers and managers gathering before work or at lunch time to study the Bible, pray, or share their faith. The CEO of one manufacturing company has hired a Vietnamese translator to enable more of his immigrant employees to engage in Bible study. The activities may be permitted by top management, or they may even be led by top management. In either case, management has to take particular care to let it be known that anyone is invited—that not attending does not in any way put a person on the outside of an "in group."

Often, top management's involvement or leadership in the activities comes about for very personal reasons. One company owner, for example, was deeply moved by and thankful for his brother's coming to the Lord. So, one morning, he asked two workers if they would pray thanks with him. They did. As weeks went by, the three of them began bringing in Bibles and engaging in study. One by one, others joined the group over time. Even former employees dropped in now and then to pray and study.

In some of the companies I studied, prayer and spiritual references are often worked into the routine of business—a natural, low-key way of blending faith and work. Management meetings may include time for prayer or even outside persons speaking on spiritual matters. Company meetings or parties are often opened with prayer. The larger and more diverse the group, however, the less likely the message comes across as Christian-only.

The Fellowship of Companies for Christ International has a variety of suggestions for "priesting" employees:

- Holding retreats to promote spiritual growth
- Sponsoring banquets and parties where the gospel can be shared

- Making tapes and books available
- Conducting marriage and family seminars
- Providing counseling assistance for people with marital or financial problems
- Scheduling a daily devotional on the premises of your business
- Paying for daycare for young mothers who work in the business.

SHARING THE FRUITS

In the Christian view, the company exists to do God's work. That means bringing to the world products or services that are of value to people—not things to be worshiped but to be used for God's purposes. The company also exists for the well-being of its members. Those leaders I studied frequently express concern that this include an equitable sharing of the financial fruits created in the process.

In the busyness of business, it is easy for managers to look at people only in economic terms—generally as a cost. Christian managers make a priority of paying people fairly, looking at that as an investment or the proper stewardship of corporate fruits. They believe they owe their employees good financial compensation while they are working and comfortable resources for retirement. This compensation can take the form of basic pay or special bonuses and stock ownership plans. The mix of packages they offer is not unlike those of other companies; they have no monopoly on clever distribution systems.

They strive to make pay as equitable and as generous as possible within the constraints of fiscal responsibility and the long-term health of the organization. Their reason for doing so is to lift people to the point where financial concerns no longer get in the way of seeking the more important fruits of working. Aside from their basic fruit-sharing systems, management also makes exceptions again and again to attend to an individual's special needs for such things as major medical treatment, leaves of absence for child care, or time off and financial support for education.

On the other hand, they don't go overboard in creating exceptions. They do not give bonuses just to stimulate the highly visible producers or sellers; they tend to recognize the contribution of any and all employees. Gary Oatey's company has a generous profit-sharing plan through which 33 percent of pretax profits go to employees. "They are the people who make the business successful—more than the shareholders," he believes. "It's a matter of making good on the promise of sharing the fruits." In every company Oatey has acquired, he has introduced profit sharing.

The matter of giving employees stock ownership in a company has received attention for decades. Yet, who owns the company's stock may not be as important to workers as who is making the decisions—the small ones as well as the big ones. In some companies where employees have acquired all the stock, the old hierarchy is replaced, the new bosses still wind up being *bosses*, and employees still do not feel ownership in the decision making.

At the same time, in companies where workers do not have stock ownership, but each worker takes on more responsibility for his own activities and decision making, workers may feel very much that they are the owners of their jobs and their lives. A worker who feels that he or she is alive and growing on the job is more likely to feel like an owner of the company than the underutilized worker with a share of stock. Stock ownership, then, is not the sole determinant of what constitutes fair treatment. Christian-led companies excel with and without stock ownership programs.

> Christian managers make a priority of paying people fairly, looking at that as an investment or the proper stewardship of corporate fruits.

SHARING THE FAITH

When we consider the Christian employer–employee covenant, we inevitably come to the delicate questions: "How much should a Christian leader share his or her faith? And how?"

A person may bring his or her faith into the workplace, but faith does not travel solely from the outside into the workplace.

Colleagues in the workplace often provide the support for those who are in the process of building their faith. The workplace may be the place where people observe at close hand, perhaps for the first time, what it means to live out one's faith. Some Christian executives report that their personal faith began, or more often, was nourished, in the workplace through a mentor or by working with a godly person.

This sharing of the faith is a personal matter and should not be an official policy, however. Bill Pollard responded to my questions about whether he shares his faith with employees: "Yes, but I don't identify that as an organizational responsibility. I think that's an *individual responsibility.* That goes to my view that I don't think that a business is a Christian organization. I think *individuals* are Christians."

He went on to make a careful distinction: "It goes back to what the Bible teaches. I think that the only organization that the Bible teaches that is Christian is the church. Everything else is either an extension of the church or it's a separate entity that functions because of economy, business, or whatever. A business organization is not Christian in my mind. I'm not going to see any Christian businesses in heaven."

At John Beckett's company, Christian talk is part of the culture. Newly married employees are given a copy of the Bible, for example. Yet, John says, "I'm pretty discreet. Our faith needs to be evident in the substance of what we're doing." By doing right over time, however, opportunities do present themselves to verbally witness for Christ. For example, when a twenty-year veteran of John's company was hospitalized, John visited him. During the conversation, the employee spoke of a void in his life. "He was reaching out," John recalls. "I simply asked, 'Do you want to commit yourself to Christ?'" The employee took John's hand and said he would make that commitment. John believes it was twenty years' exposure to the culture that made this man ready. "It's a matter of being led by the Holy Spirit as to timing," he says.

FOURTEEN

Network of Covenants

We may think of the stockholders or owners of the company as the primary, if not the only, group outside the company with which business management need be concerned. Outside the assumed boundaries of a company, however, there are other groups of stakeholders, such as customers, vendors, and the community around it, who have a vital interest in the company's success—financial, social, or both—and who *contribute* to its success.

We can find examples of both Christian-led companies and others that create financial success for stockholders. If we look at success in terms of the company's contribution to other human needs, again, both sets can do well. Regardless of which set we look at, however, it has been proven again and again that, over the long run, only those companies that respond to the nonfinancial interests of all their stakeholders perform well financially.

As we have seen, it is wrong to assume that a company with a truly Christian leaning cannot be financially successful. On the other hand, not all companies or top executives who claim to be Christian are truly Christian in their business conduct. Unfortunately, the behavior of these few may lead people to believe that all Christians are untrustworthy. When I told people I was researching a book on Christian executives and company owners, some were more than willing to offer examples of persons who claimed to be Christians, yet cheated their customers, failed to pay their bills, or took advantage of their employees.

I proceeded anyway, and I found numerous cases of companies with whom people like doing business because they feel they will *not* be cheated and where people enjoy working. In these companies, Christian executives have found plenty of ground for engagement in God's work. Their integrity weaves a network of covenants among all those with whom they have relationships. They adhere to the consistency that Wayne Alderson advocates: "What we do at work, we should do at home. What we do at home, we should do at church. What we do at church, we should do in the community. What we do in the community, we should do in the workplace. That's the only true way to live with integrity and to build character that is strong and consistent" (Alderson 1994, p. 237).

CONCERN FOR CUSTOMERS

In their dealings with the stakeholders who buy the fruits of their companies' efforts, those who walk in the company of Christ are careful to fulfill their commitments and to commit to only what they can deliver. They show their care for the customer by doing the things that make for good business—assuring product durability and dependability beyond the customer's expectations, delivering it in a personal way, attending to the customer's needs for speed and convenience, and diligently managing the costs they incur and the prices they charge.

In business, today, we hear a great deal about getting close to the customer and serving the customer's needs, but "getting close" can, and often does, mean becoming more informed about the customer's wants so that we can make sales—period. Serving the customer only as the means to an end like boosting sales is not sufficient for creating lasting success. It is only when you really care about that customer that you will ask the right questions, accurately anticipate needs, and do the right things. Techniques can help, but without a foundation of caring, they won't take you very far. It's impossible to create handbooks thick enough to teach employees to behave lovingly toward their customers. As we said earlier, love and care have been missing from many of the quality programs that have been established.

The attainment of better and better quality is more than a scheme for some companies; it is a way of life—a culture. Leadership's character is revealed in its dedication to all aspects of quality: the product or service itself, the production and distribution processes and their impact on the environment, the work lives of those associated with the product, and the social impact of the product in its usage. Quality and integrity are intertwined. When a leader is concerned only about the quality of the product and ignores the quality of the workers' lives or the impact of the business on the environment, that leader is trying to segment quality. But quality cannot be segmented.

Serving customers means treating them with dignity. This means giving them what they are entitled to in accordance with the highest moral standards. A construction contractor won a bid, and after completion of the job, returned more than $20,000 that was in excess of the total of his costs and the profit he felt was justified. On one occasion, within a few hours after John Shumate sold a real estate property, a decorative fountain on the grounds quit functioning. He called in his employees to repair it at a cost of several thousand dollars, because he didn't want the buyer to be "stuck" with something broken that he had sold.

Serving with integrity sometimes involves choosing not to serve a prospective customer. John Beckett says he was once offered a lucrative contract on the condition that he pay a kickback. He turned it down. "Profitability is not the bottom line," he says. Ray Hinderliter of Power Chemicals, Inc., has been trying to run his company "to glorify God," and that's not painless. Once, he recalls, he had to turn down the biggest deal ever to come his way because he would have had to "put money under the table."

These leaders build trust not only with the customer through good service and fair prices, but also with their employees, who know what is being done to or for the customer. The same is true of their sales techniques and advertising policies. They are very sensitive to the impact that their words can have on the world outside the company.

A construction contractor won a bid, and after completion of the job, returned more than $20,000 that was in excess of the total of his costs and profit.

Seeing relationships with customers as a covenant orients these Christian leaders to the long term, and that fits well with the demands of business today. George Seaberg points out that it takes a long time to get to know customers. His firm makes 2,000 different parts—transition components such as engine supports, brackets, plates, step assemblies—and sells primarily to one large customer. Selling has to be done at three levels: corporate, operations, and the buyer, he says. This calls for long-term efforts and consistency.

Consistency is important even in the pizza business. Tony Amato, who had worked from time to time in a family pizza business before getting into the mattress business, explains why consistency counts. "A person who spends $5 or $10 a week with you can mean as much as $5,000 in sales over ten years. There are a lot of sleazeballs in the pizza business—owners who think everybody is there to serve them. They look down on people. I look up to people and think 'I'll get your business sometime down the road.' I won't lower my standards to compete."

VALUING VENDORS

Every company is on the buying end, as well as the selling end, of business transactions. They all depend on vendors for supplies, components, equipment, or services. In recent years, many companies have begun selecting fewer and fewer vendors and relying on each of them more heavily than they did in the past, because long-term relationships can lead to the vendor's better understanding of the customer's needs and to the customer's greater awareness of the vendor's capacity and potential. By developing mutual trust over the long term, they openly share plans and aspirations and grow together.

The Christian view of relationships is well suited to this new business reality. By paying bills and repaying loans on time, a company can build trust. By showing concern for the vendor, it can enable the vendor to succeed and grow. By regarding vendors as creatures of God and partners in business, companies can help them utilize their talents to the fullest and develop new capabilities. In the long run, many of these companies find, they contribute to their own financial success.

COMMUNITY CONSCIOUSNESS

While it may be obvious that a company needs vendors and suppliers, it may not be so obvious that it needs the surrounding community—neighbors, families, schools, social agencies, government—or that the community, in turn, has needs that can be met by the company and by individuals in it.

Company leaders who are centered on Christ engage the communities around them in activities that may or may not be specifically Christian. Often, the leaders encourage other members of the company to engage in community action—both things in which they themselves are involved or activities the employees may choose.

By regarding vendors as creatures of God and partners in business, companies can help them utilize their talents to the fullest and develop new capabilities.

They live out one of those Christian paradoxes: They know good works cannot put God in our debt. But once we are right with God, we can't help but engage in good works.

They help establish businesses or social agencies that employ ex-convicts, recovering drug addicts, and the mentally or physically challenged. Some leaders are active in political affairs, campaigning for legislation that supports their faith and will best serve people, and opposing legislation that may be detrimental. They organize ongoing prayer groups with fellow executives in their cities and even on a national scale to pray for specific persons or issues.

These leaders may be part of large, highly organized social organizations or engage one-on-one to help an individual rather than waiting for grand solutions. My research did not lead me only to executives who stand out by working on headline-commanding, big projects. Others stand out even if their reach is shorter. Not all of them tackle monumental social works.

Tony Amato, for example, has become involved with an inner-city project that provides housing for homeless people, many of whom were hooked on drugs or alcohol. Tony has had just enough experience with those abuses to be able to relate well to the people being served. God placed him there, he believes. As a member of the advisory board, he was asked to head up fund-raising. He said he couldn't do that, but suggested he could help set up a company, using his experience in the mattress business. In that business, customers sometimes return mattresses. Some of his competitors accept the returns, rebag them, and resell them. Tony will sell the used mattress his company gets to a new company that will employ people being served by the project to disinfect, rebuild, and then sell the mattresses at a profit. "It's also a way to minister to my customers," he says. "They know what happens to the mattresses they bring in."

When they engage in certain community activities, these Christian leaders make an effort to ensure that the activities are identified with Christ. Gordon Heffern, the retired chairman of Society Corporation, has a long record of involvement in both secular and Christian activities in his community. In retirement, he is devoting a great deal of his time to establishing a foundation called In His Steps to fund Christian projects in northeastern Ohio. Although funds are available for many welfare and cultural activities in the area, he explains, they are not supportive of many of the Christian activities that are or could be in place.

John Shumate, who founded a Christian radio station for youth with "a lot of help from God," says, "We are getting ready to start a TV station in Columbus for the youth—just like MTV. We're going to broadcast throughout the United States over satellite, if that's God's will."

Colorado Real Estate and Investment Company is getting involved in supporting wholesome communities in the manufactured home developments it manages. This effort began with one young man who was managing one of the company's communities in the Denver area while he was attending seminary. He finished seminary and went to work as a youth pastor at a large Baptist church. Mirko Vukovich's brother asked the new pastor to get a Young Life or some sort of Christian youth group started at the company's Fox Ridge development.

The young pastor launched a youth program there as an offshoot of his church. One of the activities he launched was a breakfast club that served breakfast at the school bus stops once a week. Mirko says,

> We have been working on getting that concept established as a regular program in our communities. We are going to get this program worked up as a prototype and basically duplicate it every place that's large enough to support it.
>
> The basic idea, and there are some Christian roots to it, is that we would go to a local church and find a young couple who is interested in this type of ministry. We would provide them with a manufactured home at our cost and give them space rent-free for a three-year period. That would enable them to buy more home than they would be able to buy otherwise. What we would want is for them to run this family development program. It would involve a variety of things. It's important they're tied in to a church. This would be a ministry of the church, and we would facilitate it.

The ministry would begin with a youth group and adult Bible studies, Mirko says. "In addition to that, they would manage community activities such as a Fourth of July parade, an Easter egg hunt, Boy Scouts, 4-H Club, et cetera, so that if you were living in the community, you would have a fair amount of neighborhood activity going on.

"Our mission is to 'provide quality manufactured housing neighborhoods the working families of America can proudly call home.' *Neighborhoods* is an important part of that," Mirko believes. And it makes for good business in the long run. "I think that families, especially single parents, would move across town to raise their kids in that kind of environment. I think it's a win–win situation. There's a Christian theme behind it, but not overbearingly so."

Mirko's company has the next community in mind in another state, centering on a former youth pastor. "We're not going to be overtly related to it, but friendly to it." The only thing that will be required of the community director is a monthly or quarterly report in exchange for the company's involvement in pulling resources together.

The types of community involvement in which we find these Christian executives go beyond merely writing checks out to worthy causes. They invest their ideas, skills, and abilities to bring resources together to meet the needs of people outside the company. They are involved heart and soul. Once again, this is a way in which they reveal their integrity. They follow Christian principles not only in their internal corporate relations but in the world around them.

They invest their ideas, skills, and abilities to bring resources together to meet the needs of people outside the company.

This stands in contrast to people from business, who sometimes get involved only to serve their egos. Former President Jimmy Carter, who has been a dedicated servant in Habitat for Humanity, warns us that "service can become just another social program, or one designed to exalt ourselves. Jesus warns that we should perform acts of kindness secretly and always in the name of God rather than as a way of drawing attention or praise to ourselves" (Jimmy Carter 1996, p. 206).

THE CHALLENGE OF
BEING PROFITABLE

Because of their commitment and involvement in so many covenantal relationships, it should be clear why Christian leaders regard company stockholders as only one group of stakeholders among many. On the other hand, this does not mean they disregard the stewardship role they play for their stockholders.

In a small, family-owned company, weaving stockholders into the network of stakeholders is easier than in a large, publicly held company. In the latter, stockholders are usually connected only in a financial relationship. That too-simple relationship is not the way it always has to be, however. "There is a need to challenge the passive shareholder—the person who simply puts money in the company willy-nilly and takes it out any time he wants," says Frank Larkin. "We're afraid of them, and this causes us to do very bad things. Take a look at the companies who have taken a leadership position and said, 'We'll attract stable shareholders by doing the right thing long-term rather than kow-towing to them.' They have more stable organizations—a tighter fabric of people with a more common purpose than making money."

I do not know what the statistics would show about the ability of Christian-led companies to retain stockholders, but stockholder retention is a major concern of most top executives. "On average, U.S. corporations now lose half their customers in five years, half their employees in four, and half their investors in less than one," writes Frederick Reichheld of Bain and Company, a Boston-based consulting firm (Reichheld 1996, p. 1).

"**On average, U.S. corporations now lose half their customers in five years, half their employees in four, and half their investors in less than one.**"

There are some patient stockholders who want certain values embraced by the companies in which they invest. Some of the Christian executives I studied work to appeal to this sort of investor, not to the exclusion of financial performance but by living out certain values *and* attaining good financial returns. And that can be done. Dick DeVos of the highly successful Amway Corporation says he seeks profits not as an immediate goal but as the natural result of doing things right. John Beckett says, "The bottom line is important, but it's the result of doing a lot of things right. What falls to the bottom has been more than satisfactory at our company."

Bill Pollard says, "Profit can be an end goal or it can be a means goal. I don't take away the importance of profit by identifying it as a means goal. That means that it has to lead to something. It is not in and of itself sufficient." But how does that stance go over in the stock market? "In our environment it has fared very well," he says.

> We've had a total return on our shares in excess of 20 percent compounded each year for more than twenty years. So, in any standard of market valuation, we would stand head and shoulders at the top of the heap.
>
> We are in business and we need to excel in what we are doing. I guess what we're seeking to do is to say, "You can excel in what you are doing in business and still have a primary focus on the development of people, of seeking to do that which is right." It's not a formula. It's not something that means, if you follow each step, you will automatically be successful in business. It is what I refer to as the grand experiment of ServiceMaster. It's something we have to seek every day.

Bill raises the question, "Can those get out of balance?" His answer: "Can we spend too much time on profit and growth in our shares and not enough on people and honoring God? Yes. They can get out of balance. And they can get out of balance the other way, too. I often say to managers, 'You don't have an option of saying, "Today I'm going to honor God and I don't care about making money." Nor do you have an option of saying, "I'm going to make money and I don't care about developing people." Both have to fit in your decision-making process or something is wrong with the decision.' There is tension there. But the objective is to see that it is creative tension that will drive us to think about the best solution."

"Profit is what allows us to stay in business," Tim Conlon points out. "In our values statement we talk about how we have to give reasonable return to our shareholders—our owners. If I wanted to, I know I could turn the screws and get more out. But it is my view that, if I turn those screws and get more out for this quarter or this year or next year, in the long term, I would hurt the company. I don't see any inconsistency between maximizing long-term shareholder value and my actions because, in turning the screws, I would affect people's attitudes."

For Laura Nash's "seekers," the response to the tension between business considerations and faith actually becomes a means of expressing their faith. The paradox they face is "a creative phenomenon in that it leads to productive economic activity and to productive personal spiritual fulfillment." For this type of leader "profit is transformed from being an ultimate value to being a result of ultimate values" (Nash 1994, pp. 47). Once again, we see the paradoxical nature of being a Christian leader in business!

THE MYSTERY OF PROSPERITY

Some people believe that wealth is bad, a sign that a person hasn't lived according to eternal values. Others believe that wealth is a reward for living the good life. Which is it?

Psalm 1 says the man who delights in God's law is blessed. "He is like a tree planted by streams of water which yields its fruit in season and whose leaf does not wither. Whatever he does prospers" (Psalm 1:3). It shouldn't be surprising that a Christian can succeed in business, because when people are treated right, they respond at their best as suppliers, employees, and customers.

On the other hand, one's faith should not be seen as a guarantee of financial prosperity. A discussion card—"The Eternal Purpose," available to FCCI members—says, "The prosperity theology being proclaimed by some in our time, which promises affluence for believers, is not a New Testament teaching. The New Testament teaches that we are to 'seek first the Kingdom of God' and eternal rewards." FCCI founder Bruce Wilkinson says the notion "If you walk with God, you'll be affluent" is a misconception. "Many believers barely have enough to eat!"

Leaders who strive to follow Christ do not *use* Christ for business success. Quite the reverse. They work to glorify God and, if success comes, it is because God provides it, they believe. A confluence of relationships and events come together to create success in

ways far beyond the leader's own abilities. A plaque in George
Seaberg's office stands as a reminder of this: "All things work together for good for those who love God" (Romans 8:28).

When success brings profit, we face the question of how much
profit is enough. That's not the most relevant question, however.
For Christian leaders, the relevant questions are, "How does God
want us to use these resources? How
many jobs do we want to create or
maintain by investing profit back into
the business for equipment, training,
and other improvements? How many
good works outside the business do we
want to be able to fund from profits?"

> **For Christian leaders,
> the relevant questions
> include, "How does God
> want us to use these
> resources? . . . How
> many good works out-
> side the business do
> we want to be able to
> fund from profits?"**

There are two concepts that people
of any faith might name as Christian
tenets: 1) You cannot serve both God
and Mammon; and 2) The love of
money is the root of all evil. The
Christian overcomes the dilemma of
what to do about money by regarding it
as a means of serving God. It is not money but the *love* of money or
making money as an end in itself that is evil. Money itself is a useful
thing that can be used for good. It is not something to idolize but
something given to stewards who work for God's purposes.

PART V

Taking a Stand

FIFTEEN

Disciples in
the Marketplace

C hrist-centered business leaders know who they are. That is, they know that they, like all of humankind, have been made in the image of God. They know that God put them in this world—a Creation that God said was good—to be stewards of it. They feel called to work with the bad that we humans have created and make the world good again. They regard themselves as disciples of Christ, heeding His command to love. Equally important, they let this be known in their daily lives. They may or may not talk much about what's going on inside unless they are asked, but on the outside they clearly demonstrate where they are coming from.

CHANGE AGENTS

By living out the Christian message, Christ-centered leaders are well suited to today's business climate, in which the chief role of the top executive is to promote change and improvement. It's no longer sufficient to hold to the status quo in an effort to maintain an organization. Today, leaders have to create organizations that can continually improve their products and services and change even their corporate structure and procedures to meet a changing marketplace.

Being a change agent requires more than casting stones of criticism at the status quo. It means unleashing commitment and energy to marshal resources and lead the way—to carry a stone and show others where to place their stones to help construct the future.

The Christian executives we are looking at do not seek comfort in the world; nor do they simply attack it verbally. They are compelled to improve it—to bring it into alignment with God's plans, using the positions they have been given in trust as opportunities to be agents of change. In responding to this calling, they display one of the Christian paradoxes: Demonstrating a peacefulness while being highly energetic and forceful. They have attained "the peace of God, which transcends all understanding" (Philippians 4:7). As we saw in chapter 8, they are characterized by another of the Christian paradoxes: Standing for unchanging principles while driving change. In fact, it is their commitment to certain principles that compels them to be agents of change in the world and guides the manner in which they pursue that change.

Still another Christian paradox comes into play to enable them to earn the trust that permits change: They believe in the importance of both the individual *and* the community. Because of their paradoxical nature, these leaders are well suited to lead their organizations into change, because the employees in their companies feel they can trust that change will work in their favor as well as the company's. They are participating in the change process, confident that they will be beneficiaries, not victims of change. Above all, they can trust that the change is worthwhile.

INFECTION RATHER
THAN INJECTION

Changing corporate culture is a matter of *infection*, not *injection*. For better or for worse, a leader's character carries a message that either infects others with the desire to undergo change or thwarts it. In these chaotic times, American management faces not so much a test of skills as a test of character and integrity. Character is revealed wholeness, consistency, and selflessness.

Character is the expression of the soul as it journeys through this human life. It communicates with others at a deep level through action over time. As John wrote in his first letter, "Let us not love with words or tongue but with actions and in truth" (3:18). Leadership expert Noel Tichy says, "Leaders are motivated to set a good example for others and to improve their organizations rather than to get more money for themselves or save their own jobs" (Tichy 1997, p. 158). Effective leaders set the example of selflessness as they embody love in their official capacities and their personal lives. And that's a powerful model for others to follow.

> **F**or better or for worse, a leader's character carries a message that either infects others with the desire to undergo change or thwarts it.

Leaders can reveal their selflessness in the overarching purpose they establish for the organization—one that can be meshed with the purposes that individual employees are struggling to work out in their personal lives. We all need a dignity of purpose that can lift us from both the joys and the sorrows of daily life to a role in God's Creation. By holding up this purpose, leaders encourage people to shift their self-perceptions and see new possibilities in themselves. It helps employees shift their perceptions of their fellow workers, look for the potential in others, and share knowledge or resources that will help them. They rise from the struggle to win credit for themselves or discredit others because they share a purpose that leads them to recognize their interdependence. (Pascarella and Frohman 1989, p. 31)

"If you talked with our staff, you would see people whose lives are changing," Carole Hamm says. "To me, that's what Christianity is all about—transformation of people's lives, providing them with the same opportunities that I have for myself in spiritual growth. We have paid for people to go and experience a four-day Servant Leadership course, for example. The hope was that they would deepen their own Christian walk, which would make a difference for them in their personal lives, their work lives, and the community in which they live."

When I asked Tim Conlon of Berg Electronics how well his purpose and principles match with or are reflected in the values and practices of his company, he responded, "One of the things I learned in business school is the organization *always*—not sometimes—reflects the personality and the attitudes of the person at the top. And that's true of Berg." The chairman of his company "is clearly a force in the company, but he's not day-to-day. And so I (as Number 2 in the management structure) would say the company more reflects what he allows me to project into the company than anything else. So, do I think Berg matches my perspective on things? Yes, I think so."

When a leader works hard at tuning in to God's intentions, he or she does not let conventional business practices or laws stand in the way. In obedience to a higher law, this leader will press to the limit of man's laws or work to change them. Oatey company's belief statement, for example, contains two items relating to that: "Strive to minimize governmental and third party interference in the operation of our business. Implement affirmatively all federal, state and local laws and regulations."

Stephen Carter points out, "Integrity . . . usually means following the rules, even when following the rules costs victory. Sometimes integrity means breaking the rules, but only with a good and clear and openly articulated reason that appeals to a superior virtue" (Stephen Carter 1996, p. 170).

Most of these executives are more concerned about doing what is biblically correct than what is politically correct. When I asked one young executive about how his CEO, who is known to be a Christian in action, handles the many legalities and regulations that can block Christian efforts, he said, "Jack doesn't let that get in his way." This stance is not without risk, however. Another executive admits, "Sometimes we fail, and when we fail we sometimes get sued, and when we get sued we sometimes lose."

Bill Pollard says, "Obviously, there are restraints whenever you're a public entity. There are restraints based upon the law, but you can look at them as restraints or not restraints. I've never found them to be limiting factors. I have found them from time to time to be challenging."

RESISTANCE AND INSISTENCE

When I first set out on my research on Christian executives, a Christian consultant friend passed along a warning to anyone who aspires to step out in Christian leadership: "Be prepared to be judged." When you take your stand and let it be known what you believe, you are judged, rightly or wrongly, against what others think a Christian should be and do.

Some people will expect you to be caught up in fantasies and emotions, to believe in keeping your spiritual beliefs separate from your activities in the secular world, to be interested only in personal salvation, and dealing only with others who have been saved. On one side, you may be convicted without trial for being a fundamentalist and lacking compassion. On the other, you may be branded as too liberal in your social values. You also carry the cross of Christianity's having been identified with a blindness to ecological concerns and a mean-spirited political voice.

> When you take your stand and let it be known what you believe, you are judged against what others think a Christian should be and do.

The only way to overcome these biases is through action, not debate. "How you treat people reflects your faith," says Gary Oatey. "Your integrity has to be consistent 100 percent of the time. If you're a man or woman of your word, you make good on your promises." He says people will sometimes point to the company mission and beliefs printed on the back of his calling cards and challenge him: "Are you living up to this?" Conversely, some see him as an easy mark because he is a Christian and test his negotiating skills to see if he will give in.

Challenges to Christians' beliefs and behavior can come from inside the company as well as from outside. One upper-level executive said he feels constrained when he interacts with executives at the top corporate level. Top management doesn't share his beliefs, but his part of the organization is successful "so they leave me alone." He also meets occasional resistance from below in the unit he heads. Yet he continues to express his beliefs, and he lets it be known that people have permission to discuss their spirituality. He encourages them to search for common values about who they are and why they are at work—things that Jews, Muslims, and others as well as Christians can share. The reason for much of the resistance, he believes, is "people are afraid of losing control, of looking stupid in front of people whose opinions count."

"ANYTHING GOES?"

Although many of these Christian leaders do not draw lines around any particular belief systems, they are insistent that the people who work with them have *some* belief system—that they believe in a God who lies at the heart of the principles by which they will agree to live and work. "One of our principles is that we are truth-centered and that we believe there is right and wrong and that there is a God," says Mirko Vukovich. "I was challenged on that during a staff meeting—'Is that really appropriate to have in our statement of guiding principles?' And I said, 'Yes it is. I'm not telling you how to live your faith or that you have to share mine, but if you don't believe there is a right or wrong and there is an absolute truth, I don't want you in here because that's how we make our decisions.'

"We have had a terrible problem with our society, where separation of church and state has become separation of God and state, which was never intended," he says.

> So I feel comfortable drawing the line there, not saying "Anything goes, nobody knows, everything is relative." But you have to be a little careful if you go much further than that.

It depends on the situation. When we have our financial meetings, depending on the group that's together, we'll share some personal things and some spiritual things and then we'll go on with business. There's always a bit of a delicacy involved, a little bit of a balance. You can cause discomfort for some people who don't share your faith. People are here in their work and they're trying to earn a living; they need to have the right to do that without feeling uncomfortable about it. Unless—and this always gets a little gray—they want to compromise the biblical principles of truth and respect for each other, then you have to draw the line. You can do that without becoming preachy about it.

Christian leaders are tough—tough but not mean-spirited. The Christ they follow was not the warrior-savior the Jews had long awaited. He did not tear down the oppressive empire in which they were languishing. Nevertheless, this great revolutionary said He came to bring not peace but conflict: "Do you think I came to bring peace on earth? No, I tell you, but division" (Luke 12:51). He came to show us how we must save ourselves from ourselves; He did not say the way would be easy. He did not say there would be times when we should yield on the principles He taught.

> "**We have had a terrible problem with our society, where separation of church and state has become separation of God and state.**"

Christ had a way of avoiding conflict without yielding His ground. There were times when He asserted who he was and what was right or wrong, but He often made remarks designed to get His attackers to think through a matter for themselves. When asked what should be done about a woman who had committed adultery, for example, He said, "Let him who is without sin cast the first stone."

Christ charged his followers with being "the salt of the earth." Those who walk with Him are to be change agents in the world, to be an ingredient that enhances it. By no means did He expect them to keep their faith to themselves. He said, "You are the light of the world. A city on a hill cannot be hidden. Neither do people light a lamp and put it under a bowl. Instead they put it on its stand and it gives light to everyone in the house. In the same way, let your light shine before men, that they may see your good deeds and praise your Father in heaven" (Matthew 5:14–16). With this scriptural passage in mind, Tony Ciepiel says, "I try to be a light in the marketplace."

HOLDING TO UNIVERSAL TRUTHS

Most people welcome the light shown by a leader who leads in love. Love is a universal. In fact, most universal truths—those eternals that instruct us on how the world works—are derived from love. Honesty, respect, justice, and other principles by which we might live are all expressions of love. But there are countless ways that we humans find to disagree and destroy the chances for love to be present in our relationships. Robert Wuthnow says, "Somewhere between the absolute good and the absolute evil with which ethics is concerned lie the questions we face routinely about what should be done, what is desirable or undesirable, and which of several options may be best for us to pursue" (Wuthnow 1996, p. 52).

We can segment causes for disagreement into three categories: 1) the inability to unveil truths that we share with others but hide beneath layers of selfishness; 2) the demands of egos that are willing to ignore or defy these truths; and 3) differing descriptions of the source of our principles and our relationship to it.

Christ-centered leaders show that we can engage in meaningful discussion and even disagreement to arrive at courses of action without sacrificing our principles. Generally, what's at issue is the best way to live within these truths. These leaders are willing, sometimes even eager, to clarify and strengthen what they believe by honing those beliefs against what others believe. They could choose to ignore those differences, but they make themselves more effective in the world of action by engaging others at a deep level— at the spirit level where human and divine energy are waiting to be released. They find any disagreements are generally not over principles but over the means of determining them, and they are more able to find ways to engage in action in the business world or the world at large.

At the same time, these leaders choose certain courses of action, no matter how difficult those paths may be to follow within the prevailing culture. They are willing to take on opposition by ego-centered people who lack principle. In today's society people are more and more inclined to deny principles. They shrug off disagreements and say such things as, "Everyone is entitled to believe what he wants." "You have your beliefs and I have mine." Or, "Anything goes." This is the ego speaking!

In a democratic society, where each person is free to express his or her wants and beliefs, too many people ask, "How can a person say he knows the absolutes?" As result, many people in leadership positions are more concerned about doing what is acceptable than what is right. The Christ-centered person defies this kind of thinking, believing that we are commanded to seek what God wants rather than responding to our egos' demands.

Most of the Christ-centered leaders I interviewed believe it takes God's power to cure the world's ills—we cannot do it alone. They experience the power of Christ transforming them; they feel the power of Christ—not their own "wisdom"—directing their actions. It is Christ through whom they come to know the author of universal principles.

To sum up the positions of those I have studied:

- They accept and love all God's children.
- They work with those who share common principles.
- Most believe that Christ is the only means of transforming themselves and the world.
- A minority seems to accept that there are other ways of discovering universal truths and relating to the Author of them.
- They all believe that Christ offers a unique relationship with God.

Some of the Christ-centered leaders I encountered are inclined to work at converting people of other faiths or of no faith to the same relationship they have with God through Christ, but nearly all of them choose to do it more through action than words—by being living witnesses. Others allow that the paths to God may be many and are worthy of respect; yet they do not feel that what they themselves believe is unimportant or anything less than absolutely true.

DISAGREEMENT AND DIALOGUE

Regardless of how they regard their faith vis à vis other faiths, some of the people I studied engage in dialogue to uncover universals that they share with others. Dialogue helps clarify their values and wants—their own and others'—and holds battling egos up to the bright light of universal truths. It reveals common ground on which it is okay to disagree. Generally, they find agreement on principles and, therefore, can work together.

> **Most of the Christ-centered leaders I interviewed believe it takes God's power to cure the world's ills—we cannot do it alone.**

By no means, however, does dialogue and working together mean that they are watering down Christ's message or working toward some homogenized religion that everyone can accept. Their living and working together with people of different beliefs includes their bringing Christ to the gathering, so to speak.

Dialogue has become scarce in America. We are more interested in action or debate (preferably hostile argument). Danah Zohar's differentiation between dialogue and debate is helpful in understanding the value of dialogue. "In a debate, I know which position I am advocating or defending," she writes. "Debate is about power. Debate is about proving a point or defending a position." Dialogue, on the other hand, "is about finding out, about discussing something openly until I break through to some new knowledge or insight. Dialogue is about questions. Dialogue is about sharing. Dialogue is equal because we all have something to contribute. Dialogue is about respect. Dialogue is about exploring new possibilities" (Zohar 1997, pp. 137–40).

Joseph Jaworski points out that "dialogue does not require people to agree with each other. Instead, it encourages people to participate in a pool of shared meaning that leads to aligned action" (Jaworski 1996, p. 111). We cannot begin to participate in shared meaning unless we have clarified our own beliefs and values. We cannot arrive at shared meaning and align our actions with others unless we can understand what is meaningful to them. Thus, we need dialogue. Ironically, however, one of the things that often gets in the way of dialogue in the work setting is fear of disagreement and division. Things are moving too fast. Everyone is too busy. Therefore, there is no time for dialogue and, certainly, no time for disagreement. So, we try to "avoid conflict" and "create a calm environment."

Refraining from dialogue can deter us from deepening our own faith, being able to live it out effectively, or helping others to deepen theirs. David Musacchia laments that "some guys don't humble themselves and open up. When they have a disagreement in a group—even a Christian gathering—they walk away." On a more public scale, Dick Leggatt of the Ohio Roundtable, which is active in shaping public policy, believes principled people must have impact on the political arena, but some people go overboard in trying to impose their beliefs. For example, some Christians want to elect or appoint all Christian officeholders. They would be like Constantine, who attempted to label everything Christian, he says. "But America's founders allowed us the freedom to choose."

Dialogue has become scarce in America. We are more interested in action or debate (preferably hostile argument).

Business leaders have to find commonalities among the people in their organizations so they can work together at optimum effectiveness. This poses the dilemma of respecting others' freedom yet adhering to their own principles. In their approach to that challenge, the Christian leaders I studied reveal two key manifestations of their faith: compassion and patience. They are willing to continue loving and working at changing the world, if only a bit at a time. They demonstrate that we can engage in dialogue to share our deepest values and beliefs without intimidating others.

In the face of challenges and disagreements, nearly all of their companies have worked out statements that declare to the world their principles, values, or purpose. In chapter 16, we will look at what companies headed by Christ-centered executives say in their public statements and the process by which they arrive at them.

SIXTEEN

Guiding
Statements

"We believe that there is an absolute truth. There is a right and wrong. There is a God. Therefore, we are accountable for our lives and our choices. Each of us knows in our hearts what is right and 'how it ought to be.' Integrity is the courage to do the right thing—whatever the cost. It is to do what we say we are going to do."

That is the lead item in the "Eight Guiding Principles" of Colorado Real Estate and Investment Company. The guiding principles accompany its mission statement, which consists of a single sentence: "We exist to provide quality manufactured housing neighborhoods the working families of America can proudly call home."

The statement of mission and principles are in print for all the company's stakeholders to see and for members of the firm to live by. They explain that principles serve "to guide the thoughts, words and deeds" of the people of the organization and "characterize how we want to do business." They set the standard for "the type of reputation we want to have with ourselves, our customers, our investors, our vendors, and our communities."

Public statements about what a company stands for have become quite common in recent years. They may be called mission statements, values statements, beliefs statements, or direction statements. Some are only a paragraph; others range up to a full typewritten page or more. Some are photocopied on plain paper. Some appear in colorful brochures. Some are even cast in bronze or carved in stone.

They describe what someone in the company wants the company to be known for. That someone may be the top executive, the top management team, or essentially everyone who works in the company. They may describe certain business or financial goals, or they may cite principles and values other than financial ones. A company like Colorado Real Estate and Investment might have chosen to say something like, "We will strive to be the best manager of manufactured housing developments," or "We will provide the best housing at reasonable prices for our customers and earn the highest return in the industry for our investors." After all, many corporate mission statements take a competitive stance—to be the world's best, the leader in the industry, and so on. By choosing to say it will provide neighborhoods that families can "proudly call home," the company takes its stakeholders to a higher level of inspiration. And by speaking of absolute truth, God, and integrity, it declares itself a special kind of company—one that attaches itself to ultimate standards.

PRINCIPLES AND VALUES IN WRITING

Most, if not all, of the statements issued by firms that are headed by Christ-centered executives or owners emphasize principles and values. While these companies are not unlike many other firms that express principles, they are unusual in that their statements generally refer to *God, God's Creation, God's economy, God's purpose, our Creator*, or *Judeo-Christian principles*. Their statements go beyond simply providing for the organization's survival; they relate to some greater purpose the organization serves.

The owners of a furniture-making company, for example, tell people that their Lord was a woodworker and they operate as though He is building the furniture. There have been no objections from customers about the language or the image. After all, people are unlikely to object to trustworthy, service-oriented vendors who live out the Christian values they assert in writing.

Boehm Pressed Steel Company expresses its mission and quality policy in one paragraph:

> Through God's guidance, the Boehm Pressed Steel Company is committed to becoming the world class leader of innovative design and engineered products in the metal stamping industry. This mission can only be achieved by being highly responsible to our customers' quality, technology, cost, service, and environmental needs. Boehm will conduct all its business in an ethical manner and provide a safe, efficient and mutually rewarding environment for the employees and its community.

A corporate statement may even literally be chiseled in stone. "When you walk into ServiceMaster's headquarters," says Noel Tichy, "one of the first things you see is a marble slab engraved with its values:

1. To honor God in all we do
2. To help people develop
3. To pursue excellence
4. To grow profitably

"But the important thing about ServiceMaster is not that the words are engraved in the lobby, but that these values are engraved in the hearts and minds of everyone who works for ServiceMaster," Tichy stresses (Tichy 1997, p. 109).

ServiceMaster chairman Bill Pollard points out another important feature of the statement. The first two objectives are end goals; they are ends to be sought. The second two are means goals; they are nothing in themselves other than the means of getting to the first two. Statements such as these often deal with the means of getting there, referring to such things as hard work, teamwork, or earning a living, but they are generally put into the context of stewardship. Although they may look like the usual business objectives, they are secondary to serving some non-economic purpose.

The first two values described in Seaberg Industries' statement of seven Core Values, for example, are

We operate by the golden rule. Treat your neighbor (fellow employees, customer, supplier, or others we work with in our job) as you want to be treated. Respect the other person. Love others around you as you love yourself.

Principle above profit. We will never compromise our basic Judeo-Christian principles for the sake of financial profit. Not only is violation of these principles morally wrong, it is also financially short-sighted. However, we must never lose sight of the fact that we are in business to make money and provide a decent way of living for our families.

The other five Seaberg values have to do with work, productivity, and quality.

Quite often, you will find a company with a stated set of values that go back to an earlier generation. John Beckett says his father, a cofounder of the company, was probably the source of its present values. As the firm has grown, it has taken greater and greater effort to articulate those values, he says. "It is harder to make your values known when you're a company with a larger public to be served. We try to describe the corporate personality specifically." The company's "roadmap" publication begins with a vision:

Our vision is to build a family of exceptional companies—each of which serves its customers in distinctive and important ways—and each of which reflects the practical application of biblical values throughout.

It then lists three "Enduring Values to be embraced and applied throughout Beckett's three related companies: Integrity, Excellence, Profound Respect for the Individual." The roadmap goes on to describe the company's Guiding Principles:

Focus—We are a Biblically-based company.

People—To build and maintain solid relationships of respect among ourselves, our customers, and suppliers, encouraging the growth and well-being of each employee.

Conduct—We will conduct ourselves with dignity, adhering to the highest ethical and moral standards.

Work Environment—We aspire to be a great place to work—a progressive, dynamic and continuously improving company—embracing world-class business practices.

Stewardship—Our business is a trust, and we will be good stewards of every resource in our care.

Citizenship—We want to serve others, helping meet human needs in the community and beyond.

The profile of the company's personality deals with several specific values. Among them:

We realize we are not an end in ourselves but a part of God's larger purposes. As such, we are called upon to work as "unto Him" and to be wise and able stewards of the trust He has placed with us.

We realize we are dispensable at any time in God's economy, but that it is also possible to conduct ourselves in such a way as to please Him and find His continuing favor.

GOD LANGUAGE

Christ-oriented companies do not have trouble with their commitment to principles, but the "God language" can raise some questions or concerns. Gary Oatey's company also has a statement of beliefs that begins with "Honor God in all that we do." The corporate beliefs have been spelled out for at least the past ten years. Making them readily apparent has raised some concern in the international arena, but it has not yet been a problem, says Oatey. Domestically, it is a definite plus. "It's refreshing to some people to see a company that honors God first. We don't care if it's a problem for a few people, because it sends a message. But it can't be too big a problem because our business has continued to grow with record sales and profits year after year."

Until recently, R. W. Beckett Corporation's Guiding Principles statement described the company as "Christ-centered." At the time I visited his company, however, John Beckett said they were considering replacing that phrase with "biblically based" in order to be more accurate and less offensive. A few months later, they did so.

As business organizations operating in a diverse society, some companies have recognized that they have to allow for beliefs other than Christianity, but they stand firm in referring to God. Christian leaders and others can still hold to their principles because God is their source of principles. They will not let differences in people's paths for getting to God block their efforts to follow eternal principles in their working together with others. This doesn't mean they secularize the Christian message; they put it into language that conveys the message effectively.

Christ-oriented companies do not have trouble with their commitment to principles, but the "God language" can raise some concerns.

A public corporate statement that is out of balance and exclusively Christian is not likely to work in business. Effective Christian leaders make known what their beliefs are, but they realize it is both inaccurate and unnecessarily troublesome to claim that all the stakeholders are followers of Christ. They begin with a Christ-centered vision and then translate it into terms that will guide people's behavior. Yet they do insist on acknowledging God as the source of the principles by which the company will operate.

SEEKING GOD'S VISION

In order to construct meaningful corporate statements, FCCI recommends to all member Christian executives and company owners a process that begins with their seeking God's vision for them. From this they develop a vision for themselves and their companies that is in alignment with God's vision. This picture of a future state has three features: It allows people to see Jesus in their actions, it reflects sanctification which sets them apart, and it calls for service or stewardship—the reason for which they are set apart. The next step is to define the company Mission, looking at the current state of the company's culture, structure, capacity, and competency to determine what the leader wants the company to be known for. Alan Ross, president of FCCI points out, "All employees and suppliers can relate to your mission, but only 'the believers' can relate to the vision."

In 1997, Pam Carlson went through a Beta group for FCCI's new Masters Institute.

Our first assignment was to ask the Lord to show us His vision for our companies—not what we envisioned, but what He envisioned! I was a little fearful of what He might give me, but I decided to ask Him what His Vision was for ROC Carbon. I wrote a few things down, but there was no confirmation from the Lord. Three days before we were to return to the Master's Institute for Session Two, I was driving to work, listening to BeBe Winnans singing "All of Me." The words of that song really started stirring my heart: "Lord of my life, carry me to Your Light. Every breath that I breathe, *all* of me."

Interesting that even in that song, it's God doing the work! We will it, and He does it. God wants "all of me." I started speaking with Him. "Lord, I asked you to give me Your Vision for ROC, but I haven't gotten it yet. It's just three days before I go back to Atlanta; if You don't want to

A public corporate statement that is out of balance and exclusively Christian is not likely to work in business.

give me that Vision, it's okay. If You do, I need it now. The worst thing I can think of that could happen at ROC is that all the employees would leave, and if that happens, Lord, it's okay, because You and I together can create a far greater company than what is already there. So I'm with You all the way—no matter what happens. I give You *all of me*." With tears streaming down my face, a peace came over me with His thoughts. I went to work and typed out God's Vision for ROC:

"ROC Carbon is the premiere service-oriented Carbon manufacturer, worldwide, providing quality products and exceptional service that draws attention to the reason we exist—to know God and make Him known."

It didn't take the Lord very long to come up with His vision, but He was waiting three weeks for me and my total commitment to Him with the company he had entrusted to me.

After running her vision by the FCCI group, the next step for Pam was to present it to her board of directors, but she didn't feel ready. She didn't look forward to any confrontation or conflict.

Yet, on the morning of the next board meeting, she knew she had to make her presentation that day. She went ahead with it, and there was no confrontation. One director said, "This is good, but I do have one comment. I'm glad to see that you used the word 'God' in your statement instead of 'Jesus Christ.'" Pam looked at him and said, "I didn't put that word in there, God did! We know that God means the Father, Son, and Holy Spirit. And I think the reason He used the word 'God' is because, with all the Buddhists, Hindus, Jehovah Witnesses, and such that are part of ROC, the term 'God' is one that all can relate to in some form. And it's a beginning place to get total 'buy-in' from everyone."

The next step Pam faced was to formulate a mission and plans based on the vision—not a simple process, especially working from a vision statement that stands the usual business purpose on its head in claiming "the reason we exist—to know God and make Him known."

THE IMPORTANCE OF BALANCE

Bill Pollard cautions against going overboard in language and behavior that imply that certain people are excluded on the basis of their faith—or having no faith. "Some people in our business want to spend more time talking about God than doing their jobs," he says in his book *The Soul of the Firm*. "Others are so busy meeting their bottom-line goals that they fail in their training and development of others. We make mistakes. Our objectives do not ensure a mistake-free environment. But they do provide a constant reminder of the importance of balance" (Pollard 1996, p. 48).

He writes, "As the firm learns to accept God's mix of people, it must be inclusive and supportive, and the boundary lines of exclusion should be few." The immutables of his firm, he says, are

> Truth cannot be compromised.
> Everyone has a job to do, and no one should benefit at the expense of another.
> We should treat everyone with dignity and worth.

Our combined efforts are for the benefit of our owners, members, and customers, and not for some select group.

We must always be willing to serve. (Pollard 1996, p. 41)

While a company might go overboard in being "too Christian" in its statements and thereby be un-Christian in its regard for others, a company can remain heavily Christian-influenced without having any Christ language at all in its statements. At Applied Industrial Technologies, John Dannemiller is quite open about his Christian faith, and he says all his top management is "very spiritual"—most of them Christian. Yet the company's statement of core values is free from any God or Christ language.

At AIT, "Integrity in Distribution" had been the slogan for a long time, but John found that it didn't help people in making daily decisions; he felt something more explicit was needed. He envisioned a set of values that, perhaps, would be a takeoff from the Ten Commandments. He asked leaders in the company to list values that would describe a company they would like to work for. The list that resulted from the long give-and-take process now consists of seven core values: honesty, integrity, caring/fairness, openness, quality dedication, promise keeping, and personal mastery. The list itself was not enough, so the team went on to elaborate on each of the values in writing. The company continually holds these values up to everyone in the company. All members work through a study manual that describes, interprets, and poses questions for reflection on the values. The benefits of living by these values, the publication says, "We will be healthier people. . . . We will get more from our relationships. . . . We will make more effective contributions through our work. . . . Our customers, shareholders, and suppliers will benefit. . . . We will find more joy in our work."

> While a company might go overboard in being "too Christian" in its statements, it can remain heavily Christian-influenced without having any Christ language at all in its statements.

REELL CASE

Kenneth Goodpaster, professor of business ethics at the University of St. Thomas, shared with me his case study of a company that illustrates the diligence involved in sustaining a Christ-inspired vision through a balanced corporate statement.

Reell Precision Manufacturing was founded in 1970 by three men who shared "many basic convictions about the value of prayer, the importance of balancing work and family responsibilities, and the need to practice Christian principles in the workplace," says Goodpaster. A statement from the founders explicitly affirmed a Creator, a Redeemer, and the need for Judeo-Christian values in the work environment; and it stated the founders' "personal commitment to God, revealed in Jesus Christ."

By about 1980, some of the employees who had joined the growing company were more intense about their religious opinions than others, and this led to the beginnings of a stressful division despite considerable corporate growth and the implementation of a number of favorable developments, such as the establishment of an Employee Stock Ownership Plan, limitations on executive pay relative to others', and substantial contributions to charity.

Goodpaster says one of the founders, Bob Wahlstedt, made it clear that there were three very basic issues in his vision of the company: 1) the priority of family over job; 2) financial and job security for employees; and 3) the opportunity for each person to experience pride in what he or she does. In 1989, a broader direction statement, still with references to God, was written to explain what the company was all about. Three years later, that statement was put up for employee review, and the majority of them approved it as it stood. A small number expressed concern about references to God and Creator. They were invited to participate in meetings to discuss revisions.

Revision meetings went on for months. Objections to the God language were raised because of concern that it could be taken to mean that religious faith could be a condition of promotion. So management sought legal opinion on the discrimination issue.

"The opinion appeared to support the members of the committee who wished to remove religious language," says Goodpaster. So, the reference to the "will of God" was modified to: "By adhering to the following principles, we are challenged to work and make decisions consistent with God's purpose for creation according to our individual understanding."

But that modification didn't end the controversy. Concern arose on the other side. One member of the committee dropped out, fearing the modification was a precedent and that, eventually, references to *Judeo-Christian* and the *Creator* would be removed from the statement.

Despite the legal opinion, president Bob Wahlstedt stood his ground: "If we take out all references to God's will and our purposes, there would be nothing left beyond our own individual self-interest that we'd be concerned about here." He was also concerned about the process through which any revision should occur. In a note to vice president Steve Wikstrom, who had been heading the revision process, he said that the power of ownership suggested a majority of stockholders could choose to revise the statement, and company precedence suggested that unanimous agreement among the triad of top officers could do so, but "management style" suggested that a *consensus* of coworkers should be the basis for any revisions.

The tug of war between those for and those against God references was wearing on everyone concerned. Wikstrom worked toward closure by pointing out to the committee that consensus was not a matter of total agreement by everyone but of everyone's knowing they had been heard and supporting a decision that they could at least live with.

The Reell Precision Manufacturing direction statement stands today as revised in 1992. The first half of it:

> RPM is a team dedicated to the purpose of operating a business based on the practical application of Judeo-Christian values for the mutual benefit of: co-workers and their families, customers, shareholders, suppliers, and community. We are committed to provide an environment

where there is no conflict between work and moral/ethical values or family responsibilities and where everyone is treated justly.

The tradition of excellence at RPM has grown out of a commitment to excellence rooted in the character of our Creator. Instead of driving each other toward excellence, we strive to free each other to grow and express the desire for excellence that is within all of us. By adhering to the following principles, we are challenged to work and make decisions consistent with God's purpose for creation according to our individual understanding.

DO WHAT IS RIGHT We are committed to do what is right even when it does not seem to be profitable, expedient, or conventional.

DO OUR BEST In our understanding of excellence we embrace a commitment to continuous improvement in everything we do. It is our commitment to encourage, teach, equip, and free each other to do and become all that we were intended to be.

TREAT OTHERS AS WE WOULD LIKE TO BE TREATED

SEEK INSPIRATIONAL WISDOM by looking outside ourselves, especially with respect to decisions having far-reaching and unpredictable consequences, but we will act only when the action is confirmed unanimously by others concerned.

In 1994, Wahlstedt reported to Goodpaster: "I have heard little controversy about the statement and no suggestion that further revisions be considered. It continues to be a working document and frequent references are made to it in day-to-day discussions."

When I talked with Bob Wahlstedt in early 1998, he said there still have been no problems with the 1992 statement. That is not to say that people on both sides would not prefer something else. "There are still some who consider it watered down, and I'm sure there are some people who would want to have all the religious language out of it. But neither is being vocal about it. Everybody is, if not happy with the statement, comfortable living with it."

How well does the statement reflect his own beliefs and feelings? I asked Wahlstedt.

I think my own personal feelings are that we are not operating an exclusively Christian organization. We do not have a religious or spirituality test for hiring or promotion. And our statement must somehow live with the tension of our wanting to preserve a strong commitment to a value base that's not vague. It has to have some roots, yet it has to be inclusive enough to include the broad spectrum of people who are part of the organization. We are not saying "based on Judeo-Christian religion." We're using that as a value base reference. So, even people who don't adhere to Judeo-Christianity religion do understand the values that are espoused at least well enough to challenge you when they think you are not living up to them.

I think, probably, there will come a time when we have to revise it again to make it more inclusive—probably to go beyond "Judeo-Christian." I think, if we were doing this over again right now, I would certainly be open to it, maybe even promoting that we change it to say something like "consistent with those values that are common to the world's great religions" so as not to exclude people of other faiths. But it's still maintaining a faith base to the values. The term "God" is universal enough that, if you allow for individual understanding, it doesn't become restrictive. So I would keep the reference to "being consistent with God's purpose for creation" in our statement.

The Reell case reminds us that statements of mission, vision, or values should be living documents—both in the sense of people's ability to live by them and in the sense that they must be revised as necessary to reflect newly acquired wisdom and insight. It also presents a note of caution to the writers of such statements: They represent not only what you want the company to be, but what you yourself had better be, because you will be challenged again and again to show that you are living in accordance with your stated principles and values.

SEVENTEEN

Ambassadors of Love

"**Y**ou will know we are Christians by our love . . ." the song goes. If you say you are a Christian, you will be challenged again and again to show your love and demonstrate that you live by certain principles and values.

Leaders whose life and work are centered on Christ let it be known in the workplace and in the world outside that they are Christians. They generally have no elaborate strategy or particular skills for doing so. They begin only with the will to love because they are moved by God's love for them. The thought of Christ's life and His death for all of us compels them to bear witnesses to this love. We have seen, thus far, that they demonstrate their faith in what they do. But what about *words?* What do they say about their faith? How and when do they explain it? How and when do they try to convince others to share their faith?

"In the organization, if someone's interested, I share," Tony Ciepiel says. "People know the way you act. You don't sell anyone Christ. You can't beat them over the head with a baseball bat to convert them. The primary way people are encouraged to become Christians is by loving them into the kingdom—compassion, care, putting the other person before yourself."

He recognizes that revealing who they are and what they believe means Christian leaders take their chances on whether this becomes a handicap or an asset in business. "If people are aware of your Christian bent, you're categorized," Tony admits. He has become widely recognized as a Christian particularly since he headed up the Billy Graham crusade in Cleveland in 1994, and his pictures appeared in the papers. When his company was being acquired and he was being considered for his present position, the new parent company was well aware of his faith.

"Most people know I'm a Christian through things they've observed," says Doug Hawkins of Bristol Metal Products, Inc. He had been wearing a WWJD (What Would Jesus Do?) bracelet for several weeks when we had a long talk. When people asked about it, he had opportunities to speak of his faith. But that was just an extra boost. He frequently tells people, "I'll pray for you." On one occasion, he wrote letters to business friends, seeking leads for friends who were seeking to adopt a child. When people asked why he was involved, he had an opportunity to share the source of his love and concern. He says he has had no negative reactions to his verbal expressions of his faith, even in the few situations where he spoke out more boldly than normal and could have jeopardized his business.

I have been the beneficiary of people's praying for me, but I recall at least one time when the praying was done by a person who hardly knew me. In 1983, before giving a speech at the Cleveland Engineering Society, I met privately in a separate room with the two dozen CEOs who would be sitting on the two-tiered dais at the front of the room for an awards dinner. Gordon Heffern, chairman of what was then Society Corporation and Society National Bank, shook hands with me. We had never met. "I'll be praying for you," he said after we chatted briefly. His words stopped me—and supported me—during my speech. I had not experienced any such outward expression of faith in a business setting. Gordon did not directly tell me who he was, but he expressed concern for me. That told me a lot about him—and led me to want to know more.

Fifteen years later, I recounted to Gordon the story of his saying, "I'll pray for you." He said, "I say 'I'll pray for you' to people whether they are Christians or not because people like feeling supported."

John Dannemiller of Applied Industrial Technologies has passed out hundreds of Christian books to friends and business associates—when they have expressed interest. He shares his faith with people who have the curiosity, he says. "Most people are interested in knowing about God and eternal life," he has found.

Tim Conlon at Berg Corporation maintains a continual flow of conversation and actions that clearly lets people know he is a Christian. When he is traveling abroad on business, he will invite others in his group to go to mass with him. "My people know I go to mass every day or as often as I can," he says. "Yesterday, one of my guys came in and asked, 'Can we have a meeting?' and I said, 'No, I've got to leave for church in ten minutes.' At one of our strategy sessions, I opened with a prayer, and I've got people of all different religions—Hindus, Buddhists, and so on—who work for me." Did the prayer trigger objections from the diverse group? "No. I kept the prayer geared to 'our father' and I just sort of said 'however you want to define that.' My directors know how committed I am to my faith. My chairman knows very well. They know it's a priority for me. They also know it has never got in the way of my getting the job done."

> **J**ohn Dannemiller of Applied Industrial Technologies has passed out hundreds of Christian books to friends and business associates— when they have expressed interest.

Bill Gibson says that witnessing to his employees is not a problem, since most of them happen to be Christians. But with customers it can be "iffy." He is convinced a Christian should not raise the subject of his faith immediately on meeting someone in a business situation. "Why should anybody trust anybody in business today? You have to demonstrate what you believe. You can't just act interested in a customer; you have to really be interested."

When the opportunity presents itself, however, Bill has no problem talking about his faith. He recognizes there can be negative reactions but, he says, "We're different. We answer to a higher calling. We don't want to do business with everybody. People have a right to expect honesty from us." On the other hand, Bill says, some customers do business with him *because* they know he is a Christian and will be ethical.

"Sometimes I'm not as upfront as I should be," he admits. "Some people have a knack or skill for evangelizing and some don't. When it's done to me, it's often too much in my face—and I'm a believer! When first meeting someone, you don't want them to be offended. But I will pepper a conversation with such things as references to some Christian event or a recent sermon."

Witnessing to employees calls for special sensitivity, as we said in chapter 13. "I have shared my faith in the workplace, but I'm very careful because I'm the boss and have kind of a captive audience, and I don't want to be unfair," says Mirko Vukovich. "I have led one of my bookkeepers to the Lord. But, for the most part, I'm careful not to preach in the workplace. When I'm working, I feel that people should be able to guess I'm a Christian. I hope that my deeds and my actions are my witness more so than my having to tell people."

SPIRITUAL FORMATION

I asked Michael Prewitt how the education he is experiencing at Princeton Theological Seminary will change his witnessing if he chooses to stay in the business world after completion of his studies. "Let's use the word *formation*," he suggested.

> I think education is something where you kind of open up your head and put in a lot of concepts and then go on about your business. Formation is different from education. Formation is things are happening because you're around people who are exemplary human beings who have been shaped by the Christian tradition. You don't get that by taking a class and reading the material or cramming for the test or writing a paper. You get that by being part of a community and

bumping up against these people and watching how they react and do things.

For one thing, I'm getting to be a better listener. Getting to know when it's time to take somebody aside and say, "Are you okay?" I am nowhere near as good at that as some of the people who are unchurched, who are complete rookies in our business. In fact, I'm undoing the formation that led me to running a service-oriented business with billable time, which implied "Let's get down to work, let's be smart, let's be quick, let's do this, do that, let's forget about the human needs because they are in conflict."

We develop who we are in relationship to models that are around us—not just the intellectual stuff we put in our heads. Those models are very definitely things we see in the way other people handle situations that we also face. We watch, and we read the gospel, so we watch Jesus as a model. We watch Paul and the great Christians over time in their walk in their faith. But it mostly happens by watching real live people we're around.

MINISTRY OF RECONCILIATION

Some Christ-centered leaders are eager to talk about their faith as well as live it out. They are excited and want others to share that excitement in their lives. It may appear to others that emotion is all that is driving these people. But many of the executives I studied say they are commanded to respond to Christ's call to carry His message to others. Paul explained his determination to spread Christ's word in 2 Corinthians (5:14–20): "For Christ's love compels us, because we are convinced that one died for all, and therefore all died. And he died for all, that those who live should no longer live for themselves but for him who died for them and was raised again." As a result, says Paul, from now on we "regard no one from a worldly point of view."

Those who walk with Christ are new creations and have a new worldview that leads them to see others differently. They believe that Christ, who offered us reconciliation with God, also "gave us the ministry of reconciliation." Paul says, "We are therefore Christ's ambassadors, as though God were making his appeal through us." Those who accept the opportunity for reconciliation also accept the responsibility of telling about Christ and the opportunity He gave all of us for reconciliation with God. Thankful for having been saved from their separation from God, they want others to have the chance to end their separation, too.

Some Christians are very effective at being ambassadors through the spoken word. In one-on-one encounters or in groups, they share their faith in the hope that others will come to embrace it. John Shumate says that, in the last six years, "Probably hundreds of men have come into the kingdom in my office." John tells them about his relationship with Jesus, as opposed to the need to be "religious"; they pray and receive Jesus at that time. "No glory to me. Glory to the Lord. Sometimes during the day, two or three men will come to the kingdom of God in my office," he says. "God supernaturally sends these men in who never heard of a relationship" with God.

> Some Christians are very effective at being ambassadors through the spoken word. They share their faith in the hope that others will come to embrace it.

At the other end of the spectrum are the cases where words about Christ either fall on deaf ears or cause discomfort or anger. As several of the Christian executives, like Bill Gibson, have said, those who talk the faith without the hearers' seeing them walk it may make even other Christians uncomfortable.

EMBODYING THE VALUES

The watchword I glean from successful efforts at verbal evangelism is, Be effective. Those who are successful do not charge out into the world, demanding that it change overnight. As we consider how the Christian conveys his religious vision to others, it's important to clarify what that does *not* involve, says David Krueger, professor of business ethics at Baldwin-Wallace College. "It cannot involve the creation of an overtly Christian political economy or workplace. We cannot require that all members of our economy or our work organization convert to Christianity, much less to one particular version of Christian belief." That is "neither possible nor desirable within modern, pluralistic society" (Krueger 1994, p. 72).

He points out,

> If we are to Christianize the workplace and economic life, it will not be through directly imposing Christian beliefs on social structures or organizations. Rather, it will occur largely to the extent that we embody Christian values through our actions and behavior in our workplace. And it will occur to the extent that we can argue persuasively and non-coercively that certain values consistent with our faith are worthy of being infused into the cultures, policies, and practices of organizations. In many cases, we will have to defend our Christian values with arguments that are not explicitly Christian but in ways that make sense to non-Christians who view the world from the perspective of other religious traditions and also to people who are not religious at all. (p. 73)

Bob Wahlstedt at Reell Precision Manufacturing describes two approaches that Christians should avoid in relating their faith to business. One is to "maintain a very separate identity, so you have your faith life on one hand and your business life on the other, and there's no integration of the two." The other approach is to become too exclusive which "tends to result in some pretty bizarre behavior if you try to bring a very exclusive expression of religion into the workplace. It creates a lot of problems. We have had that with employees who take our direction statement as a license to bring in a very evangelistic agenda, for example, or a very exclusive or narrow view of what is an appropriate life style. And their behavior becomes very bizarre. We had to fire one person for that when it became a clear matter of insubordination. Others have generally gone back to that first way when they've been counseled and told 'Wait a minute. You're not doing the company any good or you any good and you're just turning people off.'"

Wahlstedt is not convinced that "the exclusivity that all religions seem to drift toward" is "*of* God." He suspects it is an individual's way of expressing a feeling of superiority to others. "There is, of course, the Scripture that says, 'I am the way, the truth, and the life. No man comes to the father but by me.' That's a troubling one," he admits. "But I believe that in business we're not talking about salvation. That's not something that I am trying to bring into the work environment.

"In terms of applying the principles of life that religions teach in a workplace setting, I see much evidence that Christianity doesn't have an exclusive handle on that. I'll leave it to the theologians to discuss what happens in another life," he quips. "All I can say is that I know people who follow Eastern religions or who are as sincere in their desire to seek and please God as I am and, at least in the way they live their life here on earth, are as effective as most Christians. As far as what we're trying to do in the workplace, relate to each other in a way that's pleasing to God, I see exclusivity working against that and inclusivity working for it. That's the only way you can integrate faith principles in a secular world."

LET THE HOLY SPIRIT DO IT

Max Stackhouse stresses two important things for Christians to keep in mind in witnessing: Allow for the Holy Spirit to work on people, and keep in mind that conversion may take a long time; it may, in fact, go beyond time. The Holy Spirit "may show up in other people in other times and places. People who do not know Christ, people who are moved by other religious traditions, people who are seekers, people who have been damaged by bad religion— when they hear the words they just turn off."

It is still possible for them to develop aspects of commitment and character that are compatible with Christianity, he says.

> What you could do is talk about the fact that, in a way, the Christian faith has sustained a kind of civilization and a kind of attitude toward others which, at its best, allows others to continue their seeking—to hold their other positions with integrity. Furthermore Christianity has generated the kind of civilizations where temples, retreat centers, mosques exist. They have the legal basis to exist. This is not because of secularization. The evidence can be clearly demonstrated, for example, that Christian theology influenced the history of democratic law in this regard. Furthermore, coming back to the more personal

level, we ought to treat all of our neighbors—even our enemies—with love.

We don't know whether some of these people, over the next twenty years, will say, "Oh, that's why you're doing it." and become converted or whether when they get to heaven they will say, "Oh that's what you meant by that Jesus stuff." In God's good time—which includes eternity as well as history—there is a possibility that we can find some reconciliation on these matters. Meanwhile, in the areas of life where we can act, we have an obligation to be tolerant and to also state our beliefs forthrightly so people don't think we're hiding anything.

Pam Carlson relates two stories about her relationships with employees that illustrate this combination of openness and patience. Pandu, a Hindu engineer in her company, attended a Baptist church with Pam's family for three years. When he was involved in a serious auto accident, he had no family here, so "we brought him home with us and nursed him back to health." Later, Pandu visited his homeland and brought back a bride. He and his wife became involved in a young couples group at the Baptist church, but eventually they dropped out and began attending Hindu studies.

> "People who follow Eastern religions or who are as sincere in their desire to seek and please God as I am are as effective as most Christians."

Their Christian friends were horrified, but Pam assured them, "It is really important that they go because they've seen the love of Jesus and they have seen the love of you reaching out to them. They need to go and see the difference of what their faith is and what they've known here."

In another case, one of her Vietnamese employees and his family was also involved in a car accident. "One little son was really touch and go," says Pam. "We let that family know that we had six hundred people praying for the family. I told the father, 'I have asked God to show you that the living God Jesus Christ cares about your family and He's real and I want you to know it.' One month from the date of the accident that little boy walked into the lobby of our company."

LET YOUR GENTLENESS BE EVIDENT

Leaders who are focused on Christ rather than on themselves do their evangelizing in a loving, compassionate way. They may not be immediately successful in passing their faith on to others, but they are in for the long haul. Their gentleness in dealing with people with whom they would like to share their faith is like that advocated in Scripture: "Let your gentleness be evident to all. The Lord is near. Do not be anxious about anything, but in everything, by prayer and petition, with thanksgiving, present your requests to God. And the peace of God, which transcends all understanding, will guard your hearts and your minds in Christ Jesus" (Philippians 4:5–7). Michael Prewitt believes, "We need to say 'No one comes to the father but by me,' but we need to say that the way Jesus would say it—with all humility and believing we minister to all those people who are on the outside. We listen to those people who are on the outside, and that's the way to take the edge off that a little bit."

George Seaberg says, "I don't want to dilute the Christian message, but I don't want to hit people over the head either. 'Tough' is a Christian term. 'Mean' is secular." As Tony Amato phrases it, "You shouldn't always ask for the order. At some time, however, you may have to knock a person off the fence," he says, recalling how a friend challenged him to get off the fence of being a Christian at certain times and not at others. But this was the action of a *friend*. Tony takes the approach of a friend in his evangelizing. "I educate, I give examples, I try to be sincere and compassionate. You can't slam people into Christianity."

Effective evangelism does not come from trying to change people but by lifting their vision, by changing not their personalities but how they see things. We may not be able to change the way people think, but we can try to help them shift the position they are thinking from. In the end, each of us has to create meaning for ourselves; no one can do it for us.

Several of the Christian leaders I talked with cautioned that "church" or "religious" language can hamper the building of relationships with the uninitiated. Words like *salvation, witnessing,* or *sanctification* can put people off. In my research, I only occasionally heard expressions like "Praise the Lord" or "If it be God's will." When I did, they seemed to flow quite naturally and appropriately. None of these persons dwelled on how good they felt about their relationship with Christ; they were more likely to express thankfulness for His dying for them and their interest in serving the needs of others or building loving relationships. They see these relationships both as ends in themselves and as channels for sharing their faith with others in a long-term process of spiritual growth for both parties.

Tim Conlon describes his approach as "'passive evangelizing'— not hands-off but clearly leading by example." Carole Hamm says she tries not to engage in verbal witnessing. "I think the best we can do as Christians is not to shout it but just live it out and demonstrate it. I think our demonstration speaks loudly whether it's the service we provide, showing a sincere caring for people, or being there for them and listening. I used to think it was important for me to do a lot of talking, and I discovered there is really a lot more to be said *to* me than *by* me. If you first demonstrate your faith, then you need to make yourself available when the questions come and be ready to take the time. Those questions can sometimes lead deeper into your faith and where you are in your own spiritual life."

> **Effective evangelism does not come from trying to change people but by lifting their vision, by changing not their personalities but how they see things.**

Certain principles transcend religion. Through the spoken or written word, we can make people intellectually aware of their existence. But only by experiencing them in action and seeing their worth will people want to bring them into their hearts and incorporate them into their behavior. Then comes the time for words. One man active in the business community cautions, "The view that the only thing that counts is leading people to Christ is too narrow. There's more to Christianity than that. You have to build relationships that become the platform for asking them to come to the Lord."

When all is said and done, effectiveness is the mark of a leader. A Christ-centered leader is, therefore, as concerned about being effective in sharing his or her faith as in business dealings. That is why you won't find one beating people over the head with the Bible or carelessly passing out religious tracts to strangers. Instead, you will see actions and hear words designed to build relationships. What counts are the tracks, not the tracts, a leader leaves behind.

PART VI

Staying on
the Path

EIGHTEEN

God or Ego Speaking?

I hope that I have not given cause for anyone to believe that the Christ-centered leaders I studied have locked on to their faith and have no doubts or uncertainties—that they roll through life as 100 percent Christian 100 percent of the time. They would not hesitate to say that they are working hard to stay in relationship with Christ and be guided by God. Most of them would insist that God does not make specific decisions for them or reveal a grand plan for the long term; these executives carefully look and listen for guidance one step at a time.

Amway's Dick DeVos says, "I believe that all people have an intuitive sense, a consciousness, of right and wrong. Personally, I believe this ability to discern between right and wrong comes from our Creator" (DeVos 1997, p. 19). Most of the executives I studied would agree. Yet many would admit that, if wisdom is a gift from God, they haven't fully acquired it. They have experienced God's love and want to be loving and charitable, but there are two ways in which they feel they need help: 1) keeping this experience of God's love in the forefront of their thinking, and 2) keeping themselves focused on the path of spiritual growth, which is an endless progression of decisions and commitments. They can be distracted in the heat of business competition or, equally, when things are going too well.

Many of these executives lament that too few answers to their daily challenges come from church or traditional sources. What they hear on Sunday mornings is not of much help from Monday to Friday, when they plunge themselves into what has been walled off as "the secular world." They do not feel that the challenges they face are being addressed enough. They do find that they can gain a great deal of support from fellow Christian executives, but as one of them pointed out, "We have not been talking to each other." As we shall see in chapter 19, however, more and more Christians in the workplace have begun talking seriously with one another about their faith.

The Christian leaders I studied are ambitious and talented people. They are not timid. They can be God's heavy artillery when they are aiming in the right direction. But how do they know when it is God and not their egos directing their actions? Daniel Hanson says he has committed to listening to God for "grace messages," as he puts it. Such insight requires deep listening. Tony Ciepiel finds guidance through prayer. He says, "Prayer is a powerful thing. God has given me wisdom that far surpassed what I could have known."

Knowing when we are following God rather than our own ego is "a problem we all have to deal with in every area, not just business," says Mirko Vukovich. "I've not found it to be much of a problem." He relates a recent case in which he had to make a decision in a gray area of ethics.

> We sold a cable system that is in one of our communities [which his company manages]. We had already sold it, and the person we sold it to was reselling it in a big package deal. The new buyer wanted the former owner's signoff on the deal, which was us.
>
> I said, "That's fine. We'll go ahead and sign that, but I want you to make sure there are no X-rated channels on this system because then I would feel like I'm selling pornography."
>
> They argued, "Well, we can't guarantee that."
>
> I said, "That's fine, but I'm not going to sign."
>
> They responded, "Well, we don't really need your signature," yet they asked that I please sign. It was a very clear issue to me. They

ended up putting a clause in that I wanted, and we signed it. Legally the sale could have gone through without my signature.

There are times when it gets a little gray and then, just like it happens in my personal life, God opens and closes the right doors and I make a decision and go forward. Most of the time there is not a lot of confusion. If you've said something, you stick to it. If you've made a mistake, you tell people. If you're responsible for the damages, you pay them. You can't be worried about whose fault it is. You've got to be willing to accept blame pretty quickly.

RIGHT FROM WRONG IS EASY

In this era, everything a manager does can be challenged by practically everyone, inside or outside the organization. This draws management more and more into the ethics arena. It raises the dual challenge of knowing what you really believe, and finding the means to get others to do things the way you believe is right. Those who lead their companies for Christ believe that, if they listen and observe the signs around them carefully enough, Christ will show them the way. Doing what's right does not present much of a problem for these executives. Like so many Christians today, they often ask themselves, "What would Jesus do?" Bruce Wilkinson advises FCCI members to "Run the business the way Christ would run it."

> Knowing when we are following God rather than our own ego is "a problem we all have to deal with in every area, not just business."

One Christian businessman who buys used equipment says the practice in that business is to pay for equipment that is being scrapped simply on the basis of its weight. It's also common to cheat the seller by understating that weight. Early in his career, he sometimes did that. After committing himself to Christ, he saw that this was unacceptable. He calculated the amount he had gained this way, doubled it, and gave it to a hunger ministry.

A common practice in business is to run out accounts payable as far as possible—to the agreed upon time limits or beyond—and, in effect, operate on the vendor's money. But David Musacchia is diligent about paying people on time. He has established a line of credit to ensure that he can pay promptly at all times, even when people are slow to pay him, so that he needn't say, "I can't pay you because I haven't been paid yet." David believes, "The way you manage your money is a true reflection of what you are. It's one of the main things you can do to show your true colors."

Another common business practice is to promise people whatever they want or to make too many promises; then the individual or company cannot help but fail to deliver. Truly Christian business people guard against getting into situations where they will be unable to follow through. They will also own up to their mistakes, no matter what the cost. One executive told me he misinterpreted a customer's request and booked an order for fifteen times the amount of product they wanted. He supplied that amount, but then took back the excess when he discovered the error. He was then sitting on a large amount of inventory that had been custom-produced. Fortunately, the manufacturer helped him by storing the inventory and doing any rework at cost so he could sell the product elsewhere over time.

Sometimes, people make tempting invitations to participate together in wrongdoings. Bill Gibson says, "We're asked to do things I could lose my license for" in the insurance business. "We're asked to pad claims, to ignore health problems so people can get coverage, and so on." One man said he would pay Bill's firm $10,000 more than the $80,000 or $90,000 premium if he could get an unqualified claim processed. Another client claimed a boat was stolen, but Bill suspected he had deliberately sunk it. He had the matter investigated. The client was found to have arranged to have it, not sunk, but "stolen," and subsequently went to jail.

"If you do something wrong that a customer asks for, you have demonstrated you are not honest. Then they will ask again and again," Bill says. "If you're in this business just for the money, you can make money, but I don't know how fulfilled you'd be. There has to be a higher calling or motivation. Sometimes people won't ask me to do things because they know where I'm coming from. If they do ask and I say 'No,' they don't ask twice. There's a connection between my answer and what I do."

Doing what's right applies to everyone in the company. Christian leaders let their standards be known and are not hesitant to counsel employees or take disciplinary measures if necessary. One Christian leader told me he had an employee who was doing other work on company time. He was getting ready to fire that person "because he is, in effect, stealing from the company."

DEFINING MOMENTS

Discussion of ethics usually deal with matters of right and wrong. For a leader, however, right-or-wrong issues are relatively easy to deal with. As many managers know, it's the dilemma in which there seems to be no *right* answer that keeps you awake at night. For example, you work for the good of the company, but you risk hurting an individual. You try to be fair to an individual worker, but you risk offending and undermining that person's boss. You try to serve customers who want your new product, but you encounter protests from environmentalists or other special interest groups. These are situations in which loving others is not the question; they are matters of justice. They call for the deepest faith, the most guidance by God, and the best business expertise. This is when the Christian executive can excel while those without a spiritual foundation flounder.

> Christian leaders let their standards be known and are not hesitant to counsel employees or take disciplinary measures if necessary.

"Positions of power carry complicated responsibilities," writes Joseph Badaracco, professor of business ethics at Harvard Business School. "On some occasions, these responsibilities conflict with each other. At other times, they conflict with a manager's personal values. . . . Often there is no way for a manager to meet every claim. These are not the ethical issues of right and wrong that we learn about as children. They are conflicts of right versus right" (Badaracco 1997, p. 4).

He calls these right-versus-right choices "defining moments," because "they reveal, they test, and they shape. In other words, a right-versus-right decision can reveal a manager's basic values and in some cases, those of an organization. At the same time, the decision tests the strength of the commitments that a person or an organization has made. Finally, the decision casts a shadow forward. It shapes the character of the person and, in some cases, the organization" (Badaracco 1997, p. 7).

David Krueger points out that, while Christians should strive to transform the world, our "efforts are always limited by our imperfection and by the inherent constraints placed on our powers to act. Ethical action is rarely an 'all or nothing' choice between moral perfection on the one hand and total moral depravity on the other" (Krueger 1994, p. 82). "Our choices are usually incremental and strategic, aiming to create measurable change, but recognizing that our power to act is usually constrained by many factors" (p. 83). The Christian has to ask, "Do I have the power to make a difference or change the situation? Should I fight this battle, or save it for another day? How much change should I be satisfied with?" (p. 97).

Joseph Badaracco pointed out in an interview with me that, if you are operating from a strong values base, you are somewhat handicapped from the start. You have certain constraints on what you can do that other people may not. It requires a great deal of pragmatism and cleverness to be effective without compromising your values. You have to act out of love with the practical or political know-how to get things done. This sometimes calls for compromise—compromise on what we get for now, not compromise of our values or our long-term intentions.

Getting things done may necessitate explaining things in terms that other people can acknowledge or that resonate with their own experience. "Ethics often ends up sort of cross-dressing as economics," Badaracco has observed. By that he means you may argue for the ethically right thing, but offer economic reasons such as "It will help our finances," or "It will keep us from being sued," rather than bluntly saying, "We ought to do it because it's ethically right." People will be insulted if they feel you view them as unethical when they disagree with you.

Loving Christians do not want to insult others. They are willing to challenge people's thinking but not by showing disrespect for them as persons. They seek a just balance between the interests of the individual and the interests of the group. When it comes down to a choice between one or the other, leaders look for ways to minimize the impact on the party who draws the short straw. They will, for example, do their best to master the technology and business practices necessary to preserve jobs so they can avoid laying off people; when he or she is forced to engage in layoffs, they do all they can to minimize the impact on the affected individuals—not simply by granting generous severance packages but by treating the employees with respect.

BIBLICAL GUIDANCE

The Ten Commandments spell out some specific rules for Judeo-Christian behavior. Christ's two great commandments of love offer broader guidance in one sense; they are open-ended rather than specific. Thus they can be more troublesome. They deal with the end, or starting point, not the means. Christians have to take the commandments to love and use them to sensitize themselves to the ethical implications in any situation, and to guide them in making the decision itself. They find direction, not rules.

To some, it appears that little guidance for today's business situations can be derived from biblical stories set in another time and culture. David Krueger points out that some Christians believe "that the Bible is a complete blueprint for ethical behavior today." At the other extreme, others "argue that the ethics of Christian Scriptures cannot be applied to modern social realities at all." Finding a meaningful middle position, he says, "I believe the general ethical themes, ideals, and values mediate between the centuries-old language of Scripture and the complex world of modern work. Identifying these mediating themes—and figuring out how to apply them to our lives—is a creative, interpretive process" (Krueger 1994, pp. 75–76).

IN THE HEART OF THE LISTENER

Christ realized that not everyone who heard His message would accept it or apply it to his or her life. He illustrated the acceptance or lack of acceptance of His message with the parable of the sower broadcasting seed. Some seed fell on the hard path and died, like the Word heard by a person with a closed mind. Some fell on rocky soil and sprouted but later withered, as God's Word withers in the heart of a person who doesn't think it through and strays away when stresses arise. Some seed fell on thorn-covered ground; at first it did well but eventually got crowded out, just as the Word can be crowded out by the many things in our busy lives—not only bad things but even things that are good in themselves. And there is the good soil in which the plant thrives, as does the Word in the person who listens, hears, and acts upon what he hears (Luke 8:5–8).

No Christian would admit to wanting to be one of the first two types of soil—the hard or the rocky. They would prefer to think of themselves as the fourth type, but they are constantly in danger of slipping into being the third type and allowing both bad and good things to crowd out their commitment to Christ's message. Christ, quite likely, chose the analogy of planting seed and the maturing of plants because faith must go through a maturing process. It requires perseverance, He said, as he explained the parable to the disciples.

The work environment can offer both good and bad situations that might distract Christians from adhering to God's Word. On the negative side, they often work in environments that are "strictly business" and rob them of the time and interest for loving others. One executive says that, in a previous job, he felt totally out of place as a Christian. He did not fit into the corporate culture. "I didn't feel that I could be authentic and I didn't feel I could be my true self." When one manager moved to an industry different from the one he had been in all his career, another manager there cautioned him about this industry's "slimy business practices," referring to the way selling was done.

It is easy to be lured into playing the corporate game, perhaps speaking the language and using the same standards of success used by those around us. We might try to do only what we must do to win at their game while insulating our true selves, but with that approach we run the risk of having no impact on the environment. Or we might simply sink into being cynical and even destructive, thereby adding to the toxic environment.

It's just as easy to slip off the path when we're doing well—when we are in a good corporate environment. We may feel we don't need God. In fact, we may not think of God at all. We may lose perspective on what it is we are doing well. We feel on top of the world because we are attaching ourselves to ephemeral things rather than doing what God wants.

Doing too well seems to trouble Christian executives more than any hardships they have to endure. What do I want to be doing when I "make it"? we heard Tim Conlon ask himself earlier. One of the executives I talked with likened his condition to that of the young ruler who asked Christ what he needed to do to get eternal life. After he had said he kept all the commandments, Christ then told him, "If you want to be perfect, go, sell your possessions and give to the poor, and you will have treasure in heaven. Then come, follow me" (Matthew 19:21).

BLESSED, NOT LUCKY

"I used to worry about providing for the family. I could do more business," David Musacchia says. "But do I want more and more and more? I'm satisfied with what God has given me. If He chooses to take it from me, that means He wants me to take a different path."

"I'm described by many people, in fact I even have a plaque that describes me, as the luckiest man alive," says Tim Conlon.

They gave me that plaque when I was leaving my last company. It had been a joke for several years about how lucky I was, how things broke my way every time, or my division's way, or my group's way, and I kind of promoted that. On this last day before my exit I said, "Let me tell you something, this is a lie. I'm not lucky at all. I've never been lucky. I've always been blessed."

I'd have to say that, personally, I have a real struggle with success. You know, it's easier for the camel to go through the eye of a needle than for the rich man to get into heaven. I have been blessed with every kind of riches there are. I've got a great wife, wonderful children, good health, my entire family has good health, my parents are still alive, no member of my family has died before the age of eighty-five. Everything I have ever set out to do in life I have achieved. That's not because of me and I know it. So I've never been tested, and this concerns me somewhat.

Some of these Christian executives have found surprising success almost without trying for it. People like Dan Hanson and Tim Conlon rose through the corporate ranks without making that the goal of their daily actions. "Yet, you must be doing something right to rise to the Number 2 spot in a billion-dollar company," I challenged Tim. He replied, "I ask, 'How many times—I'm so good at pleasing people and so good at reading what it is that's needed— did I compromise myself?' That's a real struggle. At the same time, because I'm where I am I have been able to do some things that I wouldn't have been able to do otherwise."

> "I'm not lucky at all. I've never been lucky. I've always been blessed."

When it comes to financial compensation, Tim sometimes finds himself using it as a yardstick for measuring his compensation against that of his peers in competitor companies. "That concerns me when I really reflect on it. It concerns me that I care about it. It concerns me that I care about how others perceive me from a material standpoint. And, to me, this goes right to the first commandment— What is my God? I struggle with that. I really try to only have the one true God. But I recognize that sometimes false gods creep in."

PLANS AND FAITH

Having a working relationship with Christ necessitates being open to direction day by day about using your gifts to do God's work. Most of the Christian executives with whom I spoke say they are not sure what lies ahead in their lives. They do not have a clear vision of how they will serve God next. Nevertheless, as they walk into the future on faith, they sometimes look back and see how God's work has been unfolding in their lives. "I don't always know what God's plan is, but my faith helps me to hold steadfast no matter what circumstances confront me," writes Dick DeVos (DeVos 1997, p. 69).

Talk with Pam Carlson and you can't help but be impressed with her ability to submit to God's will and God's working in her life. Again and again, as she talks about assuming the role as CEO, of changing herself to be a better leader, or selling her vision to her management team, she says she has "no idea how to do it." She expects God to do the work with her, and He has continually been faithful.

After nearly twenty years with General Electric, NCR, and McDonnell Douglas, marketing executive Shawana Johnson left her job with no vision of what God wanted her to do. Having received an attractive job offer, she resigned from the position she had at that time, but then the offer folded. "It happened for a reason, but I didn't know what it was," she says. I prayed a lot. I had always felt strongly led in where I was going. For the first time I had to step out in faith. I asked the Lord to change my life if it needed to be changed." So, she founded Global Marketing Insights. She said she would let go of her six-figure income and "trust that God will provide. He did." She adds, "I also had started this company in the last year of my work on a doctorate! All this taught me patience, which was not one of my strong suits." A high-ranking executive, traveling the world, selling her expertise, she knew what she knew, and it paid off in corporate success. "I had no gray area. Now my gray area is so big! One of my goals is to see gray."

Shawana told me, more than a year after the startup of her company, "It's easier to look back and see the path. Just let it be." Change had come to her personal life as well as her career when she met a man who fulfilled her desires "as only God could have known. I had never verbalized what I wanted." And now, she is convinced, "There is some mission for the two of us. Somehow God has a mission for us together. I don't know what."

None of the executives that I talked with spoke of predestination per se; however, several did reflect a belief that God *foreknows*. God may foreknow without *predetermining* what happens, allowing us the freedom to choose. As we struggle through time, God watches from eternity, seeing the whole picture, which has not been revealed to us.

Viewing the world in such a broad, timeless frame of reference permits these Christian leaders to focus on the short term in their daily business activities without losing sight of eternal considerations—still another of the paradoxes they embody. They operate at the soul level, not just the mental or physical level. The mind and body live in time, but the soul lives in eternity.

Does having a strong faith and trust in God mean, then, that they proceed in business without planning? Definitely not. Does planning mean, then, that they ignore Christ's instruction to "worry not"? No. There is a difference between preparing for the future and simply worrying about it. Planning is their way of ensuring that they prepare well for doing their Lord's work. They don't worry about the outcome because they involve God at the beginning of the planning process. As FCCI instructs its members, they involve God in setting the initial vision for the company. They pray to be in tune with His vision for the company. From there they set a mission that is God-centered. From that, says FCCI, options or plans flow from the leader's gifts and the gifts of associates who are joined in the mission. Yet FCCI is very specific in its prescribing careful analysis of costs, risks, benefits, and timetables.

Doug Hawkins' view on this points to another paradox with which Christian leaders live. Neither extreme—"The Lord will work it out," or total reliance on secular planning—is the answer.

Both the leader and his Lord need to be involved. "The Lord wants us to work as hard as we can and He will give us the vision."

With a vision worked out with God, leaders not only find direction for their work and guidance for their decisions, but they tap into a boundless strength to walk the path. They are supported by God as well as by the people who share the vision with them. Their organizations are, therefore, fertile soil for success, both economically and in human terms.

NINETEEN

Discipline and Accountability

C hristian executives who have a deep commitment to Christ are humble about their faith. They continually feel the need to draw closer to God and be more constant in that nearness lest they be like the plant that is choked out among the thorns. Not only do they want direction for their lives and guidance for their daily decisions at work, they know they need perseverance and patience in loving others no matter what the circumstances. They are highly conscious that we are all in sin, having drifted far from God, and they want to respond to the reconciliation that Christ offers.

Christian executives realize that staying on the path in faith requires self-discipline, so that they can stay aware of the real issues amidst the rush of stimuli. They can easily get caught up in pragmatic challenges and overlook what God wants when they are analyzing "business issues." They, therefore, use personal disciplines and outside support to focus their attention and toughen their endurance.

Randy Vesco says we have to ask continually what the Spirit is telling us about breaking away from our usual concerns. Looking at his own management consulting activities, he asked himself, "Why am I where I am?" He found the answer and set the mission of his company as "bringing clients into the Fellowship of Companies for Christ International, where Christian executives come either because they are trying to fill a void in their lives or because the Spirit is nudging them."

"God gives you talents, but you can misuse them," Tony Ciepiel realizes. He says he has learned about waiting for God. "God has given me the abilities I have. I *know* that. A lot of people are a whole lot smarter and talented, but, for some reason, God has put me in this place. God has given me strong drives and ambitions—the desire to accomplish, to achieve. I can use that talent, position, and drive for personal gain or for God."

TIME FOR REFLECTION

Leaders who walk in the company of Christ reflect on what they're doing, what's going on around them, what they've read and heard. I would not venture to say whether they are reflective by nature, reflective as the result of some deliberate effort, or both; but it does seem that reflection enables them to see the paradoxes before them rather than seeing only one side of things.

They recognize they need reflection, whether it is done in private or in the company of others. Some executives set aside certain times of the day for reflection or meditation. One with whom I talked was planning a week-long period alone in meditation and prayer! In this noisy age of multimedia, laser lights, and amplified music, we forget the language of God is sometimes heard in silence. We have lost sight of disciplines like meditation, which have been part of Christianity but nearly lost. Most of us today seek wisdom from the outside in ready-made packages when what we need is reflective experience. Truth cannot be taught; it must be sought. Then God makes it known.

> "God has given me strong drives and ambitions—the desire to accomplish, to achieve. I can use that for personal gain or for God."

We can add still another paradox to characterize the Christ-centered person: Reflection and action. Or spending time alone as well as time with others. It is the time alone in reflection that enables us to act wisely when we engage in business activities. Reflection is not an end in itself. It can prepare us for proper, purposeful action. It is built upon observation; we observe the actions of ourselves and others and reflect upon them. We see what is done, how it is done, and what the ramifications are. We compare all that with what we can determine that God wants us to do. That reflection, in turn, guides us in future action.

In business, our motto is often "Just do it." Reflection is not something in which all top executives engage, especially on the job. Michael Hammer and Steven A. Stanton observe that in today's press for time, "There is none left over for real *thinking*. Reflection must be rooted in a company's day-to-day operations. In short, reflection must be institutionalized as a business process." That would include deep thinking about customers, the environment in which the company is operating, competitors, and personal growth—self-assessment, mind expansion, assumption breaking, they say (Hammer and Stanton 1997, p. 292).

Bill Pollard says that an effective way to promote reflection in an organization and keep it in balance "is to simply ask the question whether we are [staying in balance], to look at what we're doing and ask, 'Does this measure up?' At ServiceMaster, that is something that is just part of the agenda." He refers to an education day held for his company's board of directors that included a discussion of the issue "how we perpetuate what we stand for—both in the value dissemination within the company and also in the marketplace, and how we preserve that. We concluded, you can't preserve it; you've got to perform every day. We got all the directors to think about what their role is as they review things in the business, to make sure they're asking the right questions and understanding how the dynamics of these values are working in our business and what their role is in asking the questions."

For Christian leaders, reflection is often related to their reading the Scriptures. I found, without exception, that the leaders I stud-icd are heavy Bible readers and diligent students. They read to learn the history of God's relationship with humankind and the fundamentals of Christ's life and teachings. They reflect on how these relate to their personal lives and their business activities.

To help him in his reflection and studies, Tim Conlon has associated himself with a spiritual director—"a nun who is an incredibly liberal thinker, a very intelligent woman. And she has a very Eastern orientation." His pastor,

> "**R**eflection must be rooted in a company's day-to-day operations. In short, reflection must be institutionalized as a business process."

who suggested that he meet with a spiritual director, came to him after several months and asked how the relationship was working out. The pastor said there was a Jesuit priest he could recommend if that would be more suitable "to your more Western business approach." Tim replied that the present arrangement was "perfect—somebody who brings balance to my life, somebody who pushes me in a more radical direction."

PREPARATION THROUGH PRAYER

Without exception, the executives I studied also engage frequently and regularly in prayer. Most begin the day with prayer, often rising at dawn to pray privately in their homes. They either set aside times during the day for prayer or precede certain events or decisions of the day with a quick private prayer. They may also pray publicly before a group or invite the group to participate with them at the opening of a meeting. David Musacchia starts the day with devotions, prayer, and study. "I put the day in God's hands before my feet hit the floor in the morning. Studying equips you, helps you know God better. It's our communicating with Him. From there we live our life in action," he believes. Carole Hamm says, "I've come to appreciate time in my own life for prayer. You have to find ways to feed your soul in the midst of a very busy life. You plug that into your day in some fashion. It's not unusual to find me here in my home in a very quiet manner for part or all of a day several times a week."

Tim Conlon relies on prayer in making some of his business decisions. "I definitely pray, maybe not often enough, about decisions I have to make. Sometimes when things get a little dicey, I ask for help. 'Come on, give us a break here!'" How does he know that the help he receives is answer to prayers rather than luck or smart management? "It's always answer to prayer. I'm a real believer in prayer. I've had answers to prayers and to prayers I never prayed. I don't really believe in random chance!"

Prayer is essential to our soul in its reconciliation with God and in connecting with other souls. It is a time when we allow ourselves to become conscious of God and make Him the center of our lives. It is a time of concentrated seeking out of what God wants—communication, not to change God's mind, but to prepare our minds and hearts.

What is the content of these leaders' prayers? From what I can determine from praying with them and asking them about their views on prayer, these Christian leaders' prayers are made up largely of *listening*, so that they may know God and His will. They also give thanks and offer praise to God. Prayer is, to a large degree, a form of worship for them. In a broader sense, they practice the discipline of worship not only in weekly services at church or in their time alone but amidst their daily business activities.

When they ask for things, they intercede for others perhaps more than for themselves. They ask for physical healing or for the acceptance of God's will and strength to endure the anguish of failing health or death. They ask for the healing of relationships and the wisdom to love effectively, especially in cases where they don't really want to help. They do not believe that God honors requests for creating wealth, but that they might be given financial success in order to create more meaningful fruits from it. They pray for patience, knowing that God may not give them the ability to change a situation but, instead, give them a new perspective on it.

They often ask for guidance on specific decisions so that they might run their business as Christ would. They sometimes pray about business deals so they will produce what is best for all the parties involved. John Shumate opens his business meetings with prayer no matter who is in attendance. He often brings in one or two friends to pray along with him at the signing of a contract. They pray for the persons attending, the deal about to be agreed upon, and the persons who will be affected by it. "When you believe in the Lord and He's in your heart you want to have Him involved in everything in your life and business," he explains. He believes in "the prayer of agreement" in which the parties will agree before God to do what they promise and give the "glory and honor" to God for everything. "We also pray blessings on some of these other persons who are not Christians—thank the Lord that they are there." Reminiscent of what Gordon Heffern said about praying for others and telling them so, John explains, "We do it out of a sincere heart, and that seems to make them feel like 'Wow, someone's praying for me, too.'"

These leaders value others' praying for them as well. They frequently ask others to pray for them to know God's will and to accept it. They feel supported when they know others are doing so. More significantly, perhaps, there are times when they feel support when they haven't been told others are praying for them. The power of connectedness somehow makes itself known.

SUPPORT GROUPS

Christ-centered leaders find it extremely valuable to use support groups of various types, in which Christian colleagues help one another balance their lives and tune in to God's will. One of the most popular goes under the label "Bible study." These groups center on studying the Bible and discussing its application to the situations members face in their personal lives and their work. Since the Bible provides principles rather than details for daily living, it helps to discuss various interpretations and applications. Generally, these groups go beyond Bible study to engage in group prayer in which they can give thanks, praise God, and make requests. The groups provide a safe environment for sharing personal and business concerns; members relate to and support one another by listening, sharing, and praying.

Bob Boehm says he was raised with little exposure to Bible reading. Now he is in Bible study groups on Tuesdays and Wednesdays as well as an FCCI group that meets on the second and fourth Thursdays of each month. Tom Ford, a member of another such men's Bible study group in the Cleveland area, says, "Sometimes men, say in their forties, need to know that it's okay that they haven't read the Bible, that they are struggling with their faith."

"We accept people where they are," says Bob Arciero, one of the leaders of a men's group at Saints Peter and Paul Cathedral in Providence that has been meeting on Tuesday mornings for about fifteen years. Its objectives include worship, teaching, and service. Those who attend are mostly—but not all—Catholic. Most are older men, also, says Bob. "Essentially, what has happened is that most of us have families, businesses, and so on. After any number of years and having achieved successes in those areas, we find ourselves still in need. This is the thing that brings us together—the recognition that there's something more.

> **P**rayer groups provide a safe environment for sharing personal and business concerns; members relate to and support one another by listening, sharing, and praying.

"We have free will, but we may not have chosen the path that leads us to Christ," Bob says. "That's something that's going to be missing in our lives, and we become acutely aware of it. We may not know what it is initially; for some of us it takes a lifetime to realize that this is it. What the group affords us to do is express directly to one another that we are in need and we do have faults and weaknesses. It's freeing to anyone to be able to do that and not fear repercussions. We all need that. Most of us have a recognition that we need something. We come to the realization, more so within the group, that we need one another and, most of all, we need Christ."

Even the business organization itself can be a support group. At Oatey company, where not all employees are Christian, employees have engaged in Bible studies at different times over the years. Groups read and discuss books. Each day the company's computer sign-on page carries a message that is relatively Christian-based. Two or three persons take turns providing the message. It does not appear on everyone's screen; it must be requested. The company's voicemail also has an inspirational thought for the day, although it is not always expressly Christian.

"The single thing that makes it even remotely possible to operate in the company of Christ is the people you surround yourself with," says Tim Conlon. "God sends them to me. I am surrounded. My staff are almost all faith-filled people. The controller of the company is an incredibly faith-filled person—and my HR manager. I've got really good people around me, and they help because the things we talk about, the decisions we make, are all based on being good people."

Carole Hamm likewise finds that surrounding herself with the right kind of people helps her on her Christian journey. Seeing herself as one person in a group of 350 at her company, she believes mutual spiritual support depends on creating a "critical mass" by developing more leaders who feel the same as she does about how they should treat people and deepening their own spirituality. "Whatever their faith may be, if they're demonstrating care and concern for the other individual, it still is a critical mass."

NATIONAL ORGANIZATIONS

More and more Christian leaders are showing up in business. As they step into the business-spirituality frontier, they are finding one another and creating networks around one town or city after another across the country. They gather to study the Bible, share business problems, and support one another in deepening their faith. Gordon Heffern says that when he became a top corporate officer in the Cleveland banking community in the mid-1970s he had difficulty finding other CEOs with whom he could share his faith and from whom he could draw support; today, there are many overt Christians in the area. The number has expanded dramatically, he says.

Christian groups such as Promise Keepers and the Christian Businessmen's Committee have gained attention and grown rapidly in recent years. Christianity is coming out of the closet at the top of the corporate world as well. For example, since its launch a dozen years ago, FCCI has grown to a membership of more than 1,500 CEOs and proprietors, doubling its size in the past five years. "It's a movement, not a bureaucracy. We hope the day will come when the organization won't have to exist," says Don Kline, vice president.

Most of these groups are essentially for men, addressing men's growing awareness that they have typically been overly immersed in the secular world. While Promise Keepers deals with the role of men, FCCI is concerned with issues that transcend gender. I asked Carole Hamm if the lack of comparable women's groups or groups that are more inclusive bothered her. She said, "We are what we are. It doesn't matter what gender we are." With the rise in the number of women executives, it is likely not to be long before they find their places either in extant groups or new ones.

CBMC, open to all businessmen—not especially top management—is noted for its luncheons, to which members may invite guests so they can hear testimonials by Christians who are usually well-known in one field or another. Members make follow-up visits to anyone who expresses further interest on cards handed out at the luncheons. Recognizing that commitment to God is a process that involves many decisions, CBMC's objective is to move people one step closer to the Lord, whether it be through Bible study or discussing lifestyles. It leads people into one-on-one relationships and small groups to help people develop their discipleship. "It's not a competition to see how many we can recruit," says one area CBMC leader.

Similarly, "FCCI is about discipleship, not evangelism," Don Kline points out. Its activities and programs are designed for the Christian CEO or business owner. One of its thrusts is through fellowship groups. A group typically has six to eight members who gather as peers to discuss case studies of business practices, issues, and situations that affect the way they conduct their businesses and their personal lives. Facilitators guide the meetings and keep a focus on prayer, sharing, and application of biblical guidance to the case studies or the personal issues presented by members.

Each member of FCCI is invited to have a Council of Advisors. The purpose, says FCCI: "Christian CEOs need to be sure that their perspective and the resulting witness to the world through the company reflects Christlikeness. In fact a Christian CEO's perspective is what will set his company apart from others in the marketplace." The council, with a maximum of three members chosen by the CEO, helps him clarify personal and corporate values in relationships, leadership, and stewardship and determine short-term, medium-range, and long-range needs for the operation of the company. The council meets monthly for at least the first year. Usually, no compensation is involved for the advisors. This "spiritual board of directors," as Randy Vesco calls it, meets to discuss critical issues facing the CEO, pray, and share insights and counsel. It raises questions about what the Bible says on a certain matter or what the Lord wants. It blends experience with being open to the Spirit. In short, says Randy, "It helps take the secular blinders off."

Another support for FCCI members is its Christian Business Owners Groups, in which eight to fourteen business owners take part. Led by a paid facilitator, they meet monthly in daylong meetings. The facilitator also meets with members one on one at least once a month.

In late 1997, FCCI launched its Masters Institute—a biblical approach to running a company—that sums up much of what the organization has been teaching in various ways over the years. It begins with an effort to enable executives and company owners to undergo a character change, says Don Kline. It is designed to reach three groups of members: A weekend Proprietor Program for persons owning companies with up to ten employees, an Entrepreneurs Program that runs three days a month for two months for owners and senior management of companies of up to fifty employees, and a CEO Program of nine sessions over three months for top management of companies employing more than fifty people. Following each program, FCCI sends a facilitator into each participating company for follow-up.

TRUST AND ACCOUNTABILITY

The content of formal or informal groups is of value in itself, but an important byproduct is the provision of opportunities for Christians simply to identify one another. Tony Amato notes that "there are a lot of Christian CEOs who don't know there are others around them."

The groups also, to varying degrees, provide a mechanism for accountability. We are all accountable to God, but it can be too easy to relegate that owning up to some distant time and not hold ourselves accountable day by day. We can make promises and slip a little on them, forgiving ourselves too quickly. We can also slip into measuring our success against other measures of performance than those to which God holds us accountable. Sharing and being accountable to others in small groups "helps keep you aware of what God wants," says David Musacchia. Alan Ross, president of FCCI explains, "Personal accountability requires that you willingly give another person authority to hold you accountable for specific things in your life. We need peer accountability if we are going to run excellent companies for God."

Accountability is a counterculture in this time when many of us have become more concerned with entitlement than obligation and responsibility. Yet, this is what business organizations need from their members if they are to draw upon the full human spirit. The Christian faith, at the same time, may draw more interest from nonbelievers and more support from marginal believers if it becomes *more*, not less, demanding. Self-discipline and peer accountability would enable it to counter impressions that it involves little more than dropping in for an hour on Sunday. The more effort people invest in it and the more disciplined it becomes, the more it may attract people who sense the need for something solid to which they can attach themselves.

CHOOSING A DIFFICULT PATH

People who feel Christ present within them address the challenge of changing the world by changing themselves. They work at bringing the world back in line with God's intentions by first learning to grow in their own faith and discovering those intentions.

They respond to God's offer of reconciliation by fulfilling its accompanying obligation to immerse themselves in secular affairs and serve as stewards of God's Creation.

> **P**eople who feel Christ present within them address the challenge of changing the world by changing themselves.

The business leader who centers his or her life on Christ does not choose an easy path. Maintaining the will to use the power of love in their engagement in business requires constant attention, discipline, and support in order to overcome human weaknesses and the temptations of the ego. It means dealing day by day with the many paradoxes involved in becoming what they believe God wants them to be and leading their organizations to serve God's purposes.

The joy and confidence Christ-centered leaders exhibit might lead us to overlook the steep and winding path they follow. But once they choose it, they find that they are not alone. As they pursue their high calling, they humbly recognize that their accomplishments come from God's working through them.

Christian Paradoxes

Leaders who embrace the Christian worldview are able to live with paradoxes because they are aware of deeper truths that lift them above human-made distinctions and divisions. While many of us look for simple answers in our faith, these people are willing to live with complexity. Among the paradoxes they embrace:

Being concerned for others and being effective in business

Recognizing Christ as God and human

Loving your neighbor as yourself

Knowing that we have fallen from God's grace but God has redeemed us

Living out deep obligations and enjoying unbounded freedom to be what God created us to be

Standing for unchanging principles while driving change

Being in the world but not *of* it

Acting in the present and serving the eternal

Seeking individual solutions for monumental problems

Being peaceful yet highly energetic and forceful

Honoring the individual and the community

Taking time for reflection to prepare for action

New Assumptions About the Business Organization

Throughout the industrial age, business executives and company owners have tried to fit people to organizations. Now, however, we are beginning to struggle with shaping our organizations to fit people. This means we must set aside outdated concepts of the business organization and put several new assumptions in their place:

1. An organization's productivity has *human dimensions* beyond simple output-and-input calculations of dollars and things.
2. Productivity reflects the stewardship of our *God-given talents*. It reveals the individual's skills, inventiveness, and accomplishment.
3. The organization serves not just its owners but several *stakeholder groups:* employees, customers, suppliers, and the public.
4. The organization bears considerable responsibility for the *welfare and development* of its members.
5. The organization is involved in the *ethical and moral issues* surrounding it, whether it is so directed by law or not.
6. The organization plays a major role in shaping the *values* of its various stakeholders.

7. Nurturing a *service mentality* produces both a healthier economy and more human growth than does nurturing a consumer mentality.

8. Cooperation by *growing persons* is more effective than competition among persons who have been crowded into narrowly defined roles.

9. Work and the work situation can be a rich *source of meaning, identity, personal development*, and a sense of *community*.

10. Involvement of employees in the decision-making process depends on each organization member's wanting to be part of a *unity* and feeling personally responsible for the welfare of others.

11. Terms like "cooperation" and "teamwork" are no more than slogans unless people genuinely feel a sense of unity and work out of *love for all*.

12. Free enterprise is more than competition. It is built primarily on *communities of producers creating value* for communities of customers.

13. Rapid, concurrent changes look like *chaos* to the person who wants to maintain control and stability but present opportunities for the person who plunges into change and growth with *purpose*.

14. Corporate purpose begins in the *spiritual* realm with one's worldview and deepest values.

BIBLIOGRAPHY

Agee, James. *A Death in the Family.* New York: Avon Publications Inc., 1938.

Alderson, Wayne. *Theory R Management.* Nashville: Thomas Nelson Publishers, 1994.

Badarocco, Joseph L., Jr. *Defining Moments.* Boston: Harvard Business School Press, 1997.

Beckett, John D. *Loving Monday.* Downers Grove, IL: InterVarsity Press, 1998.

"Belief by the Numbers." *New York Times Magazine,* December 7, 1997, pp. 60–61.

Bellman, Geoffrey. *Your Signature Path.* San Francisco: Berrett-Koehler Publishers, Inc., 1996.

Bennis, Warren. *On Becoming a Leader.* Reading, MA: Addison-Wesley Publishing Co., Inc., 1989.

Bolles, Richard Nelson. *What Color Is Your Parachute?* Berkeley: Ten Speed Press, 1989.

Bonhoeffer, Dietrich. *Ethics.* New York: Macmillan Publishing Co., 1955.

Briskin, Alan. *The Stirring of Soul in the Workplace.* San Francisco: Jossey-Bass Publishers, Inc., 1996.

Carter, Jimmy. *Living Faith.* New York: Times Books, 1996.

Carter, Stephen L. *The Culture of Disbelief.* New York: Basic Books, 1993.

Carter, Stephen L. *Integrity.* New York: Basic Books, 1996.

Cashman, Kevin. *Leading from the Inside Out.* Provo, UT: Executive Excellence, 1998.

Celente, Gerald. "Corporate Right Livelihood." *Trends Journal* VI, 4 (Fall 1997): 2.

Celente, Gerald. *Trends 2000.* New York: Warner Books, 1997.

de Chardin, Teilhard. *The Divine Milieu.* New York: Harper Torchbooks, 1960.

de Chardin, Teilhard. *The Vision of the Past.* New York: Harper & Row Publishers, Inc., 1966.

De Pree, Max. *Leadership Is an Art.* New York: Doubleday, 1987.

De Pree, Max. *Leading Without Power.* San Francisco: Jossey-Bass Publishers, Inc., 1997.

DeVos, Dick. *Rediscovering American Values.* New York: Dutton, 1997.

Feagler, Dick. "Spiritualism Leaves the Rules to Religion." *The Plain Dealer*, December 22, 1997, p. 2A.

Gardner, John. *Nickel Mountain.* New York: Knopf, 1973.

Gilley, Kay. *The Alchemy of Fear.* Boston: Butterworth-Heinemann, 1998.

Greenleaf, Robert K. *Servant Leadership.* New York: Paulist Press, 1977.

Hammer, Michael, and Steven A. Stanton. "The Power of Reflection." *Fortune*, November 24, 1997, pp. 291–94.

Hanson, Daniel S. *Cultivating Common Ground.* Boston: Butterworth-Heinemann, 1997.

Hillman, James. *The Soul's Code.* New York: Random House, 1996.

Jaworski, Joseph. *Synchronicity.* San Francisco: Berrett-Koehler Publishers, 1996.

Jung, Carl G. *The Essential Jung* (Selections by Anthony Storr). Princeton: Princeton University Press, 1983.

Krueger, David A. *Keeping Faith at Work*. Nashville: Abington Press, 1994.

LaBier, Douglas. "Transforming Our Lives in a Culture of Disconnection." *The Inner Edge* 1, 1 (April/May 1998): 14–18.

Lasch, Christopher. *The Revolt of the Elites and the Betrayal of Democracy*. New York: Norton, 1995.

Leider, Richard. *The Power of Purpose*. New York: Ballantine Books, 1985.

Lewis, C. S. *Mere Christianity*. New York: Macmillan Publishing Co., 1943.

Marcic, Dorothy. *Managing with the Wisdom of Love*. San Francisco: Jossey-Bass Publishers, Inc., 1997.

Merton, Thomas. *Life and Holiness*. New York: Herder and Herder, 1963.

Miller, Donald E. *Reinventing American Protestantism*. Berkeley: University of California Press, 1997.

Nagle, Bernard A., and Perry Pascarella. *Leveraging People and Profit: The Hard Work of Soft Management*. Boston: Butterworth-Heinemann, 1998.

Nash, Laura L. *Believers in Business*. Nashville: Thomas Nelson Publishers, 1994.

Pascarella, Perry. *Humanagement in the Future Corporation*. New York: Van Nostrand Reinhold, 1981.

Pascarella, Perry. *The New Achievers*. New York: The Free Press, 1984.

Pascarella, Perry. "The New Science of Management." *Industry Week*, January 6, 1986.

Pascarella, Perry. *Technology: Fire in a Dark World*. New York: Van Nostrand Reinhold, 1979.

Pascarella, Perry. *The Ten Commandments of the Workplace*. Grand Rapids: Zondervan Publishing House, 1996.

Pascarella, Perry, and Mark Frohman. *The Purpose-Driven Organization*. San Francisco: Jossey-Bass Publishers, Inc., 1989.

Pollard, William C. *The Soul of the Firm*. New York: Harper Business and Zondervan Publishing House, 1996.

Reichheld, Frederick F. *The Loyalty Effect*. Boston: Harvard Business School Press, 1996.

Ross, Alan. "Seeking to Serve God through Your Company." *Frontlines* (Spring 1998): 2

Stackhouse, Max L. *Covenant and Commitments*. Louisville: Westminster John Knox Press, 1997.

Tichy, Noel. *The Leadership Engine*. New York: HarperBusiness, 1997.

Tillich, Paul. *A History of Christian Thought*. New York: Simon and Schuster, 1967.

Vaill, Peter. *Managing as a Performing Art*. San Francisco: Jossey-Bass Publishers, Inc., 1989.

Walsh, Brian, and J. Richard Middleton. *The Transforming Vision*. Downers Grove, IL: InterVarsity Press, 1984.

Wink, Walter. *The Powers that Be*. New York: Doubleday, 1998.

Wuthnow, Robert. *Christianity in the Twenty-First Century*. New York: Oxford University Press, 1993.

Wuthnow, Robert. *Poor Richard's Principle*. Princeton: Princeton University Press, 1996.

Zohar, Danah. *ReWiring the Corporate Brain*. San Francisco: Berrett-Koehler Publishers, 1997.

Zukav, Gary. "Evolution and Business," in *Rediscovering the Soul of Business*. Eds. Bill DeFoore and John Renesch. San Francisco: New Leaders Press, 1995.

Zukav, Gary. *The Seat of the Soul*. New York: Simon and Schuster, 1989.

INDEX

A

Abraham, God's covenant with, 144
Accountability. *See also* Responsibility
  in covenantal relationships,
    150–151
  support groups for, 248
Acorn theory, 50
Actions
  doing versus being, 50, 125–126
  embodying values, 215–217, 220
  knowledge versus, 45
  transformation of, 92, 93
  values uncoupled from, 44
Advertising. *See* Marketing
Agape, 14. *See also* Love
Agee, James, 80
AIT (Applied Industrial Technolo-
    gies), 143, 162–163, 205
Alcohol problems, 165
Alderson, Wayne, 34, 172
Altrupreneurs, 4, 98
Amato, Tony
  on being a Christian leader, 164
  community involvement of, 176
  on consistency in the pizza
    business, 174
  conversion of, 84–85, 86
  on sharing the faith, 219
  transformation of, 91
Applied Industrial Technologies
    (AIT), 143, 162–163, 205
Arciero, Bob, 81, 244
Assumptions for the business
    organization, 32–33, 252–253
Attila the Hun, 54

B

Badaracco, Joseph, 229–231
Balance
  between profitability and honoring
    God, 180
  blending versus, 105, 122
  in guiding statements, 204–205
  reflecting on, 240
  work-life, 105, 115, 122
Barth, Karl, 88
Beckett, John
  commitment of company to
    God, 99
  on company guiding statement,
    200–201
  mission in life, 115
  as model Christian businessman,
    60–61, 145
  prayer service of, 131–132
  quarterly meeting of, 160–161
  on respect, 162
  on sharing the faith, 170
  success of company led by, 62
Behavior. *See* Actions
Being versus doing, 50, 125–126
Beliefs statements. *See* Guiding
    statements
Belief systems
  of Christ-centered leaders, 193
  of management, 36
  of tomorrow's executives, 40–41
  unity and, 39–40
Bellman, Geoffrey, 110
Benchmarks of success, 10–11, 62–63
Bennis, Warren, 106